Common Cause

CHATHAM HOUSE SERIES ON CHANGE IN AMERICAN POLITICS

edited by Aaron Wildavsky
University of California, Berkeley

Common Cause
Lobbying in the Public Interest

ANDREW S. MCFARLAND
The University of Chicago

CHATHAM HOUSE PUBLISHERS, INC.
Chatham, New Jersey

COMMON CAUSE
Lobbying in the Public Interest

CHATHAM HOUSE PUBLISHERS, INC.
Box One, Chatham, New Jersey 07928

PUBLISHER: Edward Artinian
COVER DESIGN: Lawrence Ratzkin
COMPOSITION: Chatham Composer
PRINTING AND BINDING: Hamilton Printing Company

LIBRARY OF CONGRESS CATALOGING IN PUBLICATION DATA

McFarland, Andrew S., 1940—
    Common Cause

    (Chatham House series on change in American politics)
    Includes bibliographical references and index.
    1. Common Cause (U.S.) I. Title. II. Series.
JK1118.M39 1984   322.4'3'0973   84-7732
ISBN 0-934540-29-2
ISBN 0-934540-28-4 (pbk.)

Manufactured in the United States of America
10 9 8 7 6 5 4 3 2 1

*Dedicated to the memory of my grandparents,
Lydia Roth Symons (1882-1977) and
Gilbert Prower Symons (1879-1956).*

Contents

Acknowledgments

This book has been a long project, and I have received much help along the way. In particular, I would like to thank Aaron Wildavsky whose encouragement was especially important for the completion of this book. I would like to thank the Social Science Research Council for a Research in Theory grant, which enabled me to think through many of the basic assumptions of this study and of my other research on public-interest groups. A Ford Foundation Individual Study Grant enabled me to stay in Washington to do the interviewing. A grant from the Russell Sage Foundation supported the preparation of an earlier draft of this book. A gift from Joseph Drown helped defray typing and xeroxing expenses. Gilbert Steiner, when director of the Governmental Studies Program of The Brookings Institution, authorized my status as a guest scholar at Brookings, where I did the research and the first stages of the writing. This provided me with a number of useful resources for research and with the friendly encouragement and advice of the personnel of the Governmental Studies Program.

Paul Quirk was a valuable — if unpaid — consultant during the writing stage. In addition, I want to thank Barry Bruce-Briggs, Henry J. Pratt, and Byron Shafer, who read an earlier version of this book and gave me many helpful comments. Edward Artinian, Don Critchlow, Martha Derthick, and Paul E. Peterson each gave me important comments on portions of the manuscript. My chief typist was Thomas Somuah, who worked carefully on drafts and redrafts of the manuscript.

Jonathan W. Siegel shared data from his survey of Common Cause members. I am sure the political science profession will benefit from the timely publication of Siegel's dissertation about Common Cause.

As leaders of Common Cause, John W. Gardner, David Cohen, and Fred Wertheimer facilitated my study. I would like to thank all the sixty-five Common Cause staffers, volunteers, and board members who took the time to be interviewed. I am thankful to the Common Cause staffers who helped in other ways, and special thanks are due to Wendy Wolff and Andrew Kneier for assisting me on numerous occasions. I am gratified that twenty members of Congress took time in their busy schedules to be interviewed.

Some Common Cause staffers and volunteers will be disappointed with my account as giving insufficient attention to their favorite phase of the Common Cause organization. I can only hope that other writers will correct any such imbalances of attention. And I alone am responsible for errors of fact and interpretation.

COMMON CAUSE

Introduction

A major change in American politics has been the increase in the number and variety of lobbyists in the nation's capital. Over 2500 trade associations and professional groups now have their headquarters in Washington, D.C., and most of them have chosen this location to facilitate their efforts to lobby the legislative and executive branches of the federal government. Other groups, not located in Washington, are represented in the capital by one or more of the thousands of lawyers, public relations experts, and outright "lobbyists" who attempt to influence the policy process for a fee. Such influence is difficult to measure, but it is considerable.

Not only the sheer number of lobbyists has increased; the quality of lobbying has also changed. Particularly in attempts to influence members of Congress, lobbyists now generally try to involve the citizenry, the members' constituents, in their efforts. Of course the involvement of constituents is not entirely new; politically active constituents in the 1920s and 1930s occasionally received requests from interest groups "to write your congressman." But advances in technology have made the coordination of constituents' activity and efforts of lobbyists much easier. Many lobbyists, for instance, have available computerized lists of names and phone numbers of group members that can easily be arranged by congressional district or state. Address labels can be printed automatically, or members can be called by WATS line from a group's headquarters. For example, friends of a member of Congress can be called and urged to telephone the member on behalf of a bill. The overall effect of such efforts is to coordinate the political skills of the Washington lobbyist with messages from "the voters back home." Millions of people have been involved in Washington lobbying efforts in this way, although such political involvement extends only to a relatively small fraction of the citizenry—probably under 5 percent.

A particularly interesting example of the new form of Washington lobby is Common Cause, the lobby founded by author and ex-HEW Secretary John W. Gardner in 1970. This organization concentrates on lobbying for good-government measures, such as the public funding of presidential and congressional elections, mandating open meetings of decision-making bodies ("sunshine laws"), regulating the activities of lobbyists, and disclosing nongovernmental sources of income of members of Congress and higher civil servants. At one time or another 800,000 persons have contributed to Common Cause, and by 1984 the lobby had spent $80 million. The money was generally spent effectively, and Common Cause has had a significant impact on government.

Common Cause's effort to represent "public interests" to balance the power of "special interests"—to achieve "civic balance"—is not a new goal. It is in line with a tradition of good-government reformers that extends at least back to the Progressives at the turn of the century. But the nationwide political organization is a new phenomenon within the tradition of government reform. As such, the organizing and lobbying techniques of Common Cause are of interest to students of American politics because the cause of good government is evidently a permanent part of our politics.

Common Cause was a pioneer in developing the new organizing and lobbying methods that involve citizens in campaigns to influence Congress. Regardless of one's opinions about the organization's goals, a few hours devoted to the study of Common Cause can provide a basic introduction to mass-membership political lobbies in Washington, particularly those that rely on members whose contributions spring from a belief in a cause.

The structure of this book reflects a duality of concerns. First, I have a very robust curiosity about how politics works in America. This curiosity has led me to places like the Goldwater Hospitality Room at the 1964 Republican National Convention where, even though I was not a delegate and indeed supported Lyndon Johnson, I circulated, drinking "Gold Water" and eyeing participants wearing "I'd rather fight than switch" buttons. This curiosity has led me to question those who influence politics: What do lobbies do? How do they do it? Which ones will last? The answers to these questions lie in an understanding and appreciation of organizational and lobbying techniques, and the lobby I analyze is Common Cause.

Accordingly, chapter 1 provides a brief history of Common Cause; I leave it to someone else to eventually write a fuller history. In chapter 2, Common Cause is viewed as part of the tradition of political reform in America. The third through the fifth chapters deal with the Common Cause organization: Who joins? Why do they join? What is the structure of the organization and what are its processes? How is the organization governed? Chapter 6 describes sixteen techniques used in Common Cause's lobbying activities. Chapters 7 and 8 treat the core of the Common Cause program of reform. These chapters detail the organization's lobbying activities through time and its impact on society as a whole. The final chapter asks a question, Will Common Cause endure? and answers it in terms of a changing environment for American reform organizations.

My second concern is to make some contribution to the discipline of political science. This need not contradict my desire to satisfy my own curiosity. Indeed, the day that curiosity about politics and political theory are separated will see the end of a science and the beginning of an assembly line of academic production quotas.

At least eight facets of this book are of interest to scholars of political science.

1. *The case study.* Common Cause is a significant political phenomenon in itself. In addition, it serves here as a model for a systematic description of the new methods of Washington lobbyists.

2. *Entrepreneurs and the formation of interest groups.* Using an analogy to economics, various political scientists have stressed the key role played by individuals in organizing interest groups.[1] Such individuals invest their own political resources in an organization in the hope of increasing their political "capital." The role of John W. Gardner in organizing Common Cause is a particularly striking instance. Gardner's "profit" was not money but the continuing possibility of influencing American politics, either directly as chairman of Common Cause or indirectly through the actions of the institution.

3. *Communication theory and lobbying.* My first experience with lobbying was reading Louis Anthony Dexter's path-breaking chapters in *American Business and Public Policy.*[2] Essentially Dexter viewed lobbying as the communication of political information through networks of interaction among participants in politics. This view of lobbying fits Common Cause very well and is presupposed in my descriptions of the organization and its lobbying techniques. Even more than Dexter, I stress the role of friendship in lobbying. I depart from Dexter's work somewhat in emphasizing the importance of forming coalitions with friendly members of Congress in order to influence undecided members on particular issues.

4. *"Civic balance" belief system.* Apparently, a set of beliefs plays an important role in mobilizing citizens to contribute to "cause groups." By "civic balance" I refer to the belief that "special interests" control some areas of governmental policy and that "public interests" ("the people") must organize to balance the power of those special interests. The need for a civic balance permeates the press releases, magazines, and statements issued by Common Cause.

5. *Political learning.* Social scientists seem to vacillate between these two extremes: the hope that their research will affect society in a major way and the despair that their work will have no effect at all. Despairing social scientists will be cheered to know that scholarship in the fields of political science and history seems to have had some effect on Common Cause. In particular, Common Cause seems more determined to use practical political techniques,

to engage in the hurly-burly of political bargaining and compromise, than was
the norm among earlier generations of reformers. This may be due to Gardner's reading of V.O. Key, Jr., and David Truman. The leaders of Common
Cause are generally aware of the scholarly criticisms of previous good-government reformers—an awareness one would expect from people who were social
science majors or law students in the 1960s and 1970s. Common Cause demonstrates that the social sciences can have an effect on political behavior, producing an increase in political sophistication.

6. *Applications of language philosophy to empirical research.* Others have
applied Hanna Pitkin's *The Concept of Representation* to the understanding
of representation within such political bodies as presidential nominating conventions, Community Action Councils of the Johnson poverty program, and
the Health System Agencies (HSAs) that allocate licenses for hospitals and other health facilities.[3] Pitkin's work is applied here to understand several dimen-
sions of representation within Common Cause's organizational structure.

7. *Middle-class social movements.* Politics in America has been vitally
affected by middle-class social movements. Among other things, these movements have spawned lobbies to help pass legislation that has had an important
effect on public policy. Common Cause, a pressure group originating in social
movements, has represented the "establishment" side of various public-interest
movements since the 1970s. As such, the experiences of Common Cause can
help us understand relationships among the middle class, social movements,
lobbies, legislation, public policy, and countermovements.[4]

8. *Political parties and political participation.* This book demonstrates the
potential for political power that Common Cause and several dozen similar
lobbies may exercise on American politics in the future. The current vitality
of liberal and conservative "cause groups," which involve middle-class contributors in effective lobbying campaigns to influence Congress, the executive, and
public opinion, can lead to a concern about the future representation of blue-
collar workers, minorities, and others not active in these groups. Common
Cause ironically demonstrates the significance of political parties as institutions of participation, for political parties and election campaigns bring together Americans of various classes and life styles into groups working toward
common political goals.[5]

As a citizen, I have a third concern in this book. To what extent do the
activities of Common Cause bring about a better politics and a better society?
I think that we are better off with them than without them. But I believe I have
supplied enough data to provide plenty of grist for the mills of those grinding
out the opposite conclusions.

NOTES

1. See note 42 to chapter 6.
2. Raymond A. Bauer, Ithiel de Sola Pool, and Lewis Anthony Dexter, *American Business and Public Policy* (New York: Atherton, 1963).
3. See notes to chapter 5.
4. See note 5 in chapter 9.
5. I share the views on the need to strengthen the political parties expressed in the President's Commission for a National Agenda for the Eighties, *The Electoral and Democratic Process in the Eighties* (Englewood Cliffs, N.J.: Prentice-Hall, 1982). I was the staff co-author of this volume.

1. Common Cause: A Concise Description

Common Cause was founded in August 1970 by John W. Gardner and his associates.[1] Gardner had headed the Carnegie Foundation, had written two best-selling books,[2] had chaired a presidential commission on education policy, and had served as Secretary of Health, Education, and Welfare under Lyndon Johnson from July 1965 until January 1968.

After leaving the cabinet, Gardner led the Urban Coalition, an organization that attempted, rather unsuccessfully, to coordinate the efforts of community leaders to alleviate the "urban crisis" and the dissatisfaction of urban blacks. The most successful aspect of the Urban Coalition, in Gardner's judgment, was its lobbying arm — the Urban Coalition Action Council. But when the Tax Reform Act of 1969 forbade foundations to contribute to lobbying organizations, it eliminated a financial basis for the UCAC.[3] Gardner decided to seek a mass financial base for the UCAC, which would be then cut loose from the Urban Coalition. Thus, Common Cause was launched in a series of newspaper ads and by a mass mailing.

In the summer of 1970 middle-class people were especially upset with American political institutions; events abroad, in Cambodia, and at home, at Kent State University, were painful recent memories. The response to Gardner's invitation to found a "people's lobby" was enthusiastic. Within six months there were 100,000 members; by the beginning of 1972 the membership had doubled.

In January 1970 Gardner had had to borrow money to meet the payroll of the UCAC. A year later, he and his associates headed something called Common Cause, the incipient organizational expression of widespread enthusiasm and hope. Something more than an urban-oriented lobbying organization had developed.

It took two years for Gardner, Lowell Beck (a former American Bar Association lobbyist), Jack Conway (Walter Reuther's long-time political aide), Tom Mathews (a public relations consultant), David Cohen (once a lobbyist for Americans for Democratic Action), Georgianna Rathbun (a former editor for

Congressional Quarterly), Robert Gallamore (a recent Harvard Ph.D. in economics), and other founders to think through the nature of the new organization, although certain basic decisions were reached almost immediately.

Common Cause would be a "people's lobby" to combat the undue power of special interests. Common Cause would be "pro-politics"; it would not shy away from using the experience of Washington insiders to apply "pressure" for the public interest. Common Cause would be an "action" organization, not an "education" organization. Lobbying would be its main goal, not the political education of its members.

Common Cause would not be a "research" organization; it would rely on the research of others except when original research was necessary to pursue particular objectives. Common Cause would be an organization of experts, who would be paid professional salaries, rather than an organization staffed by low-paid youthful workers. The new lobby would have a legal arm, but the legal division would have a lower priority than the congressional lobbying effort. And Common Cause would give its members a voice in organizational decision making. As Gardner noted five years later: "A lot of reform groups, historically and today, have operated with self-perpetuating boards and non-voting memberships. We chose the route of an elected board, referenda on issues, and other paraphernalia of participation, with an awareness that it involved enormous effort and some risk of organizational paralysis."[4]

These basic decisions were made shortly after the initiation of Common Cause. There were other aspects of the organization, however, that were not so easily decided.

What issues should Common Cause pursue? Gardner knew that Common Cause would founder if it pursued every issue that had some appeal to its constituency. The orginal prospectus for Common Cause contained a wide-ranging list of fifteen issue areas including antiwar, government reform, urban concerns, welfare, and the environment. Priorities had to be set, or lobbying activity would be dissipated.

Another unresolved question was organizational structure. Gardner did not have state governments in mind when he launched Common Cause. Almost immediately, enthusiastic members proposed that state affiliates be formed to work for state government reform. The organizational founders, who had clearly decided that national lobbying was the main purpose of Common Cause, could hardly forbid enthusiastic members from pursuing Common Cause goals at the state level. This relationship of national goals to state goals has never been solved and has remained the principal organizational problem of Common Cause. It is an inherently irresolvable problem because limited resources must be allocated among national and state activities.

From the beginning, Common Cause's subscribers tended to be upper-middle-class whites; they were well educated, middle-aged, financially secure, and disproportionately from Eastern Seaboard and Pacific Coast states. In 1976, pollster Peter Hart, at the behest of Common Cause, conducted a random sample of 4000 members that received a 44.25 percent response (1770 persons). Of the respondents, 58 percent were *over* fifty years old, 50 percent held a postgraduate degree, and 65 percent had been members for more than two years. Sixty-two percent of the respondents were men; this contradicted two earlier surveys, in 1971 and 1974, that showed a nearly equal division between the sexes. In 1976, Common Cause membership figures indicated that 36.7 percent of the members lived along the Eastern Seaboard (New England, New York, New Jersey, Pennsylvania, Maryland, Delaware, and the District of Columbia), while 23.5 percent lived in the five states bordering on the Pacific Ocean (California, Oregon, Washington, Hawaii, and Alaska). A 1982 survey showed almost the same percentages of members living in these two regions.

A careful study of Massachusetts members in 1974 by Marttila and his associates indicated a typical family income of $23,000 per year.[5] A 1971 national survey, and the 1974 Massachusetts survey, indicated that the partisan breakdown of members was about 10 percent *more* Democrats than the sampled population, 10 percent *less* independents, and about the same number of Republicans.[6] Virtually all the Republicans were so-called liberal Republicans identifying at the time with the party's Rockefeller-Percy wing rather than its Nixon-Ford or Goldwater-Reagan wings.

Common Cause's early surveys, then, revealed a membership with characteristics similar to the usual impression of Common Cause as an organization of upper-middle-class professionals. But there were two interesting facts. First, Common Cause members were older than might be expected. Second, if liberal Republicans were about 7 percent of the national population, they were overrepresented within Common Cause (20 percent of the members).

In 1971-72 the reform-minded, upper-middle-class members of Common Cause each contributed $15 in yearly dues to an organization with a number-one lobbying priority: to oppose the Vietnam war. Beginning in 1973, Common Cause's number-one priority became the "structure and process" issues of government reform: the Campaign Reform Act of 1974, open meeting laws, changes in congressional seniority, and so forth. State organizations of Common Cause, established in 1972, were initially limited to state versions of government reforms: disclosure and ceilings on campaign donations, control of lobbyists, open meetings of government bodies, and disclosure of finances by government officials. Consensus on national and state versions of structure and process issues unified the membership and minimized the internal conflict. Of course, persons who did not care much about government reform did not join Common Cause.

Common Cause Issues

Of the principal issues on which Common Cause has had an impact, five stand out:

1. Support for the Federal Election Campaign Amendments of 1974, which established limits on contributions to presidential and congressional elections and established the present system of matching funds for presidential candidates (see chapter 7).

2. Common Cause's suit in 1972-73 against the Committee to Re-Elect the President (CREEP) forced the disclosure of massive contributions to the Nixon campaign, which provided the cash basis for the illicit Watergate efforts and indicated a need to control corporate gifts to presidential campaigns.

3. Common Cause acted as the "outsider" lobbying coordinator (as opposed to "insider" lobbying by members) against the Vietnamese effort in the House of Representatives in 1971-72. The House had never voted "up or down" on the war until 1971 because of a lack of orchestrated constituent pressure and the relative tactical inferiority of antiwar members (see chapter 8).

4. Since 1974, Common Cause state organizations have played an important role in lobbying for the torrent of good-government reforms recently passed by all state legislatures.[7] Such reforms have concentrated on the disclosure of and ceilings on campaign contributions, the control of lobbyists, open meeting laws, and the disclosure of personal finances by state officials. It is still not clear whether the impressive quantity of state reform laws will have an important substantive effect, whether the effect will be in line with the intentions of reformers, or whether such laws will remain unenforced and constitute a body of "symbolic politics."[8] State organizations of Common Cause have been active in initiating lawsuits to facilitate the enforcement of state reform laws.[9]

5. During the 1970s Common Cause had an important impact on the reform of Congress, particularly on the House of Representatives. However, in my judgment Common Cause did not play as central a role in congressional reform as it did on the other four issues because the main impetus for change in Congress came from change-oriented members of Congress.[10] Common Cause *was* the most important "outsider" lobbying force in such matters as unseating committee chairmen in the House who were widely thought to be unresponsive to the public; reforming the committee assignment process in the House; and attaining a relatively strict ethics code regarding the use of cam-

paign contributions for other than electoral purposes, the pursuit of outside income, the use of congressional office funds, and the acceptance of gifts from lobbyists.

Common Cause had a major lobbying impact on two other important issues: lobbying against the oil depletion allowance and lobbying against federal subsidies for the SST (the supersonic transport airliner) in 1971. Common Cause claims a large share of the credit for the abolition of the oil depletion allowance for major oil companies in the spring of 1975; it probably deserves the credit, for other liberal or reform lobbyists (except for Nader organizations) did little actual lobbying on this occasion. Common Cause generated a great deal of mail in opposition to the SST subsidy, which was a contributory (although secondary) cause of its defeat. The SST had an additional importance for Common Cause because it demonstrated for the first time that Common Cause could generate a significant amount of grass-roots pressure on Congress.

In the mid-1970s Common Cause continued to emphasize structure and process issues. At the national level its main priority was the adoption of public financing for congressional campaigns on a 50 percent matching federal funds basis. In 1976 Congress passed a "sunshine act," providing that most meetings of federal boards and commissions be open to the public. Common Cause had actively lobbied for this legislation. In early 1977, both houses of Congress adopted "ethics codes," which mandated disclosure of financial holdings of congressmen and limited their income from speaking and consulting fees. Common Cause pressed for the extension of such ethics codes to the top levels of the bureaucracy in 1978. During these years, Common Cause continued its campaign to control lobbyists more strictly and force them to disclose their expenditures, and lobbied for the enactment of structure and process legislation at the state level that had not yet been enacted. (Common Cause ordinarily does not lobby at local levels of government.[11])

In early 1975 the organization launched an exploratory program to extend its government reforms into the executive branch. The most important aspect of such lobbying was the initiation in Congress of "sunset legislation," which would call for the abolition of agencies after a set term unless they were specifically renewed by Congress (see chapter 8). Other executive lobbying activities emphasized the need for top federal executives to "log" contacts with extra-agency people as an index to special-interest power.[12]

Another Common Cause activity was to try to influence presidential campaigning in the direction of greater issue orientation. "Campaign '76" activities included the compilation of 150-page booklets citing the candidates' stands on issues at three different points in the primary campaign. They also invited people to submit lists of questions that they wanted candidates to answer; Common Cause compiled the questions in order of frequency and then publicly requested that candidates answer them.

With the close of the Vietnam war, Common Cause continued to take stands on issues, although these stands typically got less public attention than its government reform proposals. In 1975 Common Cause temporarily gave priority to energy issues.[13] It was the only major lobbying organization to back the ill-fated Ullman energy bill of 1975, which would have raised the federal gasoline tax by 20 cents a gallon to conserve energy.

Common Cause also lobbied against "subsidies" as a way to combat the powers of special interests and inflation. On these grounds it worked against the oil depletion allowance, grants to the maritime industry, high price supports for milk producers, and the proposed B-1 bomber. During the 1970s, polls of the membership indicated a great interest in so-called tax reform, but the membership was divided on what this meant in respect to specific measures (abolition of capital gains, abolition of charitable deductions, and so forth).

In the 1970s, Common Cause put forth a minor lobbying effort on a surprising number of measures. By "minor" is meant that Common Cause joined a lobbying coalition on some measures, lent its name to proposed actions, and contacted some congressmen who were close to Common Cause. But Common Cause did not commit its entire grass-roots network to such efforts.

Common Cause frequently joined lobbying coalitions for measures that were designed to promote fairness for minorities within the American political process. Common Cause lobbied for renewal of the 1965 Voting Rights Acts in 1972 and 1982; for measures to discourage banks from refusing to grant mortgage loans on the basis of geographical location—the practice known as "redlining"; for the just treatment of minorities under revenue-sharing programs; for full voting rights in the District of Columbia; and for the rights of the Menominee Indian tribe.[14] Common Cause supported major environmental bills, such as the Clean Air Amendments of 1977 and the Udall strip-mining-control legislation of 1977.

Lobbying for these measures is popular with reform and minority lobbies in Washington. Such efforts ordinarily attract little attention and thus do not provide much conflict within Common Cause. Nevertheless, members wrote to the Common Cause national headquarters in 1975 to protest the organization's stands against the B-1 bomber and for a moratorium on the construction of nuclear power plants. Farm-bloc congressmen resented lobbying efforts against higher dairy subsidies. Such events clearly indicate that Common Cause would pay a considerable price in lost support if it took stands on several controversial issues in addition to its government reform positions. Thus, giving top priority to lobbying on procedural issues is a wise decision from the stand-point of organizational prestige and cohesion.

The Emphasis on Structure and Process Issues

If a public-interest group lobbied on every issue on which general interests seem to need representation, it would soon collapse. One lobby cannot represent unorganized public interests on all consumer, environmental, good-government, and taxpayer issues. The lobby's resources would be spread so thin that the group might not be effective on *any* issue. Such lobbying would necessitate hir-ing a large staff to provide the expertise needed to understand all the issues. Conflict would develop as consumer, environmental, energy, good-government, and tax specialists and lobbyists struggled for the organization's scarce resources.

Most public-interest groups solve this problem by concentrating on one issue area of public-interest politics, be it consumer, environmental, or what-ever. Beyond this, many groups specialize on particular issues within an area. For example, the Environmental Policy Center specializes in strip-mining legis-lation and coal policy, and other public-interest groups look to the EPC for expertise and lobbying leadership on these matters. But, obviously, a public-interest lobby established with many purposes in mind has a different organiza-tional history than do more specialized lobbies.

This was the situation when Common Cause decided in 1970 to "repre-sent the people," to balance special-interest power, and to work for "a better quality of life" (meaning environmental and urban legislation). John Gardner realized that Common Cause could founder by getting involved with too many issues. But over a period of three years, this problem was resolved. Polls and other evidence indicated that the membership cared most about lobbying to oppose the Vietnam war, and this became the organization's number-one prior-ity until the war ended. During this period, Common Cause staff became in-creasingly involved with "structure and process" issues, that is, reforms of gov-ernmental institutions and procedures. Once the war in Vietnam was over, governmental reform issues took first priority. These issues had the virtue of maintaining organizational unity; few Common Cause members objected to this priority. And emphasis on governmental reform provided a rationale for Common Cause's avoidance of extensive involvement on a wider range of is-sues. Given limited resources, the most effective way to represent the public, or so Common Cause leaders maintained, was to reform the institutional prac-tices that "stack the deck" against public interests.

In Gardner's words, by the end of the third year ". . . it had long been apparent to some of us that the 'systemic' issues had other virtues—not wholly foreseen. They had no party label on them and could provide a solid non-partisan theme for a citizens' movement. And they solved the 'multi-issue problem' perceived by every shrewd early observer of Common Cause. Most of the historic examples of successful citizen movements were single-issue movements (women's rights, conservation, population), so there was little potential for internal divisiveness: if you weren't for that one issue you didn't join that particular movement. Observers wondered whether Common Cause could ever achieve that sort of consensus with a 'varied portfolio' of issues. Clearly the remarkable consensus of our members on issues of government accountability provided a possible solution to that difficulty."[15]

The history of the League of Women Voters is similar in this respect. During the 1930s, the league emphasized government reform as a way of holding together the multipurpose organization. Before the women's liberation movement, reforming governmental institutions was the league's number-one priority in lobbying.[16] Apparently, one way to hold together a citizens' lobby that initially advocated many different policies is to emphasize reforms of political procedures and institutions.

From 1977 through 1981, during the Carter administration and the first year of the Reagan Presidency, events seemed to demonstrate what some Common Cause staff called "the adversity theory of Common Cause." By this they meant that political events perceived to be adverse, such as the war in Vietnam and the Watergate affair, had the effect of increasing the number of Common Cause members. A reverse prediction was that the Common Cause membership would decline when such adversity was lacking, as in the Carter administration. In accord with this theory, the Common Cause membership dropped during the Carter years, from 260,000 to about 220,000. This theory continued to hold during the Reagan administration when membership once more reached 255,000. Potential members of Common Cause were particularly aggravated by Reagan's arms buildup and by his lack of concern about the role of special-interest contributions in congressional elections.

Sociologist Robert Mitchell of Resources for the Future has demonstrated that an important motivation for joining an environmentalist group is a perception of a threat to a wholesome environment. Mitchell's observation is analogous to the adversity theory of Common Cause leaders; people join Common Cause because they are threatened by some sequence of events.[17]

During the Carter years, the leadership of Common Cause changed, but the organizational structure remained much the same. In April 1977, founder and chairman John Gardner resigned, largely because he believes in the value of changing activities every decade or so, and because he felt that the Common Cause organization could carry on without him. The Common Cause governing board elected as its second chair Nan Waterman, a member of the board who had been particularly active in fashioning organizational networks and resolving conflicts between various units. Mrs. Waterman served as "chair-woman" (her preferred term) until 1980, when she resigned and was succeeded by Archibald Cox, the well-known Harvard law professor fired from his position as special prosecutor by the Nixon administration during the Watergate scandal. In the Carter years, David Cohen served as president (i.e., organizational manager) of Common Cause. He resigned in May 1981 and was succeeded by Fred Wertheimer, who was senior vice-president of Common Cause and had been its chief lobbyist before that.

The organizational structure remained essentially the same during this period. The elaborate complex of a national headquarters, various state headquarters, and committees and telephone chains within local congressional districts stayed in place. The tactics of coordinating lobbying in Washington with communication from Common Cause members also stayed the same (for a description of these tactics, see chapter 6). The budget for the national Common Cause organization remained roughly constant at about $5.5 to $6.0 million a year during the Carter era. Of course, this meant that, by 1981, Common Cause had about 45 percent less to spend because of the shrinking buying power of the dollar. The national management was able to devise many ways of saving money as they gained greater experience in running the organization. Still, salaries lagged behind inflation, and the number of paid full-time employees at national headquarters declined from 100 in 1977 to 75 in 1981. Nevertheless, Common Cause leaders did not regard the decline in the real dollar value of their budget as a major obstacle to success in lobbying the U.S. Congress.

By the late 1970s, Common Cause had lobbied successfully for two of its five major institutional reforms at the national level. The federal Sunshine Law, which provided for public access to most federal meetings, was enacted in 1975. In 1978 Congress passed the Ethics in Government Act, which attempted to lessen the incidence of conflict-of-interest situations for higher civil servants and judges by requiring them to report sources of outside income and limit their acceptance of gifts from lobbyists, and precluded them from accepting employment within a year after leaving government service from persons they had regulated while working for the government. In addition, Congress in 1977 and 1978 enacted ethics codes to apply to itself. Such legislation restricted the personal use of congressional office funds, limited the acceptance of gifts from lobbyists, and restricted the amount of income allowable from such sources as the practice of law and giving speeches for fees.

Common Cause did not succeed in its lobbying campaigns for the other three major institutional reforms: public funding for congressional elections, the regulation of lobbying of the federal government, and the enactment of a sunset law applicable to many federal agencies. Efforts for public funding of congressional elections received a severe setback in the summer of 1977 when Senate Republicans decided to oppose the measure as favoring incumbents (then predominately Democrats) and threatened a filibuster.[18] Republicans in the House were not so unified against the concept of public funding, but it seemed useless to fight for a measure in the House that was nearly certain to be defeated in the Senate. Consequently, Common Cause and its allies concentrated on gaining passage of a bill to limit the amount of funds a candidate for Congress could receive from Political Action Committees, known as PACs, the political fund-raising units associated with corporations, unions, professional associations, and ideological groups. One such measure, known as the Obey (Dem-Wisc.)-Railsback (Rep-Ill.) bill, passed the House in the fall of 1979; the Senate refused to consider it, even though the bill applied only to elections to the House. During the Reagan administration the prospects for an immediate adoption of public funding measures or bills to control Political Action Committees were dim.

A similar fate occurred to regulation of lobbyists and sunset measures. By 1978 it was clear that sufficient support to pass a law regulating the conduct of lobbyists would be extremely difficult to get. Political support for enacting a government-wide sunset law seemed stronger then, but by 1980 congressional support for a sunset law had diminished (see chapter 8).

Common Cause achieved considerable success in sponsoring institutional reform measures at the state level. Laws establishing some form of public funding for state elections increased from five in 1976 to seventeen in 1980.[19] The passage of ethics codes for state government employees was also frequent. From 1977 to 1980, Common Cause was more successful at the state level in lobbying for its "structure and process" reform than at the national level.

Common Cause was active during the Carter years in pressing for the enactment of several other institutional reforms. The organization worked hard in support of President Carter's Civil Service Reform Act of 1978. Common Cause took the lead in organizing members of the House to censure Robert Sikes (D-Fla.), a powerful senior member who used his position to enrich himself in various legal ways (see chapter 6). Common Cause was somewhat slow to support the Equal Rights Amendment, but since 1977 has put considerable resources into the effort to gain ratification of the ERA. A staff member worked full-time in pursuit of ERA ratification. Common Cause also gave free office space and telephoning privileges to members of the coalition for ratification of the proposed constitutional amendment to grant the District of Columbia full voting rights in the Congress.

Common Cause put a modest amount of resources into lobbying for other institutional reform measures. Examples of such lobbying activities included Common Cause support for establishing a public prosecutor who would be mandated to investigate charges of corruption of top-level federal officials; promoting the selection of federal judges according to merit criteria; congressional censuring of Charles Wilson (Dem-Cal.) for the diversion of campaign contributions to personal expenditures; maintaining procedures of the congressional budgeting reform of 1974 and strengthening this measure by the adoption of "reconciliation" procedures in 1980 by which Congressional Budget committees could mandate expenditure ceilings in various budgetary categories; and backing the Democratic leadership's effort in the House to consolidate authority over energy legislation into a new energy committee, an effort that failed in 1980.

At least two internal conflicts occurred in conjunction with activity on institutional reform measures. In February 1978 the national governing board of Common Cause refused to lend its lobbying resources to the campaign to press Congress to extend the seven-year limit for the ratification of the Equal Rights Amendment. A majority on the board thought that such an extension was inappropriate. Some board members worked vigorously for the reversal of this decision, and at the next board meeting the decision was reversed by a close vote.

A second difference of opinion occurred in 1977 when a majority of Common Cause board and staff opposed the Carter-Mondale measure to repeal provisions of the Hatch Act that preclude federal civil servants from active participation in federal electoral campaigns. The majority felt the provisions effectively protected federal employees from political pressure; a minority considered the act to be an abridgment of the citizenship rights of civil servants.

During the Carter years, Common Cause state organizations expanded activities to include lobbying for the adoption of statutes to provide for the reapportionment of political districts by "impartial" boards, a practice followed in Canada and Great Britain. A major priority of some state organizations was the adoption of changes in state budgetary processes, particularly to provide greater access for the public to a state's budgetary process.

In November 1978 the national governing board voted to make combating inflation a major priority for Common Cause. Staff and board agreed that lobbying against government subsidies, tax breaks, and regulations beneficial to "special interests" would be an appropriate strategy for Common Cause to combat price increases. In fact, Common Cause was already doing this on an ad hoc basis. For example, Common Cause supported the abolition or reduction of the oil depletion allowance in 1975 and joined the campaign for the deregulation of the airline industry in 1976. Common Cause played a key role in the successful lobbying effort to oppose a federal rule that the percentage of imported oil carried in U.S.-constructed and -operated ships be increased from 3 percent to 9.5 percent, as the Carter administration requested in 1977.[20] Such an increase would have cost the public $610 million a year, according to an estimate by the General Accounting Office.[21]

As part of its anti-inflation program, Common Cause opposed increases in subsidies to milk producers and sugar growers. In 1980 Common Cause lobbied against a successful proposal to enable Congress to veto rulings of the Federal Trade Commission. Common Cause expected that such vetoes would occur because, after losing an FTC case, interest groups might successfully lobby Congress to reinstate inflationary price-fixing practices. In 1983 the Supreme Court declared such legislative vetoes unconstitutional. In addition, Common Cause lobbied to protect the FTC budget from major slashes proposed by agency opponents on Capitol Hill.

Also in 1980, Common Cause was active in lobbying for the deregulation of the trucking industry, a move proposed by the Carter administration and adopted by Congress in that year. Joint lobbying by Common Cause and the Chamber of Commerce for trucking deregulation surprised and impressed members of Congress. (Common Cause did not lobby for deregulation of oil and natural gas because such activity would not have had the support of a majority of the staff, board, and membership.)

Common Cause lobbied to oppose the construction of the Tennessee-Tombigbee Canal, an expensive public works project that was difficult to justify using cost-benefit criteria. By the middle of 1983, Common Cause staff and board were discussing the possibility of opposing dubious expenditures in the defense procurement area. In addition, Common Cause support for the revamped congressional budgeting process, which was intended to help attain a balanced budget through putting an overall ceiling on thirteen appropriations bills, was part of Common Cause's lobbying campaign against inflation.

In November 1978 the governing board voted to give a major lobbying priority to working for a Senate ratification of the SALT II treaty in addition to the priority given to lobbying against inflation. A poll indicated that Common Cause members supported SALT II by a margin of 79 to 9 percent, but it seemed that many more groups would lobby for the defeat of the treaty than for its ratification. As SALT II was not considered on the floor of the Senate, Common Cause did not get the opportunity to test its lobbying capabilities in this area.

Common Cause leaders have usually considered energy policy to be an area appropriate for lobbying activity because it is particularly necessary to mobilize the cause of general or long-run interests to combat the influence of special interests. Yet Common Cause activity in energy has been sporadic. In 1975, for instance, Common Cause was active in opposing the oil depletion allowance, in supporting a measure to reduce oil imports through taxing gasoline, and in formulating a general statement on energy policy.[22] But in 1976 and 1977 Common Cause was not active in energy as public concern waned. The governing board expressed a renewed interest in energy in the spring of 1978 (a year before the second round of major increases in oil prices). In 1978 and 1979 this concern led to support for appropriations for development of solar power and the conservation of energy. In addition, Common Cause supported measures to limit the authority the Carter administration would have given to a federal Energy Mobilization Board to suspend federal and state laws slowing down the construction of coal gasification and other "synfuel" projects. (Congress refused to authorize such a board.) But after 1980 Common Cause activity in energy again lapsed.

At the beginning of the Reagan administration, most of the leadership of Common Cause believed that a new political era had begun and that Common Cause would have to change to meet the demands of the 1980s. Indeed, much of the top leadership of Common Cause changed during 1980-81. Archibald Cox assumed the position of Chair in February 1980. In May 1981 Fred Wertheimer became president (organizational manager) of Common Cause. He reorganized the national headquarters, and several long-time leaders of the national staff resigned.

A number of organizational innovations began to appear at this time. The major Common Cause publication—the tabloid-sized, bimonthly publication Frontline—had been thoroughly revamped in the fall of 1980 and was replaced by a sprightly magazine, Common Cause, printed in bright colors on glossy paper and featuring article-length investigative reporting. It was hoped that the new publication would attract members, but this apparently has not happened to a great degree. (This provides some evidence that Common Cause members generally regard their dues as a "contribution," much like a contribution to health research or to feed the poor, and are relatively indifferent to the receipt of tangible rewards from Common Cause.)

In 1981 Common Cause began to experiment with ways to enhance its lobbying capacity by fielding teams of highly motivated members within districts of key members of Congress who tended to be uncommitted, "swing" voters on issues of concern to Common Cause (see the discussion of "action teams" in chapter 6). Wertheimer also initiated measures to give the state organizations autonomy in drawing up their budgets, which had been closely supervised by the national organization.

that public-interest groups pursue benefits for the entire public, while civil rights groups pursue equality for a minority group.

5. Gardner, memorandum to Common Cause staff, 21 October 1975, 2. On the cover page of this memorandum, Gardner wrote: "A number of staff members who have not been with Common Cause since the beginning are not fully aware of how we came to the present emphasis on the process and structure issues. In the attached memorandum I have tried to explain it from the beginning."

16. John Grumm, "The History and Function of the League of Women Voters" (M.A. thesis, Department of Political Science, University of California, Berkeley, 1952). This thesis is deposited at the main library at the University of California, Berkeley.

17. Robert Cameron Mitchell, "National Environmental Lobbies and the Apparent Illogic of Collective Action," in *Collective Decision Making*, ed. Clifford S. Russell (Baltimore: Johns Hopkins University Press, 1979), 89-136.

18. The definitive treatment of the relationship between incumbency and public funding of candidates is Gary C. Jacobson, *Money in Congressional Elections* (New Haven: Yale University Press, 1980).

19. *The Book of the States, 1980-1981*, vol. 23 (Lexington, Ky.: Council of State Governments, 1980), 53.

20. *The Congressional Quarterly Almanac,* vol. 33 (Washington, D.C.: Congressional Quarterly, 1978), 537.

21. Ibid., 536.

22. McFarland, *Public Interest Lobbies*, 57-66, 117-29.

At first it seemed that Common Cause might have serious problems during the Reagan era. Congressional support for such measures as public financing for congressional campaigns, the regulation of lobbyists, and a widely applicable sunset law was much less in 1981 than a few years earlier. Would Common Cause's lobbying efforts become less relevant during the Reagan administration?

The answer became apparent almost immediately. The Reagan administration and its allies in Congress provided Common Cause with a new issue, one that was popular with the Common Cause constituency: lobbying in defense of legislation enacted with the backing of Common Cause or other public-interest groups in the 1970s. For example, in 1981 Common Cause lobbied for the retention of the powers of the Federal Election Commission, established by a Common Cause-influenced election act of 1974. Common Cause also lobbied against major changes in the Freedom of Information Act and the Clean Air Act (generally supported by environmentalists). Other examples included opposition to proposals to change the Voting Rights Act, opposition to the proposal to eliminate the Legal Services Commission (which provided legal services to the poor), and opposition to various congressional measures that would redefine the jurisdiction of the federal courts, such as redefining "life" to include the fetus, thereby overruling the Supreme Court's abortion decisions. (In the latter case, Common Cause pointed out that it was not taking a position on abortion but was objecting to what, in the opinion of Archibald Cox, would be an abridgment of constitutional separation of powers.)

Many Common Cause members were quiescent at first about the policies of the Reagan administration because they wanted to give the new President his chance. By 1984, however, the "adversity theory" seemed to be confirmed. Membership went back up to 260,000, largely because of a major increase in the returns from Common Cause's mailed solicitations for membership, which generally stressed the theme of federal policy going in the wrong direction. This membership increase was largely responsible for a one-third increase in the Common Cause budget—from $6 million to $8 million per year.

In February 1982 the national governing board voted to make lobbying for nuclear arms control a top priority for Common Cause. While the leadership of Common Cause generally favored arms control measures in the tradition of the SALT negotiations, Common Cause subsequently lobbied Congress on behalf of a nuclear freeze, on the grounds that such resolutions were useful in pressuring the Reagan administration into conducting serious negotiations with the Soviets. Taking action for arms control was enthusiastically received by Common Cause activists, and was opposed by practically none of them.

NOTES

1. This material is based on my field work at Common Cause national headquarters. Seventy-nine interviews were conducted with national staff, state activists, former staff, and members of the U.S. House of Representatives. In addition, numerous informal conversations were held. Activists from seven states were interviewed; representatives from fifteen other states presented reports to the national staff and board. Some field work was conducted in Massachusetts, California, and Arizona. Common Cause staff memos were made available to me, as was poll data.

There is a dearth of published work on Common Cause. The only scholarly article known to me is Joel L. Fleishman and Carol S. Greenwald, "Public Interest Litigation and Political Finance Reform," *Annals of the American Academy of Political and Social Science* 425 (May 1976): 114-23. My *Public Interest Lobbies: Decision Making on Energy* (Washington, D.C.: American Enterprise Institute, 1976) contains a chapter on Common Cause. *Congressional Quarterly* and *National Journal Reports* contain useful information on Common Cause. See, for example, Al Gordon, "Public Interest Lobbies: Nader and Common Cause Become Permanent Fixtures," *Congressional Quarterly* 34 (15 May 1976): 1197-1205; and Theodore Jacqueney, "Common Cause Lobbyists Focus on the Structure and Process of Government," *National Journal Reports* 5 (1 September 1973): 1294-1304. A Ph.D. dissertation on Common Cause has been completed: Paul Lutzker, "The Politics of Public Interest Groups: Common Cause in Action" (Political Science Department, John Hopkins University, 1973). Two papers on Common Cause delivered at American Political Science Association conventions preceded my own: Paul Dawson, "On Making Public Policy More Public: The Role of Public Interest Groups" (delivered at the 1973 annual meeting of the APSA at New Orleans); and Carol S. Greenwald, "The Use of Litigation by Common Cause: A Study of the Development of Campaign Finance Reform Legislation" (delivered at the 1975 annual meeting of the APSA at San Francisco). Mary Topolsky's "Common Cause?" *Worldview* 17 (April 1974): 35-39, is a trenchant critique informed by a scholarly perspective, although written in a journalistic style. Common Cause published bulletins for its membership ten times a year: *Report from Washington* (1970-75) was superseded by the alternating periodicals, *In Common* and *Frontline*. In 1980 these periodicals were replaced by *Common Cause,* which appears six times a year. John W. Gardner's *In Common Cause* (New York: Norton, 1972) presents his early thoughts on Common Cause in a somewhat polemical fashion. Lawrence Gilson, *Money and Secrecy: A Citizen's Guide to Reforming State and Federal Practices* (New York: Praeger, 1972), was written by a Common Cause staffer and reflects the Common Cause point of view. Jeffrey M. Berry's *Lobbying for the People: The Political Behavior of Public Interest Groups* (Princeton: Princeton University Press, 1977) contains more than a dozen references to Common Cause. Norman J. Ornstein and Shirley Elder, *Interest Groups, Lobbying, and Policymaking* (Washington, D.C.: Congressional Quarterly, 1978), contains more than a score of references to Common Cause. Carol S. Greenwald, *Group Power: Lobbying and Public Policy* (New York: Praeger, 1977), also contains many references to Common Cause. At the political science department of Stanford University, Jonathan W. Siegel is writing a Ph.D. dissertation about Common Cause that emphasizes a comparison of its activists with other members.

2. John W. Gardner, *Exellence* (New York: Harper & Row, 196 (New York: Harper & Row, 1963).

3. See *Congressional Quarterly Almanac,* vol. 25 (Washington, D. Quarterly, 1970), 591.

4. Written response to the author's interview questions, August 1975.

5. Marttila, Payne, Kiley & Thorne, Inc., of Boston, Massachusetts, co phone interviews with 400 randomly selected Common Cause memb random elapsed members.

6. In the fall of 1971 a telephone survey of a random sample of the national ship (1164 completed interviews, original sample now unavailable) condu Daniel Yankelovich Inc. indicated that 57 percent of Common Cause member tified as Democrats, 21 percent as Republicans, and 22 percent as Independ The 1974 Marttila poll in Massachusetts indicated that 49 percent of memb in that state identified as Democrats, 16 percent as Republicans, and 32 perce as Independents. The partisan breakdown of all voters in the state was roughly 43 percent Democrat, 17 percent Republican, and 40 percent Independent.

7. Common Cause's field staff in 1977 believed that Common Cause played a significant role in enacting 160 state government reform bills.

8. Murray Edelman, *The Symbolic Uses of Politics* (Urbana: University of Illinois Press, 1974).

9. Cf. Paul Sabatier, "Social Movements and Regulatory Agencies: Toward a More Adequate—and Less Pessimistic—Theory of 'Clientele Capture,' " *Policy Sciences* 6 (September 1975): 301-42.

10. David Cohen and some other Common Cause leaders would disagree with this statement. I adhere to the usual view that the 92 new members of the House of Representatives elected during the Watergate year of 1974 were especially desirous of decentralizing power in Congress during the year after their election. Academic sources for this view can be found in *Congress Reconsidered,* ed. Lawrence C. Dodd and Bruce Oppenheimer (New York: Praeger, 1977). Because of the extraordinary desire by the members for changes in congressional procedures in the fall of 1974 and in 1975, it can be argued that reforms of this period would have passed even if Common Cause had not existed.

11. At first, Common Cause's national leadership tried to prevent lobbying of local governments because they feared such activity would disperse the organization's resources so that Common Cause would not be politically effective at either state or local levels. But it proved impossible to restrain state units from lobbying at the city level, and by 1982 local Common Cause units, with the approval of national staff, had lobbied for government reform issues in at least ten major cities.

12. See McFarland, *Public Interest Lobbies,* chap. 4.

13. Ibid.

14. A distinction between "structure and process" issues and "civil rights" issues is not a logical one, but it is a conventional one in American political culture. The term "political reformers" as used by journalists or academicians is not normally understood to refer to the black civil rights movement, for instance. Common Cause, on the other hand, is not referred to as a "civil rights group," even though its main goal is to enhance the power of the individual citizen vis-à-vis the power of political elites. Perhaps this conventional linguistic distinction relies on a perception

2. The Civic Reformers

Common Cause is not unique; it can be placed within the reform tradition of the Progressives and with local government reform groups.[1] Common Cause is a recent manifestation of the mobilization of elements of the American middle class who attempt to enhance democracy and effective government through the adoption of procedural reforms supported for reasons other than clear-cut economic gain. This has been an important political phenomenon since 1890.[2]

While there were similar groups before the Civil War, the middle-class civic reform tradition began after 1865 in reaction to the rapid industrialization and urban growth in northern and midwestern cities.[3] American traditions of local government did not provide ready answers to the problems of devising new or greatly expanded systems of sanitation, transportation, lighting, and public health and safety. Citizens of rapidly growing cities much preferred an extraordinary fragmentation of formal institutions of city government to the centralization of power under the authority of a strong mayor, an elite civil service, or local patrician families in alliance with the newly rich. Nevertheless, in most cities a political "machine," controlled by "bosses," got control of portions of local government by trading jobs and material goods for votes. Such bosses then made deals with individual entrepreneurs to provide trolleys, gas lighting, and even water systems. The result was frequent scandal and waste of public money. Local politicians and their franchise-holding friends were not averse to enriching themselves at the expense of the public. The result was what Lord Bryce called "the one conspicuous failure of the United States."[4]

By the 1890s, local political movements to end corruption, check the power of political bosses, and rewrite city charters were common. The author of *Municipal Reform Movements in the United States,* published in 1895, described seventy such movements.[5] There is little doubt that they were primarily middle class in character, although there is dispute about the amount of upper-class and working-class participation in urban government reform movements of the 1890s and later during the Progressive era (1901-14).[6]

During the Progressive years, the political activities of reformers in the cities were paralleled by similar activity by reformers at state and national levels.[7] The reform proposals of Progressive politicians, who based their power primarily on middle-class support, set the terms of political debate during the administrations of Theodore Roosevelt and William Howard Taft, and for the first two years of Woodrow Wilson's Presidency.

As part of their battle against the bosses and monopolistic "trusts," Progressives tried to reform political institutions so that government would be more responsive to the popular will. But their registration laws curbed voting turnout,[8] and their institutional forms did not appeal to immigrants, whom many Progressives regarded as ignorantly lacking the Anglo-Saxon appreciation of *the* public interest. The Progressives bequeathed to us primary elections and the popular election of U.S. senators, reforms that have pleased later generations. But they also left us with the initiative, the referendum, and devices to recall public officeholders, institutions whose merits are dubious to many observers. Progressives began the development of the city manager system of government, which was designed to place city administration in the hands of a professional manager and remove it from the grasp of patronage-oriented mayors and aldermen. Cities were run more efficiently and taxpayers saved more money, but at the cost of lessening the access of the ordinary person to the policy-making process because professional managers, unlike ward aldermen, were remote figures. Similarly, Progressives instituted nonpartisan local elections to undermine the power of their rivals, the party bosses. Nonpartisan elections often hurt the cause of political chieftains, but they also made voting more difficult for the average person, who was confronted with a welter of names on a ballot but no party label. Local celebrities and minority party leaders did better under this system of election, which few political scientists would now defend.[9]

Overall, the Progressives' reforms of government procedures are not an impressive contribution to the American heritage of democracy because their failures were about as great as their successes. The mixed record of the Progressives in the area of government reform is an underlying reason why some political scientists adopt a very critical attitude toward middle-class groups that aim to reform the procedures of government.[10]

The Progressive era ended as a great European war absorbed the political attention of Americans. After World War I, the political mood of the country was dominated by a return to "normalcy," and the 1920s were generally antireform, laissez faire, and probusiness years.

Nevertheless, middle-class-supported good-government groups at the local level continued to exist as a significant element in the panoply of political groups active in city politics. For example, New York City's Citizens Union, founded in 1897, has continued to press for such good-government measures as charter revisions, city government reorganization, the permanent registration of voters, greater autonomy by the city government in relation to state government, and air pollution control. The Citizens Union has used such tactics as endorsing candidates for city office, communicating its positions to news media, doing research on issues and candidates, attending City Council meetings, and lobbying city officials.[11] Founded in a reaction against machine government in the 1920s, the Charter party of Cincinnati has defended good-government measures for over fifty-five years and has made the City Council elections in Cincinnati a three-party affair. Established in 1920 to institutionalize the woman's suffrage movement, the League of Women Voters has since given its top priority to the political education of its members through discussion and action on political issues. Around 1930, the league began the practice of disseminating to the community the results of its studies, and by the late 1930s it devoted considerable effort to lobbying for the passage of government reform measures at local and occasionally national levels.[12]

Common Cause and the Reform Tradition

Placing Common Cause within the Progressive reform tradition offers two kinds of meaning. First, it underlines the realization that political movements and social changes in America are frequently initiated and supported mainly by elements of the middle class. This violates an expectation that is widespread in our culture: that it is the most deprived who are the most active in movements for social change. Second, viewing Common Cause as part of a Progressive reform tradition implies that the Common Cause program can be compared to the program of the Progressives.

The Common Cause program is subject to most of the problems incurred by the Progressives' good-government reforms and programs of local civic reformers. But this does not mean that some sort of inevitable logic of failure is at work. A major antidote to the repetition of the mistakes of the Progressives is the scholarly criticism of the Progressives' government reform program. True, the Common Cause leadership does not cite Richard Hofstadter or Robert K. Merton to one another in staff conferences, but most of the leaders have excellent educational backgrounds and have been lectured on the failures of Progressive reform by earnest historians, sociologists, and political scientists. Certainly all the leaders of the national staff are familiar with such basic ideas as procedural changes might have no effects, might have unanticipated negative consequences, might advantage the middle classes at the expense of the working classes, and so forth.

John Gardner was very concerned that Common Cause not repeat the mistakes of other reform groups. Gardner was influenced in his outlook on politics by David Truman's *The Governmental Process* and by the writings of V.O. Key, Jr., and Daniel Bell, who were familiar with Progressivism. [13] Moreover, Gardner was influenced by his experiences as head of HEW and the Urban Coalition. He determined that lobbying Congress was the most productive activity of the Urban Coalition. Common Cause was organized to carry on and expand the lobbying activities. As Gardner wrote: "All experts on government accept lobbying as a legitimate part of the political process. The problem is not that it exists but that it is almost always carried on in behalf of special interests. Everybody's organized but the people."[14] One criticism of civic reformers and the Progressives is that they were too inexperienced and too moralistic to engage in the hurly-burly of interest-group political bargaining for any significant length of time.[15] Gardner, aware of this problem, took care to give influential roles in Common Cause to experienced lobbyists and organizers in order to give Common Cause political sophistication and staying power.

Thus Common Cause emerged as a Washington-based lobbying organization. Nothing quite like it had existed in the turn-of-the-century Progressive era, nor had local civic reformers ever federated to lobby Congress. While placing Common Cause within the Progressive reform tradition, we must recognize that Common Cause embodies a new phenomenon within that tradition.

As an attempt to be a national lobby, combining idealism with a respect for pragmatic action and political skill, Common Cause was able to profit from the examples of labor, civil rights, and environmentalist lobbying. Gardner was impressed with civil rights and "conservationist" lobbyists when he was at HEW and had these organizations in mind when he established Common Cause.[16] He did not have labor in mind as a model, but within a year of the new organization's founding, he gave former labor lobbyists and organizers Jack Conway, David Cohen, and Jack Moskowitz influential positions. These men were certainly willing to use labor lobbying and organizing tactics that were appropriate for Common Cause.

Mistakes of the Progressives

Progressives' and civic reformers' mistakes may be repeated by Common Cause in the future, but so far it has avoided making most of them. Yet many people who know little about Common Cause caricature the public-interest lobby by assuming it repeats the mistakes of other reformers: "Common Cause is not effective," "Common Cause is too moralistic to engage in wheeling and dealing," and so forth. History need not repeat itself in precise fashion. Let us examine some of the mistakes of the Progressives and local-level civic reformers in relation to the activities of Common Cause.

The Error of Being Above Politics. In addition to being willing to engage in political bargaining, Gardner and his associates were willing to make alliances with former opponents, did not believe that passing laws ipso facto would solve a problem, and did not believe that establishing new governmental units or reorganizing old ones would accomplish much unless outside political pressure was applied. Some state leaders of Common Cause, however, have not been as flexible as the national leadership.

Belief in an Objective Public Interest. Citing the need to represent widespread but hard-to-organize interests provides a persuasive rationale for civic reform. Many Progressives went beyond this idea, however, to argue that they were representing *the* public interest in various situations.[17] Such an attitude tends to be associated with political inflexibility, which leads to failure in the politics of bargaining. Gardner and his associates thought of themselves as providing a countervailing power instead of representing *the* public interest in a situation. Such an attitude helped Common Cause lobbyists talk in a friendly way with such conservative legislators as Senators Barry Goldwater and William Brock, as well as the former head of the House Republicans, Representative John Rhodes.

Scientific Administration. The Progressives were suspicious of political bargaining. Accordingly, they were attracted to organizational schemes designed to help administer public policy in *the* public interest. Commission government and city manager government at the city level, planning, comprehensive budgeting schemes, formal devices such as the "span of control," the expansion of the civil service, and the like were lauded as "scientific" administration for "economy and efficiency."[18] But such ideas often had dubious merit because they presumed that political conflicts could be avoided; they tended to lessen the influence of lower-income groups that could not get access to "scientific" administrators; they demanded too much of human rationality in incredibly complex situations. Common Cause has proposed no scientific administration schemes as yet. But Common Cause could well make this mistake in conjunction with its "sunset" proposals and other ideas to reform public administration.

More and More Elections. The Progressives sought to increase the influence of the general public by increasing the number of elections. They instituted the direct election of senators and primaries, but they also established the initiative, referendum, and recall in many state and local jurisdictions. The Progressives also initiated nonpartisan elections, often for obscure positions, in many jurisdictions.[19] Their reliance on increasing the number of elections, in combination with strict voter registration practices, confused the ordinary voter and did not enhance his influence.

During the 1960s and 1970s, reformers seldom sought an increase in the number of elections, except in the case of the presidential primary after 1968. Common Cause staff and members generally approve of the increase in the number of presidential primaries after 1968, but Common Cause did not pressure state legislatures for this change. Accordingly, Common Cause should not be criticized for the negative aspects of having so many presidential primaries: that is, for decreasing the power of local party organizations, virtually requiring a candidate to campaign for a year before the nominating convention, and so forth.

The Anglo-Saxon Ethos. The Progressives and civic reformers have been frequently described as disproportionately of Anglo-Saxon background, which has enabled observers to freight descriptions of Progressivism with all sorts of interpretations (e.g., Progressives were "public-regarding" in their political attitudes rather than "private-regarding," [20] Progressives were "really" trying to reduce the political power of immigrants,[21] civic reform is "really" an expression of neopuritanism[22]). There is some truth to these interpretations. But I do not see how it can be helpful in understanding Common Cause to apply the Anglo-Saxon ethos interpretation, at least until more data are gathered about Common Cause. It is more useful to focus on the upper-middle-class aspects of Common Cause than its ethnicity.

Nevertheless, while the national staff of Common Cause contains many persons of Jewish and Catholic heritage, the national image projected by John Gardner had much in common with the figure of the Yankee minister fighting for the "social gospel" or the abolition of slavery, or with the Progressive figure of an intellectual-activist of the Woodrow Wilson ilk, coming from a staunch Protestant background. Moreover, two of Gardner's books, *Excellence* and *Self-Renewal,* stressed the personal virtues of striving for quality and achievement in the manner of traditional Protestantism.[23] But since there is no evidence that the Common Cause membership underrepresents those who are not Protestants, except insofar as they are underrepresented in the upper middle class, it might be observed that the image of the reform-minded intellectual Yankee appeals to many upper-middle-class Jews and Catholics (see chapter 3). It was, after all, Admiral Hyman Rickover who suggested to Jimmy Carter the maxim "Why not the best?"

Distance from Lower-Income Groups. The Progressives championed some reforms that helped the working classes: factory safety laws, workmen's compensation measures, and the regulation of child labor, for example. But the Progressives and civic reformers were insensitive to the fact that lower-income groups did not fare as well under Progressive good-government measures as did high-income groups. There had been more upward communication from the poor to the political machine chieftains than there was between the poor and a city manager or officials elected in nonpartisan elections.[24]

One of John Gardner's failings was that he did not sufficiently consider the possibility of conflicts of interest between elements of the Common Cause program and lower-income groups. Two possible conflicts are whether the regulation of lobbyists would weaken labor lobbyists and whether public funding of congressional races (possibly combined with low ceilings on campaign expenditures) might be a disservice to labor (see chapter 7). A former leader of Common Cause, David Cohen, *was* concerned about such questions, as we would expect from a one-time labor lobbyist. Cohen admitted that there were conflicts between Common Cause and labor lobbyists, such as disagreements over the Bolling-Martin congressional reform proposals;[25] California's Common Cause-sponsored government reform initative, Proposition 9, in 1974; the Ullman bill to tax gasoline;[26] and proposals to make lobbyists note in a log all their conversations with congressmen. Still, Cohen observed that Common Cause had few conflicts with the interests of labor as defined by reform-minded leaders of the United Auto Workers (the UAW), the American Federation of State, County, and Municipal Employees (AFSCME), and the American Federation of Teachers (AFT).

In sum, the national leaders of Common Cause have been generally successful in avoiding the mistakes of the Progressive reformers. Nevertheless, Common Cause has tendencies that could lead it to engage in scientific administration rhetoric and avoid considering whether its program would weaken the spokespersons for the working class. Some state organizations are more prone to repeat the mistakes of the Progressives than is the present national organization.

Why Common Cause Began in 1970

Given the existence of an American Progressive reform tradition and numerous local civic reform groups, one might wonder why a national good-government lobby was not founded before 1970. After some examination, it becomes evident that organizing a national government reform lobby is more difficult than might be imagined. The National Municipal League was founded in 1894 as a federation of persons concerned about government reform in their various cities of residence. But the NML concentrated its efforts in research and in communicating ideas among scholars and city officials; it was not a lobby.[27] The League of Women Voters, established to institutionalize the woman's suffrage movement after the extension of the franchise, did lobby Congress for good-government measures, but its impact has not been strong there in the institutional reform area. The league's first priority has been the civic education of its members and other voters in the local community. Moreover, the league has probably put more resources into lobbying for good government at state and local levels than at the national level. Thus the league has not had a lot of organizational resources to devote to lobbying Congress for procedural reforms. The establishment of a mass-membership national lobbying group for the reform of government in 1970 represents a significant novelty within the Progressive tradition.

Common Cause was started by the right man at the right time. When it became known in June 1970 that John Gardner was planning to found a mass-membership citizens' lobby in the public interest, almost everyone in Washington thought the idea would not work. Even some in Gardner's immediate circle at the Urban Coalition Action Council expected failure.

August 1970 turned out to be a particularly propitious time to launch such an effort. As we know now, the constituency for a general-purpose citizens' lobby would be predominately upper-middle-class professionals, generally holding to liberal social beliefs. At that time, during the second year of the Nixon administration and shortly after the turmoil created by the American "incursion" into Cambodia and the shootings at Kent State University, the potential constituency for Common Cause was extremely disaffected from the federal government. Many were looking for new ways of expressing their dissatisfaction, but they were not attracted to demonstrations or more radical protest.

The summer of 1970 saw at least one other effort to form an organization that might have resembled Common Cause. Andrew Maguire, formerly a Democratic congressman from New Jersey, and a group of friends started an organization of young professionals to lobby for peace and to "reorder our national priorities," as it was called at the time. (This was before Maguire was elected to the House.) One of the people Maguire consulted about how to form such an organization was David Cohen, then a lobbyist for Jack Conway's Center for Community Change, a lobby for urban issues. But Maguire and his friends, in all about fifty people, merged their incipient organization with Gardner's Common Cause because they recognized that Gardner was trying to do much the same thing as they, but was much farther along in the process of organizing.[28]

Maguire's experience indicates the critical importance of Gardner's role in founding Common Cause. Even among those who thought a national citizens' lobby could be formed, few besides Gardner could have raised $250,000 or more for mailing and newspaper advertisements, inspired confidence among the constituency of educated professionals who would be attracted to such an organization, commanded outstanding speaking and writing skills, and been able to assemble the competent staff that coalesced around the Urban Coalition.

Another circumstance was propitious for the founding of Common Cause. The country was pulling out of a minor recession, and so the potential constituency for Common Cause was not especially worried about finances. The early 1970s were good years for getting the public to contribute to public-interest lobbies. Getting contributions in later years was more difficult as people worried more about the economy and their financial futures.

Technology also helps explain why Common Cause developed in 1970 rather than in 1960, 1950, or even earlier. Three technological developments were important in the initiation and maintenance of Common Cause.

The expansion of national television news during the 1960s contributed to the vividness of experiencing faraway events. Among well-educated professionals accustomed to effective action, vividly experiencing repugnant events frequently produced a desire "to do something," which was alleviated by sending a check of $15 to Gardner and engaging in Common Cause's letter-writing campaigns. During the late 1960s, reform-oriented liberals had to watch on their television screens the Vietnam war, assassinations, riots in ghettos and on campuses, and environmental desecration. Their preferred political candidate—perhaps a liberal Democrat or a Republican like Rockefeller or Lindsay—was to lose out to Nixon and Agnew, whose visages appeared daily on the news. Later, the spectacle of Watergate on television enhanced the tendency of many people "to do something" by joining Common Cause.

Another technological development that facilitated the founding of Common Cause was computer-based direct-mailing.[29] By the end of 1983 Common Cause had sent out about 82 million solicitations to join the Cause. This would have been extremely difficult to do without the computerized mailing lists acquired from current-events periodicals and membership groups. Computers also keep track of the Common Cause membership, breaking down members by congressional district, which facilitates local organizing. Local leaders are provided with a monthly list of members living in their district, and with a list of those who have moved out of or into the district. In addition, by means of computers, Common Cause can readily send mailings to members residing within a given state in order to get letters sent to the two U.S. senators or the state legislature.

A third technological breakthrough that facilitated the organizing of Common Cause was relatively cheap, reliable, and quick long-distance telephone communication. Common Cause depends on coordinating the observations of its Washingtonian "insider" lobbyists with its capacity to organize letters and other pressures in individual congressional districts. In 1981 Common Cause rented eleven Wide Area Telephone System (WATS) lines at monthly flat rates to communicate with its local branches. Had the Washington headquarters and local units been forced to communicate by mail and telegram, the organization would have lost much of the liveliness and immediacy induced by regular conversations between local and headquarters personnel. In addition, some Common Cause "alerts," requests to pressure congressmen, must be carried out by telephone because the mails are too slow to deal with the exigencies of parliamentary maneuvering. Telegrams might do, but they are prohibitively expensive because complex legislative situations cannot be clearly summarized in a few words.

Once Common Cause had some lobbying success, in its solicitations for membership it could portray itself as a politically effective lobby, a description that helped get more members. The new members in turn strengthened the lobbying effort. Thus the initial successes of the citizens' lobby, once established, helped produce further successes in gaining members and influence.

Common Cause was not originally intended to be a government reform lobby. As we noted, Common Cause was organized to lobby for a wide range of goals including government reform, an end to the war in Vietnam, environmentalism, social welfare measures, and rights for minorities. But had Common Cause originally advertised as a lobby for procedural reform, in the context of widespread anger over Cambodia and Kent State, many people would never have joined. Such a program would have seemed irrelevant and dull. Many became members because of their dislike for the Nixon administration, and remained members because they became convinced of the need for a major lobbying effort to reform governmental institutions.

The establishment and maintenance of Common Cause says much about the decline in people's trust in our national political institutions. The data in tables 2.1 and 2.2 show this decline graphically. While there is a possibility that the distrust is not as deep-seated among the upper middle class as among other groups, polls taken of Common Cause members indicate that they tend to respond in a fashion similar to national random samples.

The increasing distrust of political institutions among Americans is reflected in a significant tendency to respond to the mailed solicitations of Common Cause, which stress a "you can't trust our government to do what's right" message. It should be noted that although a person might state his low trust in government to a survey researcher, this does not necessarily imply that the respondent will drop out of politics. On the contrary, he might become active in support of a candidate who expresses a skeptical point of view and who appears to be different from the usual breed of "untrustworthy" politicians. Sending Common Cause $15 is another type of political action such a citizen could take.

In sum, Common Cause was formed in 1970 but could not have been founded earlier. The right leadership, technological advances, an initial success that promoted the image of political effectiveness, and a growing distrust of national political institutions followed a disastrous war and a scandal-ridden administration to produce the optimum moment for the creation of a national citizens' lobby.[30]

TABLE 2.1

Decline of Popular Trust in Social Institutions:
Harris Survey Responses

Question: I want to read you some things some people have told us they have felt from time to time. Do you tend to feel or not feel:

	Percentage of Voters Agreeing			
	1966	1972	1973	1974
The rich get richer and the poor get poorer?	45	68	76	79
Special interests get more from the government than the people do?	n.a.[a]	n.a.	74	78
The tax laws are written to help the rich, not the average man?	n.a.	74	74	75
The people running the country don't really care what happens to you?	26	50	55	63
Most elective officials are in politics for all they personally can get out of it for themselves?	n.a.	n.a.	60	62
What you think doesn't count much anymore?	37	53	61	60
You feel left out of things going on around you?	9	25	29	32

SOURCE: "Public Disaffection at Record High," *The Harris Survey,* released 27 June 1974. Cited by Jack Dennis, "Trends in Support for the American Party System," *British Journal of Political Science* 5 (April 1975): 227.
    a. n.a. = not available.

TABLE 2.2

Decline of Popular Trust in Government: Survey Responses (in percent)

Question: How much of the time do you think you can *trust* government in Washington to do what is right—*just about always, most of the time,* or *only some of the time?*

Response	1964	1966	1968	1970
Always	14.0	17.0	7.5	6.4
Most of the time	62.0	48.0	53.4	47.1
Only some of the time[a]	22.0	31.0	37.0	44.2
Don't know	2.0	4.0[b]	2.1	2.3
total	100.0	100.0	100.0	100.0
(N)[c]	(4658)	(1291)	(1557)	(1514)

Question: Would you say that the government is pretty much run by a *few big interests* looking out for themselves or that it is run for the *benefit of all* the people?

Response	1964	1966	1968	1970
For benefit of all	64.0	53.0	51.8	40.6
Few big interests[a]	29.0	34.0	39.2	49.6
Other; depends; both checked	4.0	6.0	4.6	5.0
Don't know	3.0	7.0	4.3	4.8
Total	100.0	100.0	100.0	100.0

Question: Do you think that people in the government waste *a lot* of the money we pay in taxes, waste *some* of it, or *don't waste very much of it?*[d]

Response	1964	1966	1968	1970
Not much	6.5	—	4.2	3.7
Some	44.5	—	33.1	26.1
A lot[a]	46.3	—	57.4	68.7
Don't know; not ascertained	2.7	—	5.3	1.5
Total	100.0	—	100.0	100.0

Question: Do you feel that almost all of the people running the government are smart people who usually *know what they are doing,* or do you think that quite a few of them *don't seem to know what they are doing?*[d]

Response	1964	1966	1968	1970
Know what they're doing	68.2	—	56.2	51.2
Don't know what they're doing[a]	27.4	—	36.1	44.1

TABLE 2.2 *(continued)*

	1964	1966	1968	1970
Other; depends	1.9	—	1.8	2.3
Don't know; not ascertained	2.5	—	5.9	2.4
Total	100.0		100.0	100.0

Question: Do you think that *quite a few* of the people running the government are a little crooked, that *not very many* are, or that *hardly any* of them are crooked at all?[d]

Response	1964	1966	1968	1970
Hardly any	18.2	—	18.4	15.9
Not many	48.4	—	49.3	48.8
Quite a lot[a]	28.0	—	24.8	31.0
Don't know; not ascertained	5.4	—	7.5	4.3
Total	100.0		100.0	100.0

a. Indicates response interpreted as "cynical."
b. Includes 1 percent coded "It depends."
c. The sample size for each of the years applies to all five items. The 1964 N is weighted.
d. These items were not included in the 1966 election study interview schedule.

SOURCE: Arthur H. Miller, "Political Issues and Trust in Government: 1964-70," *American Political Science Review* 68 (September 1974): 953. The data were compiled from national sample surveys of eligible voters conducted by the University of Michigan Survey Research Center. Used by permission of the American Political Science Association.

NOTES

1. My interpretation of Progressivism relies heavily on the perspective of Robert H. Wiebe, *The Search for Order* (New York: Hill and Wang, 1967). Also influential in determining my point of view is Richard Hofstadter's *The Age of Reform: From Bryan to F.D.R.* (New York: Vintage, 1955), and a variety of work emphasizing politics: George E. Mowry, *The Era of Theodore Roosevelt, 1900-1912* (New York: Hill and Wang, 1958); Arthur S. Link, *Woodrow Wilson and the Progressive Era, 1910-1917* (New York: Harper, 1954); John Morton Blum, *The Republican Roosevelt* (Cambridge, Mass.: Harvard University Press, 1954); and idem, *Woodrow Wilson and the Politics of Morality* (Boston: Little, Brown, 1956).
2. See Wiebe, *The Search for Order*, 111-95, esp. 149; Hofstadter, *The Age of Reform*, 164-214; Clifford W. Patton, *The Battle for Municipal Reform* (College Park, Md.: McGrath, 1969); and Edward C. Banfield and James Q. Wilson, *City Politics* (Cambridge, Mass.: Harvard University Press, 1965), chap. 11.
3. Wiebe, *The Search for Order*, chaps. 1-7.
4. Cited in Hofstadter, *The Age of Reform*, 176.

5. William Howe Tolman, *Municipal Reform Movements in the United States* (New York: F. H. Revell, 1895), cited in ibid., 165.

6. Some have argued that Progressivism was substantially upper class in its character. See James Weinstein, *The Corporate Ideal and the Liberal State, 1900-1918* (Boston: Beacon, 1968); and Samuel P. Hays, "The Politics of Reform in Municipal Government in the Progressive Era," *Pacific Northwest Quarterly* 55 (October 1964): 157-69. Others have pointed to urban working-class support for Progressivism. See J. Joseph Huthmacher, "Urban Liberalism and the Age of Reform," *Mississippi Valley Historical Review* 44 (September 1962): 231-41; and John D. Buenker, *Urban Liberalism and Progressive Reform* (New York: Scribner's, 1973). Thelen has stressed the community-wide support for municipal reform in cities and towns in Wisconsin in the 1890s. See David P. Thelen, *The New Citizenship* (Columbia: University of Missouri Press, 1972).

7. Wiebe, *The Search for Order,* 164-81, 196-201.

8. Stanley Kelley, Jr., Richard E. Ayres, and William G. Bowen, "Registration and Voting: Putting First Things First," *American Political Science Review* 61 (June 1967): 359-77, esp. 374.

9. Banfield and Wilson, *City Politics,* chap. 12.

10. For example, see Nelson W. Polsby and Aaron Wildavsky, *Presidential Elections,* 4th ed. (New York: Scribner's, 1976), chap. 6 and p. 19.

11. Wallace S. Sayre and Herbert Kaufman, *Governing New York City* (New York: Russell Sage, 1960), 497-502.

12. John Grumm, "The History and Function of the League of Women Voters" (M.A. thesis, Department of Political Science, University of California, Berkeley, 1952).

13. David B. Truman, *The Governmental Process* (New York: Knopf, 1951); V.O. Key, Jr., *Politics, Parties, and Pressure Groups,* 5th ed. (New York: Crowell, 1964); Daniel Bell, *The End of Ideology,* rev. ed. (New York: Collier, 1962).

14. John W. Gardner, *In Common Cause* (New York: Norton, 1972), 80.

15. While I have heard political scientists express this opinion, it does not often get into print. But it is a reasonable extrapolation from such sources as Hofstadter, *The Age of Reform,* 203-14; and Alexander L. George and Juliette L. George, *Woodrow Wilson and and Colonel House: A Personality Study* (New York: John Day, 1956). A similar argument has been applied to the liberal Democrats of reform clubs by Wilson and to supporters of Barry Goldwater, Eugene McCarthy, and George McGovern by Polsby and Wildavsky. See James Q. Wilson, *The Amateur Democrat* (Chicago: University of Chicago Press, 1962); and Polsby and Wildavsky, *Presidential Elections,* 29-40.

16. In addition, Tom Mathews, Gardner's public relations consultant, pointed out the relevance of the fund-raising success through direct mail appeals of the Center for the Study of Democratic Institutions (then in Santa Barbara, California).

17. Hofstadter, *The Age of Reform,* 257-61; Banfield and Wilson, *City Politics,* 139-40, 153-55.

18. Wiebe, *The Search for Order,* 169-77; and Dwight Waldo, *The Administrative State* (New York: Ronald, 1948).

19. Hofstadter, *The Age of Reform,* 257, 258, 266.

20. Banfield and Wilson, *City Politics,* 38-45, 154-55, 234-40.

21. Hofstadter, *The Age of Reform,* 174-86. But John D. Buenker chronicles cases in

which immigrant-supported political machines backed Progressive reforms, either because they alleviated harsh conditions in the factory or because they served the interests of urban machines in struggles with rurally based politicians for control of statewide political parties. See Buenker, *Urban Liberalism and Progressive Reform.*

22. Hofstadter, *The Age of Reform,* 204-14.

23. See David C. McClelland, *The Achieving Society* (Princeton, N.J.: Van Nostrand, 1961).

24. See, for example, Robert K. Merton, *Social Theory and Social Structure,* rev. ed. (Glencoe, Ill.: Free Press, 1957), 70-82; Banfield and Wilson, *City Politics,* chap. 9; and Hays, "Politics of Reform in Municipal Government." Hays is the only one of the three who explicitly contrasts the position of the poor under machine politics with their position under the reform systems of the Progressives.

25. "Major House Reform Rejected," in *The Congressional Quarterly Almanac,* vol. 30 (Washington, D.C.: Congressional Quarterly, 1975), 634-40.

26. See *The Congressional Quarterly Almanac,* vol. 31 (Washington, D.C.: Congressional Quarterly, 1976), 207-19.

27. Frank Mann Stewart, *A Half Century of Municipal Reform: The History of the National Municipal League* (Berkeley: University of California Press, 1950).

28. Interview with Congressman Maguire, July 1975.

29. See Robert Cameron Mitchell, "National Environmental Lobbies and the Apparent Illogic of Collective Action," in *Collective Decision Making: Applications from Public Choice Theory,* ed. Clifford S. Russell (Baltimore: Johns Hopkins University Press, 1979).

30. A similar but more general discussion of why public interest groups organized nationally appears in Andrew S. McFarland, *Public Interest Lobbies: Decision Making on Energy* (Washington, D.C.: American Enterprise Institute, 1976), 12-24.

3. The Members

Who would wish to join a nationwide civic reform association? What are such Americans like? What characteristics do they share? Let us begin our examination of the Common Cause membership by looking at the graph depicted in figure 3.1. The ebb and flow of membership over time can then be briefly described.

There was a rush to join in the beginning; 100,000 became members in the first six months, and six months later, 200,000 were members. Membership fell about 15 percent during 1972 and then rose markedly at the beginning of 1973. New members continued to join until Nixon's resignation in August 1974. Membership then declined by about 40 percent over the five-year period up to the summer of 1979. For the next three years, membership fluctuated between 203,000 and 220,000, and then began a rapid rise in the spring of 1982 to the present level of over a quarter million members.[1]

We can infer why people join Common Cause from changes in the number of members, from the content of direct-mail solicitations and newspaper advertisements, and from data gathered by surveys. Recall from our overview in chapter 1 that we are discussing a constituency that is largely over fifty years of age, upper middle class, well educated, living on the Northeastern Seaboard or the Pacific Coast, liberal in opinions, and probably has a significant number of liberal Republicans. An analysis of the solicitations mailed by Common Cause is relevant to an understanding of reasons for joining because all such mail is pretested. That is, various themes are pretested, the most successful theme is selected, and then various presentations of the successful theme are also pretested. Thus direct-mail solicitations are the result of experiments devised to determine which appeals draw the largest response from the public.

One theme that is common in recruitment mailings from Common Cause can be traced back to the Progressive reformers of the early twentieth century, who frequently reiterated the view that *the* public interest needed representation to counteract the corrupt influence of political machines and corporate trusts. A continuity in the Progressive reform tradition is that Common Cause (and other public-interest groups) use similar rhetoric in their call for the need to represent "public interests" to balance the political power of "special inter-

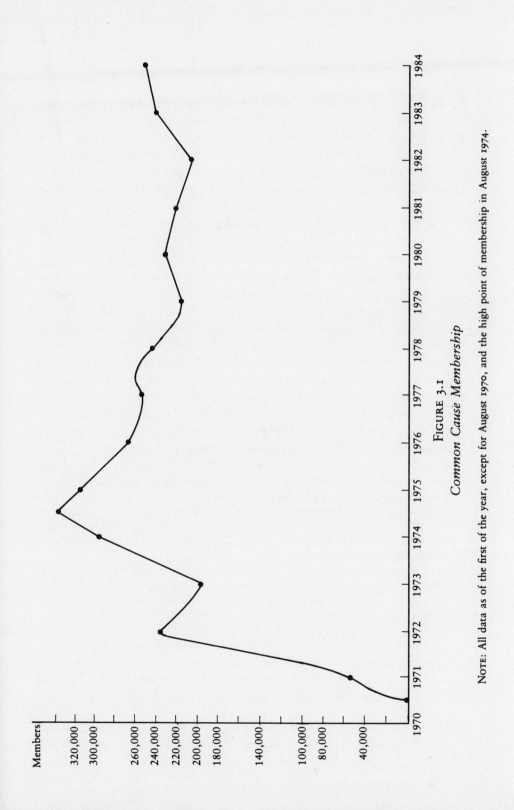

FIGURE 3.1
Common Cause Membership

NOTE: All data as of the first of the year, except for August 1970, and the high point of membership in August 1974.

ests." This language springs from a view I have called the theory of "civic balance."[2]

Civic balance is an interpretation of American politics and the power structure. Speakers and writers from lobbies, consumer groups, and environmentalist groups constantly refer to conflicts between special interests and public interests. They claim that special interests tend to control particular areas of policy unless public interests are organized. The role of public-interest groups, in this view, is to intervene in politics to redress the balance of power to the benefit of the public.

To illustrate what is meant by this, let us examine some mass mailings sent out by Common Cause. These mailings represent a major financial investment; they are written with great care; they are pretested on sample groups of the intended target population. Such mailings are at least moderately successful in persuading upper-middle-class Americans to contribute money to a public-interest group.

An early Common Cause mailing, designed to attract new contributors, was headlined: *Common Cause: Modern Americans Fighting for Principles as Old as the Republic.* The text was printed on an elegant ten-page brochure designed to fit inside a standard business envelope. Almost 2 million copies of the brochure were mailed. From the beginning, the text carries the theme of special interests versus "people's" interests and stresses the need for citizens' organizations to attain a more representative form of government. I have italicized such emphases within the quoted material.

> Our nation's founders did not leave us a completed task . . . they left us a beginning. It is our obligation to define and dislodge the modern obstacles to the fulfillment of our founding principles. Because, as visionary as they were, our founders could not have foreseen *how dominant special interests would become* through the accumulation of wealth and power, and through skillful secret dealings with government officials.
>
> In the face of this, people like you and me — people who reject apathy and cynicism — must join forces to fight for open and accountable government. How? By joining Common Cause and supporting our efforts to create direct and immediate changes in the political system.

The message continues, accompanied by a full-page picture of one of America's founding fathers, Benjamin Rush, Treasurer of the U.S. Mint, who is quoted as saying that "the influence of wealth at elections is irresistible." The text that follows is a particularly direct statement of the civic balance belief system:

> THANKS TO COMMON CAUSE, THE INFLUENCE OF WEALTH IN ELECTIONS IS SHRINKING. In Benjamin Rush's day, money could influence elections. A century and a

half later, it could dominate them. By lavishing contributions on candidates, well heeled *special interests* came to exercise decisive leverage over the outcome of elections. Matched against this enormous power, the principle of fair elections often proved a feeble challenger.

That is, until Common Cause changed the odds by strengthening the *people's interest* through election reforms.

Our members threw themselves behind the cause of campaign finance reform. Our highly skilled lobbyists *pressured* Congress. Our volunteers monitored campaigns throughout the country. And our staff disclosed the cozy relationships between candidates and *special interest* contributors.

It should be noted that John Gardner became uneasy over connotations of the term "the public interest" and substituted "the people's interest." It is also noteworthy that Gardner referred to Common Cause as having "pressured" Congress, indicating the expressly political orientation of Common Cause, in contrast to the apolitical Progressive reformers, who advocated "scientific management" in the "public interest" (see chapter 2).

Civic balance is further expounded on the next page of text, where it is applied to Congress:

> Congress was never intended to be a bulwark against *the people's interests*. But a self-perpetuating system of favors and rewards caused its committee structure to become just that. Committee chairmen who favored *special interests* were richly rewarded with campaign contributions. With better financing than their challengers, they repeatedly won re-election. In turn, they used the power of their seniority to side with *the special interests*. Common Cause was determined to dismantle this structure by toppling its two strongest pillars: seniority and secrecy.

Gardner, who closely supervised membership solicitations, stressed civic balance ideas from the beginning, as is evident in an *Everybody's Organized but the People* newspaper ad of 1970, which was extremely successful and was the prototype for much subsequent Common Cause solicitation. A framed copy of the ad hung in the conference room at Common Cause for a decade. At the top of the page was the headline (quoted above). In the middle of the page was a medium-size picture of Gardner bearing the caption: "After spending the last five years in Washington as Secretary of Health, Education, and Welfare and as Chairman of the Urban Coalition, John Gardner is convinced that only an aroused and organized citizenry can revitalize 'the System' and change the nation's disastrous course." The text of the ad read:

> John Gardner asks you to join him in building a mighty "Citizen's Lobby," concerned not with the advancement of special interests but with the well-being of the nation.

. . . [Common Cause] is not a third party, but a third force in American life which upholds the public interest against all comers, particularly the special interests that dominate our national life today. Common Cause does not support candidates; it confines itself to issues.

Wherever you touch the public process in this country today, almost without exception, you will find a failure of performance. The air we breathe is foul. The water we drink is impure. . . . We take the phrase "Common Cause" seriously. The things that unite us as a people are more important than the things that divide us. No particular interest group can prosper for long if the nation is disintegrating. Every group must have an overriding interest in the well-being of the whole society. . . .

One of our aims is to revitalize politics and government. The need is great. State governments are mostly feeble. City government is archaic. The Congress of the United States is in grave need of overhaul. We can no longer accept such obsolescence. . . .

Thus early Common Cause ads and mailings stressed ideas about special-interest rule, the need to reform government, the need to reorder national priorities, the positive symbol of John Gardner as a man of integrity, and implicitly, the failure of the Nixon administration to deal with society's basic problems.

I think it is safe to hypothesize that most members of Common Cause share Gardner's civic balance beliefs. Themes that stress the undue power of special interests have been effective in getting people to contribute to Common Cause. In addition, a poll of the members (cited more fully later in this chapter) found them to agree overwhelmingly with three items that are closely related to civic balance beliefs. Thus, 83 percent of the members agreed that "there is too much waste and giveaway programs at the expense of taxpayers." Second, 89 percent agreed that "big business has too much influence on how the country is run." A massive 93 percent agreed that "there's too much bureaucracy and favoritism." But members were divided over the question whether the federal government was uninterested in the welfare of the citizenry. In response to "people in the federal government are looking out for themselves and their friends and aren't interested in people like myself," 53 percent agreed and 44 percent disagreed, with 3 percent uncertain.

In addition to the theme of civic balance, the early recruitment mailings stressed joining Common Cause as a way of working to end the war in Vietnam. Polls of members in the fall of 1970 indicated that they were overwhelmingly opposed to American involvement in Vietnam. This corresponded to the opinions of the staff and the first national board. Accordingly, in 1971 Common Cause heavily stressed opposition to the Vietnamese war in its solicitations. In another Common Cause ad that was framed and hung in the organization's conference room, an antiwar pitch is made so heavily that Common

Cause is not even mentioned in the first sixty lines of copy, even though the purpose of the ad was to persuade people to join. The ad is headlined by a typical citizenship message: *Only One Person Can End the War.* Then, after a space and in smaller type, the answer appears: *You.* In the center of the ad, a framed box announces: "A recent Gallup poll showed: 73 percent of the people want all our troops home by the end of this year. Can you imagine what would happen if they all spoke up?" The text of the ad reads:

> Yes, you. The average American who has felt so powerless up until now.
>
> As a matter of fact, the more average-American you are, the more power you have to influence events at this crucial moment in American history.
>
> The Gallup poll of January 31st [1971] showed that 73 percent of the American people want all U.S. troops brought home from Indochina before the end of this year.
>
> 73 percent of the people. You can't get much more average-American than that. Now all you have to do is *ask for it.*
>
> If you speak up, it means that other Americans like you will speak up. But if you remain silent, you have no right to expect anyone else to open his mouth.
>
> Congress can and should act.
>
> The battle of public opinion has been won. Now we must organize for a legislative end to the war. . . .

A Yankelovich poll of Common Cause members in the fall of 1971 indicated that "getting out of Vietnam" was the choice of a plurality of members as their lobbying priority. This was the choice of 39 percent of Democratic members, with structure and process reforms coming in second among Democrats with 24 percent. Republicans were also antiwar, but somewhat less so, as 33 percent of Republicans preferred good-government reforms as the top priority, with 32 percent preferring the antiwar effort. Still, these data indicate that a significant motivation for joining Common Cause was the disgust felt by antiwar liberals, Republicans as well as Democrats, with the Nixon administration.

An inference can be made that "bridging the generation gap" on the Vietnam issue was an important motive for joining Common Cause in 1970 and 1971. There is no direct information to support this observation, but it is probable from these and other data. In the early 1970s the typical Common Cause member was a liberal upper-middle-class person, middle-aged and educated, who lived in metropolitan New York or a California suburb. Such people were frequently the parents of college students alienated from the Nixon administration and vociferously opposed to the American involvement in Vietnam. To the parents, joining Common Cause may have been a gesture (or a heartfelt action) to demonstrate to their children that "we too care" but that obnoxious policies should be opposed by action "within the system."

The Yankelovich poll of the early Common Cause membership found that 90 percent of those polled agreed that Common Cause was "unique," and 65 percent agreed that it was "neither establishment nor protest" in nature. These findings indicate that as many as half of the members regarded Common Cause as an unusual organization and that they were attracted to it as a means of expressing opposition to the Nixon administration in an orderly way.

Opposition to the Nixon administration's Watergate policies was a powerful incentive to join Common Cause in 1973 and 1974. Membership had fallen 15 percent during 1972, but it began rising in early 1973 and continued to rise until August 1974. Solicitations stressed joining Common Cause as a means of opposing the Nixon administration's conduct on Watergate. Except for the first rush to join in 1970, they were the most successful in the organization's history. During the Watergate period, getting new members was so easy that it was difficult for the national staff of Common Cause to adjust to the need for working hard to retain members after Nixon's resignation.

In the spring of 1971, Common Cause literature began to stress joining the organization as a means of effective participation in national politics. Participation messages were efficiency oriented—join Common Cause and use your time and money effectively to make an "impact" on decisions—rather than face-to-face participatory. This kind of participation motivation was frequent; 28 percent of respondents in one poll gave participation responses in stating their chief reason for joining Common Cause.

An example of an early participation message is this mailed solicitation sent at the end of 1971:

> We invite you to join us. We are Americans who don't believe that mere complaining gets results. We intend to *do* something to get this nation back on its course. Many things are wrong. Many things must be done to correct them. And wishing *won't* make it happen. Action will. Our institutions don't move unless we push them—and push them hard.
>
> So we're pushing.
>
> . . . *On political campaign spending*—Common Cause has filed a suit against the major political parties for evading the present laws concerning campaign spending ceilings. . . .
>
> . . . *On congressional reform*—Common Cause was a major factor in making the tyrannical and archaic seniority system in Congress a national issue, and is credited by both Congress and the press with helping produce the first real crack in that system.
>
> . . . *On voting rights*—Common Cause was the chief citizen organization lobbying for the Constitutional Amendment to give 18-year-olds the right to vote. After the Amendment overwhelmingly passed both the Senate and the House, we fought for ratification state by state. No Amendment was ever ratified more swiftly.

> . . . *On the Vietnam war* — Common Cause has sought legislative action to name a date certain for withdrawal from Indochina — and has pursued that goal through an extensive advertising campaign and a television program to bring the message to the people. Common Cause also organized the first effort in the House of Representatives for withdrawal from Indochina.
>
> . . . *On the SST* — "Common Cause deserves a world of credit for the tremendous job it played in rallying opposition to the SST and winning the fight." — Senator William Proxmire. . . .
>
> As you have gathered by now, we don't just take positions. We enter into battle and there are a lot of battles that need to be fought. . . .

Such solicitations follow the custom of favorable letters of recommendation — they are based on truth but stretch the truth somewhat to the benefit of the recommended party. For examples, the statements in the quote are accurate in regard to activity on campaign spending, Vietnam, and the SST, but the congressional reform assertion would have been "truer" if it stated that Common Cause was the major group, outside Congress, working to reform the seniority system. Common Cause's major successes on congressional reform occurred three years after this letter. Similarly, the amendment to lower the voting age would have passed without trouble even if Common Cause had not been in existence.

Some of the Common Cause membership might be called "public contributors." According to one Common Cause source about half of the contributors to Ralph Nader's Public Citizen also give to Common Cause. (This works out to about one-fifth of Common Cause members giving also to Nader.) Many of the Common Cause contributors — in Massachusetts, about 10 percent — also give to the American Civil Liberties Union. And in the mid-1970s, 15 percent of Common Cause members were also members of the League of Women Voters.

Common Cause rents the membership lists of public television and radio station contributors, who, they feel, are among those most likely to join Common Cause. In fact, there seem to be 100,000 households in the country that contribute a total of at least $75 a year to three or more of the following: Common Cause, Nader's Public Citizen, LWV, ACLU, public television/radio, and environmentalist lobbies. Such contributions buy the right to participate in LWV discussions or Sierra Club fringe benefits (charter air fares and so forth), but usually these contributors get little more than moral satisfaction in return. A culture of public contribution has grown up among such households, perhaps for reasons similar to those underlying the rise of public-interest lobbies — a civic balance belief system, personal prosperity, a belief in the effectiveness of such groups, and a generally high educational level. The idea that a household should contribute significant amounts annually to public-interest organizations surely has benefited Common Cause.

The specific membership of Common Cause is interesting. About half of those who join do not renew their membership at the end of the first year (45 percent in 1982). Yet the renewal rate is 78 percent for all members, indicating that long-time members renew at a high rate (see table 3.1).

TABLE 3.1
Renewal Rates of Membership

Length of Membership	Percent Renewal
1 year	55
5 years	83
6 years	85
10 years	92
11 years	94

Common Cause has a hard core of particularly loyal contributors, who have given every year for several years (see table 3.2).

TABLE 3.2
Length of Consecutive Membership

Length of Membership	Number of Members	Percent
0-1 year	81,600	34
2-4 years	52,800	22
5-9 years	69,600	29
10-12 years	36,000	15

NOTE: The number of members was calculated from a rounded number of 240,000, the approximate number of members in December 1982. As the table indicates, the typical member has contributed for four consecutive years.

By January 1978, 375,000 people who at one time were members of Common Cause had dropped their membership. Common Cause had about 250,000 members at that time, and so this meant that for every two current members, there were three former members. In all, about 625,000 people had contributed to the organization at least once. This figure excludes 112,000 spouses in "Mr. and Mrs." memberships. In 1977 the organization, realizing how large a number of former members it had, began telephoning former members and asking them to rejoin. This proved to be an effective way to maintain membership levels.

Multiyear members (more than three years of consecutive membership) become part of a "Common Cause culture," a phrase used by the national staff. In other words, whatever their original motivations for joining, such relatively permanent members come to share the organization's definitions of political situations and the worthiness of the responses to such situations. The Common Cause culture can be summarized as a civic balance belief system and its program as the attempt to control special interests through structure and process reforms.

During the 1970s, a Common Cause member who belonged to the group for three years received 18 organizational bulletins, 12 pamphlets on specific issues, and 20 other pieces of communication (e.g., bulletins about state units, special appeals, and the annual package of materials for electing the national board).

One interesting poll taken in 1974 (see table 3.3) indicates why people had joined Common Cause in the early 1970s. Many of these people are, of course, still Common Cause members.

TABLE 3.3
Why Did You Join Common Cause?

	Total Percent	Members	Former Members
Someone suggested it	7	5	11
John Gardner	13	13	14
Watergate/national issues	11	12	9
Believe in aims	23	26	19
One way to fight lobbies	3	4	3
Wanted to feel had say in government	28	27	30
Impressed by literature	3	3	1
Other	8	8	8

The most striking fact is the 28 percent of the people who joined Common Cause wanted to have a feeling of participation in government. The survey also confirmed my impression that belief in John Gardner was an important reason for joining. When the poll was conducted, all the solicitations by mail were still signed by Gardner.

At least two other political scientists are now further exploring the reasons people give when they explain why they joined Common Cause.[3]

One factor that facilitates joining Common Cause is the relatively high income of the membership. Thus in one of its own polls, Common Cause found in 1982:

TABLE 3.4
What Was the Total Income of Your Family?

	Percent
Less than $20,000	17.7
$20,000-$39,999	38.2
$40,000-$59,999	20.9
$60,000 or more	17.4
Don't know	3.0
No response	2.8

The median Common Cause member had a family income of about $37,000 at a time when the national average family income was about $20,000 per year. This ratio was almost the same according to a 1974 poll, and probably has been the same throughout the organization's history.

In sum, Common Cause members joined because of a civic balance belief system, Vietnam, Watergate, a desire to participate effectively in national politics, a belief in John Gardner, as public contributor households, and to bridge the "generation gap." Joining and renewing membership is facilitated by the high incomes of most Common Cause members.

Demographic Characteristics

Sex. A 1982 poll showed 56.5 percent men and 43.5 percent women comprised the Common Cause membership.

Education. The typical Common Cause members is very well educated. In 1982 a poll showed:

TABLE 3.5
What Is the Highest Level of Education You Have Completed?

	Percent
Some high school	1.6
Completed high school	6.1
Some college	14.9

TABLE 3.5 *(continued)*

	Percent
Completed college	18.7
Some graduate or professional school	14.5
Completed graduate or professional degree program	42.6
No response	1.5

Very similar results were found in polls taken in 1974 and 1978.

Age. Common Cause members are mostly middle-aged and older. One survey in 1976 indicated a median age of 52; another in 1982 showed a surprisingly old median of 60 years. A careful survey by political scientist Jonathan W. Siegel revealed the age distribution shown in table 3.6. In citing these statistics, Common Cause might be regarded as a vehicle for political participation by senior citizens.

TABLE 3.6
Common Cause Membership, by Age

Age	Percent
18-25	2
26-30	4
31-40	14
41-50	12
51-60	21
61-65	14
66-70	11
Over 70	22

SOURCE: Jonathan W. Siegel, Stanford University Political Science Department; personal communication. The data were gathered by a mail survey of a random sample of 1596 Common Cause members; 950 completed the questionnaire, for a return rate of 60 percent.

Occupation. The senior quality of the Common Cause membership is again confirmed by the "occupation" category; almost one-third of the members are retired (see table 3.7). Another interesting characteristic is that about

one-third of those who do work are *not* employed by large organizations; they
are self-employed or are professionals. More members are teachers or academics than work for private business firms; the number working for the government is not especially large; and the number of blue-collar workers is quite
small.

TABLE 3.7
Which of the Following Best Describes Your Occupation?

Occupation	Percent
Business executive/salaried employee	10.0
Nonprofit or voluntary organization executive/salaried employee	3.8
Skilled worker/wage laborer	2.5
Government official/salaried employee	4.5
Homemaker	7.6
Academic/teacher	12.1
Professional (doctor, lawyer, etc.)	13.8
Self-employed	6.0
Retired	32.1
Student	1.4
Other	5.0
No response	1.2

Political Party. Common Cause wants to have an image of being nonpartisan. Its lobbyists want to work with Republican legislators, a goal that would
be undermined if it was learned that only a tiny proportion of its members
are Republicans. Early polls in 1971 and 1974 showed that the number of Republican members was similar to the number of Republicans in the country
at large. After that, Common Cause stopped asking members about their partisan identification. However, as the major Common Cause issue, public funding for elections, came to be viewed as a partisan issue (see chapter 7), there
are some grounds for belief that the number of Republican members has declined. Siegel's data from 1981 appear to confirm a decline in the number of
Republican members (see table 3.8 on page 51).

At any rate it is clear that most members see themselves as political liberals
or moderates. In 1982, 43.3 percent saw themselves as "liberal"; 9.6 percent
as "very liberal"; 36.3 percent as "moderate"; 6.9 percent as "conservative"; and
.4 percent as "very conservative" (3.6 percent gave other answers or did not
respond).

TABLE 3.8
Political Party Identification

	Percent
Strong Democrat	14
Weak Democrat	13
Lean Democratic	40
Independent	14
Lean Republican	12
Weak Republican	4
Strong Republican	3

SOURCE: See table 3.6.

Race. Unfortunately there is no racial breakdown of the Common Cause membership, although it is believed that about 1 percent of the members are black. I saw very few blacks at Common Cause meetings or volunteering at the national headquarters. Nevertheless, critics of Common Cause should not exaggerate the importance of so few black members. It is well known that upper-middle-class blacks prefer to give political contributions to black political organizations (e.g., the National Association for the Advancement of Colored People) and other black institutions. Apparently no mass-based public-interest group has ever claimed to have a substantial number of black contributors.

Ethnicity and Religion. Some observers think of Common Cause as a WASP organization because of the public image of John Gardner and preconceptions arising from the history of reform movements in eastern cities. Siegel's survey reveals a more complex picture. The self-stated religious preference of the 950 Common Cause members indicated 45.2 percent Protestants, 10.9 percent Catholics, 16.7 percent Jewish, and 15.8 percent agnostics; 11.4 percent declined to state a preference.

It thus appears that the proportion of white Protestants in Common Cause is similar to the proportion in the country as a whole, if one presumes that about half the agnostics and those who declined-to-state come from Protestant backgrounds. Catholics are about half as common among the members as among the U.S. population; Jews, on the other hand, are much more common. The most striking finding about religion in Siegel's survey is the extreme paucity of fundamentalist Protestant members. His survey produced only 3 self-identified Southern Baptists and 2 other fundamentalist Protestants in a group of 950 respondents.

Geographic Dispersion

Data from 1983 continued to verify the earlier data on members' place of residence, and indicated that 35.4 percent of the members lived along the Eastern Seaboard (New England, New York, New Jersey, Pennsylvania, Maryland, Delaware, District of Columbia) and another 24.1 percent lived in Pacific Coast states (California, Oregon, Washington, Hawaii, Alaska). Only 15.4 percent of the members lived in the South. Thus we can say that three out of five members lived along the Eastern Seaboard or on the Pacific Coast.

Common Cause members are, on the whole, "metropolitan." In fact, 49.1 percent live in California, New York, Pennsylvania, Massachusetts, Illinois, and New Jersey. Table 3.9 indicates Common Cause membership by state.

TABLE 3.9
Common Cause Membership by State

17 Largest		17 Middle		17 Smallest	
California	48,727	North Carolina	4,143	Oklahoma	1,197
New York	30,451	Colorado	4,135	Louisiana	1,152
Florida	14,133	Missouri	3,549	Delaware	924
Pennsylvania	13,468	Arizona	3,485	Montana	875
Massachusetts	12,306	Dist. of Col.	3,327	Alabama	858
Illinois	11,134	Indiana	2,995	South Carolina	843
New Jersey	10,536	Iowa	2,551	Nebraska	833
Maryland	8,015	Georgia	2,287	Utah	824
Ohio	7,846	Kansas	1,909	Arkansas	760
Washington	7,276	Tennessee	1,880	West Virginia	688
Michigan	7,194	New Mexico	1,838	Alaska	580
Virginia	6,661	New Hampshire	1,751	Idaho	566
Connecticut	6,628	Maine	1,448	Nevada	496
Texas	6,518	Hawaii	1,413	Mississippi	441
Minnesota	5,677	Vermont	1,337	South Dakota	349
Oregon	4,336	Kentucky	1,315	North Dakota	342
Wisconsin	4,210	Rhode Island	1,267	Wyoming	293

Given the description of Common Cause members up to this point, their place of residence is not surprising. But a few comments are called for. A basic source of Common Cause support is in suburban areas along the Pacific Coast — not only in suburbs of San Francisco, Oakland, and Los Angeles but also suburban San Diego, San Jose, Portland, and Seattle. Washington and Oregon have fairly high membership rates. The Florida organization is active in recruiting members; many Common Cause members can be found among retirees from the North. The 6500 members in Virginia include 4000 from the suburban Washington, D.C., area in northern Virginia. Otherwise the Virginia membership would be relatively sparse, as is the pattern in the South.

A tabulation of Common Cause membership *as a percentage of a state's population* is interesting. In particular, Pennsylvania, Illinois, and Ohio fall from the top of the chart; they are not Common Cause strongholds (see below).

TABLE 3.10
Common Cause Membership per Capita by State

1. District of Columbia	18. Alaska	35. Nevada
2. Vermont	19. Rhode Island	36. Indiana
3. Massachusetts	20. Maine	37. Utah
4. Connecticut	21. Arizona	38. Nebraska
5. California	22. Virginia	39. North Dakota
6. Maryland	23. Pennsylvania	40. South Dakota
7. New Hampshire	24. Montana	41. Texas
8. New York	25. Illinois	42. Georgia
9. Washington	26. Wisconsin	43. Tennessee
10. Oregon	27. Iowa	44. Oklahoma
11. Delaware	28. Kansas	45. Kentucky
12. Hawaii	29. Michigan	46. West Virginia
13. New Jersey	30. Ohio	47. Arkansas
14. Minnesota	31. Missouri	48. Louisiana
15. Colorado	32. North Carolina	49. South Carolina
16. Florida	33. Idaho	50. Alabama
17. New Mexico	34. Wyoming	51. Mississipppi

Vermont has fifteen times as many members per capita as Mississippi, which ranks last.

Note that midwestern states are concentrated in the middle of the table, with a few at the low end. Only one midwestern state is in the top third of states in membership per capita. That state, Minnesota, is usually considered to be the midwestern state that is currently the most friendly to governmental reform. Ten of the lowest twelve states are in the South (counting Oklahoma and Kentucky as southern). The top thirteen states, as expected, consist of Eastern Seaboard and Pacific states. Florida and New Mexico both have a relatively high proportion of retirees from the North. In addition, Common Cause is strong in the nuclear and high-tech industrial area around Los Alamos, New

Mexico. Colorado has become a stronghold of environmentalist political action, which has helped Common Cause attract members there.

Three other items related to membership per capita should be cited. First, easy correlations between centers of Progressive era reform (1900-1914) and centers of Common Cause membership are not possible because Progressivism was strong in the Midwest (Wisconsin, Iowa, Michigan, and Ohio are usually mentioned), while Common Cause is not. Second, there is no absolute correlation between the number of members, or even members per capita, and the degree of influence exercised by the Common Cause state organization. Some high-membership states have had mediocre success in lobbying their state legislatures, while some lower-membership states have been notably successful (Michigan, Montana). Third, Common Cause has found that the smallness and geographical compactness of a state correlates with the organizational vitality of state units, which in turn correlates with the number of members. This is a reason why Vermont is second in members per capita, New Hampshire is seventh, and Hawaii is twelfth.

In respect to congressional districts, it is not surprising that the greatest concentrations of Common Cause members are in upper-middle-class suburban areas: Westchester County (New York), Montgomery County (Maryland) and Fairfax County of Virginia (Washington, D.C.), Berkeley-Oakland (California), and also in California, the "high-tech" area around San Jose and Stanford University, Beverly Hills and the UCLA area, Marin County (San Francisco), and so forth. Some concentrations are in lesser-known areas adjacent to such cities as Seattle, Portland, and San Diego. It is generally accurate to characterize Common Cause members as "suburban."

Attitudes toward the Federal Government

A survey by the Peter Hart polling organization gathered some interesting data about the very critical attitude of the members of Common Cause toward the federal government in the 1970s. Years later, some of the percentages in table 3.11 have surely changed, but the overall direction of members' attitudes is probably the same, because dislike for the Reagan administration would maintain such critical attitudes.

Members were overwhelmingly critical of big business as having "too much influence on how the country is run." One inference is that a large majority of the members agree that corporations often influence public policy in a direction that is detrimental to the interests of the general public.

The poll conducted by Peter Hart in 1976 did not ask members what they thought of the power of big labor. Perhaps this question was not asked because the Common Cause staff did not want it to be asked. Finding that Common Cause members are also critical of "big labor" would put pressure on the national staff to lobby for measures to limit the power of labor unions, which would preclude the possibility of cooperation between Common Cause and the unions. While there has been conflict between Common Cause and labor over such proposals as the regulation of lobbyists, Common Cause and labor frequently join forces in lobbying coalitions in Washington. Pressure from members critical of labor would put the Common Cause staff in a difficult position because labor support is valuable in passing much legislation that has been endorsed by Common Cause.

TABLE 3.11
Members' Responses to Hart Poll

Instructions: You have probably heard many criticisms about the federal government lately. Listed below are some typical criticisms. For each one, please indicate whether you would tend to strongly agree, agree with reservations, partially disagree, or disagree.

	Strongly Agree	Agree with Reservations	Partially Disagree	Disagree	Not Sure
There is too much waste and giveaway programs at the expense of taxpayers.	51	32	12	3	2
Big business has too much influence on how the country is run.	64	25	7	2	2
There's too much bureaucracy and favoritism.	67	26	4	1	2
The federal government has become too wasteful and inefficient. It seems unable to come to grips with the country's problems.	58	30	8	2	2
There's nothing wrong with the federal government. The trouble is with those who run it.	17	35	27	15	6

TABLE 3.11 *(continued)*

	Strongly Agree	Agree with Reservations	Partially Disagree	Disagree	Not Sure
People in the federal government are looking out for themselves and their friends and aren't interested in people like myself.	15	38	32	12	3
Too much power to make decisions is centered in the federal government.	21	35	25	14	5
The federal government is encroaching on the rights and freedoms of the individual person.	28	39	20	11	2
The present political system doesn't work. We need a new system such as socialism.	5	11	16	62	6

The question referring to "a new system such as socialism" is a particularly interesting one. Note that 62 percent disagreed with the question asking whether we need "a new system," whereas only 5 percent "strongly agreed." This indicates that 5 percent of the membership might be termed "radicals." Thus one characteristic of Common Cause, and perhaps of some environmental groups as well, is that they violate our usual expectations by attracting support from all parts of the left-right ideological spectrum (although obviously not to the same degree from each part of the spectrum). According to this survey, when the federal government is referred to in the abstract as "bureaucracy," members are overwhelmingly negative. But when the question refers to "people in the federal government," more than 40 percent of the members decline to be critical. The majority of Common Cause members surely have relatives, former classmates, or friends who work for the federal government. Such members would not be inclined to criticize "people in the federal government."

Most Common Cause members are active in political campaigns. It cannot be said that the typical Common Cause member is "alienated" from politics.[4] The typical member appears to be someone who has been active in politics but has become very skeptical about the effectiveness and fairness of the federal government. Yet the person is inclined to act, not to withdraw; at least to act to the extent of contributing to Common Cause. Many members contribute to other political groups, and they write their congressman occasionally at the behest of Common Cause. Table 3.12 shows the findings of a 1974 poll on Massachusetts members' participation in political campaigns.

Siegel's 1980 national sample confirmed these results. He found "[n]early three-fourths of the members reported giving money to a political campaign in 1980; almost a fifth of the membership sample and a third of the activist sample worked in a political campaign; and substantial numbers endorsed a candidate or asked someone they knew to support one."[5]

TABLE 3.12
Members' Political Participation (in percent)

	Total	Members	Former Members
Ever Volunteered in Political Campaign			
Yes	56	57	56
No	43	42	42
Contributed to Political Campaign			
Very frequently	26	27	24
Occasionally	43	43	44
Almost never	20	21	19
Never	10	9	12

The Logic of Collective Action

Olson's influential book about collective action stressed the difficulties of getting individuals to contribute to lobbies aimed at obtaining collective goods—if one person in an area has them, then by their very nature, everyone in the area must have them.[6] For example, if a Common Cause program is successful, then it obtains better government for all citizens (a collective good), not just for the members of Common Cause. This means that a citizen can reap the benefits of an organization's political action whether or not he contributes to that organization. Why, then, have 800,000 people ignored this logic of collective action and, at one time or another, contributed $80 million to Common Cause?

A number of factors have been mentioned that led people to join and maintain membership in Common Cause: Gardner's public appeals, Vietnam, Watergate, disagreements with policies of the Nixon administration, a civic balance belief, increasing civic skepticism, the perception of Common Cause as politically effective, technological advances, personal prosperity, and a desire to participate in decision making through some national organization. One can give a fairly complete description of why people joined Common Cause without referring to Olson's book. But *The Logic of Collective Action* alerts us to the role of cost-benefit calculations made by individuals when they decide to join.

Members receive no tangible economic goods from Common Cause except for publications. During the 1970s members received about ten organizational bulletins a year for their $15 contribution. After 1980, bulletins were sent only to the 5 to 10 percent of the members most active in the organization, while the others for their $20 contribution received six times a year a forty-eight page magazine covering Common Cause activities and the power of special interests within the political process. Surveys showed that a majority of the membership found the bulletins and *Common Cause* magazine to be of some interest. But there is no evidence to indicate that many people join Common Cause to get the magazine. In 1983 about 1 percent of the new members joined through sending a coupon from the magazine. Although no doubt others found the magazine a significant inducement to join, this is still only a small fraction of newly joining members.[7] (The magazine probably has more impact on members' decisions to renew their membership.)

But, obviously, people do not join Common Cause without any regard to economic motivation. Cost-benefit calculations do come into play. Income is an important factor affecting whether people will renew their membership. In terms of opportunity costs (what one foregoes by an expenditure), membership in Common Cause costs less for its typical top 15 percent income-group family than it would for a median-income family. Because of this economic factor, future organizations like Common Cause will retain their preponderantly upper-middle-class membership. Cost-benefit reasoning has a place in an analysis of who joins Common Cause.

In addition to the problem of getting people to contribute to the provision of a collective benefit, Olson's book also shows that there is an incentive problem in organizing an interest group. Few collective benefits are so worthwhile that a person will be motivated to spend all his work time to organize a lobby and gain the benefit. As Salisbury and Frohlich point out, however, an entrepreneur may be willing temporarily to bear the costs of organizing because of the possibility of some long-run gain. Such a gain may be broadly interpreted to include status, influence, or altruism.[8] John W. Gardner clearly played such an entrepreneurial role in the founding of Common Cause, a theme developed further in chapter 9.

NOTES

1. Common Cause compiles a monthly table of its members by state. Researchers should be aware that there are two categories of members, a division initiated in December 1978. Eighty-five percent are regular members, who pay $20 dues per year. Fifteen percent are "family members," couples who pay $30 dues per year and receive the privileges of being polled separately and casting separate ballots in Common Cause elections. The concept of family membership is an effective organizational device; it enables Common Cause to increase its income by at least $150,000 a year and at the same time follow the precepts of feminism. This concept is not unique to Common Cause and is used by many voluntary associations.

2. Andrew S. McFarland, *Public Interest Lobbies: Decision Making on Energy* (Washington, D.C.: American Enterprise Institute, 1976), 6-12.

3. See Constance E. Cook, "Membership Involvement in Public Interest Groups" (paper delivered at the 1983 annual meeting of the American Political Science Association). In addition, a forthcoming Ph.D. dissertation by Jonathan W. Siegel, Department of Political Science, Stanford University, will treat this topic.

4. Common Cause members exhibit a variety of styles of citizenship. But surely some members are similar to a type of citizen discussed by Paul Sniderman—people who are quite critical of the present state of American democracy but who are yet loyal to the ideals of democracy, as their critical responses to survey questions indicate a commitment to the norms of democracy and well-reasoned reflection about the present condition of democracy in America. See Paul M. Sniderman, *A Question of Loyalty* (Berkeley: University of California Press, 1981).

5. Jonathan W. Siegel, "Summary of Common Cause Survey" (memorandum on file at Common Cause national headquarters, July 1982). Quoted with permission of the author.

6. Mancur Olson, Jr., *The Logic of Collective Action* (Cambridge, Mass.: Harvard University Press, 1965).

7. Compare the benefits of joining environmentalist groups as charted by Robert Cameron Mitchell, "National Environmental Lobbies and the Apparent Illogic of Collective Action," in *Collective Decision Making*, ed. Clifford S. Russell (Baltimore: John Hopkins University Press, 1979), 106.

8. See Robert H. Salisbury, "An Exchange Theory of Interest Groups," *Midwest Journal of Political Science* 13 (February 1969): 1-32; Norman Frohlich, Joe Oppenheimer, and Oran Young, *Political Leadership and Collective Goods* (Princeton: Princeton University Press, 1971); Jeffrey M. Berry, *Lobbying for the People* (Princeton: Princeton University Press, 1977), 18-27; and idem, "On the Origins of Public Interest Groups," *Polity* 10 (Spring 1978): 379-97. On 389, Berry cites Common Cause as a case of the formation of a group by an entrepreneur. Also see Terry M. Moe, *The Organization of Interests* (Chicago: University of Chicago Press, 1980), chap. 3. A similar sociological perspective is known as the resource mobilization theory of social movements. See John D. McCarthy and Mayer N. Zald, "Resource Mobilization and Social Movements," *American Journal of Sociology* 82 (May 1977): 1212-41. Political entrepreneurs, of course, are persons who mobilize political resources.

   In this volume, the political organization and lobbying tactics of Common Cause are emphasized. The question why persons should contribute to the production of a public good when they will benefit anyway, even if they don't contribute, is now attracting a significant amount of attention from social scientists. One answer is provided by the entrepreneurial theorists, cited above. Others who have written on this problem include James Q. Wilson, *Political Organizations* (New York: Basic Books, 1973); Russell Hardin, *Collective Action* (Baltimore: Johns Hopkins University Press, 1982); Kenneth Godwin and Robert Cameron Mitchell, "Rational Models, Collective Goods and Nonelectoral Political Behavior," *Western Political Quarterly* 35 (June 1982): 161-92; Mitchell, "National Environmental Lobbies;" John Chamberlin, "Provision of Collective Goods as a Function of Group Size," *American Political Science Review* 68 (June 1974): 707-16; Harriet Tillock and Denton E. Morrison, "Group Size and Contributions to Collective Action," *Research in Social Movements* 2 (1979): 131-49; and David Marsh, "On Joining Interest Groups: An Empirical Consideration of the Works of Mancur Olson, Jr.," *British Journal of Political Science* 6 (1976): 257-72. Because of the great interest in Olson's work, others have begun to study the reasons why individuals contribute to Common Cause in relation to the "collective action problem." See Cook, "Membership Involvement in Public Interest Groups."

4. The Structure of the Organization

Common Cause as a Technical Organization

A national reform organization is necessarily complicated and requires considerable technical expertise among its staff. Members' letters to Congress must be coordinated with the Washington lobbying effort; lobbying efforts at the state level must be coordinated with activity at the national level; multimillion-dollar budgets must be drawn up and executed; the organization must register as a lobby and a nonprofit fund-raising organization in thirty states; accurate membership lists must be maintained and new members recruited; and involved lobbying strategies for passing legislation must be planned. In addition, a favorable relationship with the press must be maintained; newsletters must be written and mailed to members; research on political issues must be carried out; in the case of Common Cause, a legal office is busy with complex litigation; and volunteers must be found, taught, and encouraged.

The functions performed by Common Cause are similar in complexity to the tasks that must be performed in a nationwide presidential campaign. While a campaign is harder to manage because of the great pressure of time, Common Cause managers face the necessity of renewing resources year after year—finding *new* members, *new* volunteers, and *new* lobbying programs. Many people who visit the national Common Cause headquarters for the first time comment that it looks like a campaign headquarters. On a typical day, perhaps fifty persons, without obvious distinctions between staff and volunteers, are working in the open portion of Common Cause's main floor. They are making phone calls, conferring in small groups, typing, or pouring over memoranda. (Others are working in enclosed offices or on another floor.) The most common wall decorations are maps of states marked into congressional districts. Desks are everywhere. The headquarters is carpeted, air-conditioned, and located in a new office building; thus it is more plush than most campaign headquarters. Common Cause state headquarters do resemble the offices of impecunious campaigns, however; they often consist of a few rooms in a dilapidated building.

In 1982 Common Cause had the equivalent of 80 full-time employees (75 working full-time and 10 working half-time) at its national headquarters. At the time of the largest budgets, there were 110 full-time employees at national headquarters. An average of 166 volunteers a month performed services equivalent to 37 full-time employees. An estimate is that volunteers at state headquarters contribute services equivalent to 25 full-time employees.

Common Cause is capable of activating phone networks among its members in about 300 congressional districts in almost every state. Members call other members to write their congressman on an issue. In addition, there is some form of statewide organization in almost all the states. During the late 1970s, about 14 percent of the members, or 35,000 people, were part of a local telephone network. Common Cause identified 11,000 out of approximately 252,000 members as "activists." Such activists ordinarily respond to Common Cause headquarters requests to write a letter to Congress. Of the activists, an estimated 4000 were members of congressional district steering committees or state committees (PACs). These 4000 members sent an average of 15 letters each to Congress every year. The other 7000 activists sent an estimated 8 letters per person. Perhaps another 20 percent of the members write Congress occasionally. This activity in the late 1970s is summed up in table 4.1.

TABLE 4.1
Estimated Number of Letters to Congress

Participation Category	Percent of Members	Number of Members	Letters per Year
Very active	1.6	4,000	60,000
Active	2.8	7,000	56,000
Occasionally active	20.0	50,000	100,000
	24.4	61,000	216,000

Of the 35,000 members organized into telephone networks, 11,000 were activists and 24,000 were in the "occasionally active" category. One estimate is that about 40 percent of the members have written Congress at least once for Common Cause. The remaining 60 percent have done no more than contribute dues and look at the Common Cause bulletins.

According to this estimate, 435 representatives, 100 senators, and the D.C. delegate receive an average 403 letters a year from Common Cause members. Of course this average conceals a great range of variation in letters received by members of Congress. Some southern representatives receive a hundred in a year, while some senators receive several thousand. Viewed one way, 216,000 letters to Congress is an impressive total. But from another perspective this total is less than the number of members (250,000) used to compute the estimate. However, 216,000 letters sent to the right members of Congress at the right time are more effective than 2 million letters sent without any coordination and organization of effort. In addition, Common Cause activists write many thousands of letters each year to state legislatures.

Common Cause is a large organization; to succeed, it must amass and utilize a variety of technical know-how. A major reason for Common Cause's success in this respect was John Gardner's concern for the technical aspects of the organization. Gardner respected technical skill and communicated that respect to the technicians. Gardner's concept of managing an organization meant that he enacted the morale-building roles, while "a strong right arm" fulfilled the more technical management functions. At the Department of Health, Education, and Welfare the "right arm" was Wilbur Cohen, who briefly succeeded Gardner in the secretaryship in 1968. At Common Cause, long-time labor official Jack Conway was the chief of management, or "president" of Common Cause (as opposed to Gardner's chairmanship), from the summer of 1971 until January 1975. Conway was succeeded by his protegé, David Cohen.

Common Cause's national staff includes people in the following technical roles: lobbyists, writers, editors, printers, data processing and direct-mail specialists, lawyers, a legal secretary, policy analysts (who do "issue development"), bookkeepers, accountants, a comptroller, a budgeting specialist, and public relations experts. Common Cause has been one of the major centers in the country for compiling and organizing data on the financing of political campaigns. It is also a center of information about recent good-government reforms in the states and about conflict-of-interest questions in American government.

The role of technique in Common Cause is emphasized to dispel the notion that political reformers are amateurish intellectuals who discuss politics while drinking tea in parlors or scotch in private clubs. Common Cause is an organization founded by a man who had previously managed one of the world's largest bureaucracies and who designed Common Cause to bring together technical and political skills in the pursuit of lobbying and agenda-changing goals. While Common Cause resembles local civic reform organizations in its purposes, its differences from other reform organizations are symbolized by its in-house computer; its eleven WATS telephone lines; and its nine budgeters, accountants, and bookkeepers. And perhaps by the fact that its name was suggested by a New York advertising agency. American writers have been fond of depicting charming, proletarian Irish machine politicians outwitting the cold, intolerant WASP reformers; indeed, this often happened. But such mythic political tales should not lead us to expect that a national, upper-middle-class reform group would be staffed by bunglers and amateurs. Common Cause is led and staffed by the same hard-working, well-educated, technically trained, and frequently innovative people who compose the American upper middle class, which pays for the organization.

Insider-Outsider Lobbying

What Common Cause calls "insider-outsider lobbying" coordination is a central task of the organization. Essentially this means that communication from members to congressmen—"outsider lobbying"—should be coordinated with the activities of Common Cause "insider" lobbyists to achieve maximum impact. A basic task of the Common Cause national staff is to make sure that the right *messages* get to the right members of Congress at the right time. The process of legislation in Congress is very complex: bills may take years to travel in and out of committees in either house, deals are made, amendments occur, and complicated conferences are held. Few citizens will know who to write when and about what bill in most instances. Writing one's congressman usually has an effect, even if the letter arrives after a bill is passed or is sent to a member who already favors a measure. Such letters contribute to a congressman's impressions about the climate of his district's opinions on issues. But the ordinary letter to a member of Congress does not have the influence of the letter sent to the right person at the right time. This is what Common Cause tries to get its members to do.

Four years of experimentation were necessary to develop the present organizational pattern to coordinate insider-outsider lobbying, which now is effective, particularly on governmental reform issues. This pattern is called "the Washington connection" and refers to the connection of Washington lobbyists, field staff, and volunteers with the various congressional district groups via long-distance WATS lines. Essentially, a headquarters volunteer telephones a congressional district coordinator to tell about the need to lobby Congress on some issue, and then the coordinator passes the message along via his local telephone networks.

Common Cause tried several other patterns of insider-outsider coordination, which were successively modified. In an initial period of enthusiasm but disorganization, later recalled by senior staffers with laughter, national volunteers and staff in communal efforts would telephone members directly in what might be termed "calling-bees," frontier fashion. Calling-bees were obviously inefficient, particularly because of the lack of knowledge as to which members were most likely to respond by writing to Congress. And then the number of members got too large. During the first year of Common Cause, two or three letters were sent to the entire membership urging them to write their congressman in support of the Nedzi-Whalen antiwar measure and against the SST. But it soon was apparent that sending first-class letters to all members on every "alert" would be too expensive and second-class letters would take too long to get to the members for them to write Congress at the strategic times.

Next, Common Cause tried telephoning requests to members to write Congress out of four regional headquarters — Boston, New York, Denver, and San Francisco — and out of Washington, D.C. The incipient congressional district steering committees were contacted from these five places. But the regional headquarters frequently did not understand the details of what was happening in Congress and could not respond satisfactorily to questions from local members. This kind of coordination was abolished. Experience also indicated that another pattern — the national office calling the state offices, which could then call local steering committees — would not work because state offices would also get confused about events in Washington.

The present pattern of insider-outsider coordination, the Washington connection, evolved in 1973. In this pattern, Common Cause lobbyists decide the strategy on a legislative issue in conjunction with the organization's chairman and president. Such strategic decisions include when to call an alert on an issue. An alert can be a "membership alert," in which all members are asked to write their congressman, or an "activist alert," in which some or all of those on the list of 11,000 activists are asked to write Congress. There are about fifty alerts a year — that is, requests to some of the Common Cause members to write Congress. But only three or four of these fifty are requests to activate the local telephone chains (14 percent of the members). Perhaps a dozen of the fifty will be alerts to the entire list of activists.[1] The remaining number of alerts are "specialty alerts" — requests to subdivisions of the list of activists to write Congress. When Common Cause lobbyists want to put pressure on Congress, they ordinarily are not concerned about the entire Congress, or even the entire House or Senate. The key political maneuvers in passing legislation usually involve persuading a committee to report a Common Cause-sponsored bill. Accordingly, many specialty alerts are attempts by Common Cause headquarters to get the activists residing in the districts of the members of some committee to write their congressman. Other specialty alerts involve getting activists residing in the districts of uncommitted, "swing" votes to write such congressmen.

Sending out an alert necessitates the use of letters and long-distance telephoning. In most cases an activist alert can be sent by first-class mail in an "action-gram," a dramatic-looking letter that resembles a telegram. The two or three pages of information in the action-gram explain the alert and request a letter be sent to Congress. The Common Cause computer sends the action-gram only to activists in the appropriate category (residents of states of members of the Senate Finance Committee and residents of districts of members of the House Judiciary Committee are likely examples). Headquarters volunteers in telephone conversations tell the appropriate congressional district coordinators that an alert is coming in the mail. Headquarters also reminds the coordinators about the alert after it has been received by the district organization.

Occasionally, rapid action is needed because of some unexpected amendment or other parliamentary maneuver in Congress. In such situations, the mails are too slow, and Common Cause headquarters volunteers must telephone the coordinators and ask them to send a telegram to their congressman in behalf of the local Common Cause organizations and urge the congressman to take the position favored by Common Cause. At other times, there is no need for hurry. For example, Common Cause likes to get as many co-sponsors as possible for its major legislation. Members are informed in Common Cause publications at the beginning of a congressional session that they should write their congressman and request him to co-sponsor some Common Cause-sponsored bill. At the same time the local telephone networks may be activated by telephone and mail messages from Common Cause headquarters. In this situation, lobbying strategy provides several months to get the co-sponsorships on record, and there is no need for rushed action.

Volunteers at headquarters are the key to the operation of the Washington connection system of relaying messages from lobbyists to members in the congressional districts. Each volunteer in the Washington connection is assigned to four or five congressional districts and is responsible for maintaining telephone communication with the Common Cause coordinator in each district. The Washington volunteer ordinarily will talk to the steering committee coordinator or some other Common Cause member once every week or two. Usually a feeling of friendship grows between these two. Discussion of what is happening to Common Cause in Washington helps the district coordinator understand the reasons for a Common Cause alert when it is called. The Washington volunteer, who is briefed in meetings with Common Cause lobbyists, is capable of explaining the details of Common Cause-sponsored legislation and the reasons why Common Cause thinks it is needed. The regular telephone conversations provide an opportunity for Washington to remind the district units to take action after they have received instructions for an alert by mail.

On the other hand, the Washington connection enables the district coordinator to ask for further information about alerts or other Common Cause activities. If the coordinator has serious reservations about the worth of a Common Cause action, he can express these to the Washington volunteer liaison. This, in turn, gives Common Cause some feedback about organizational problems. For example, in 1975 the national headquarters realized that district coordinators and members in local telephone networks usually would not write Congress if they were previously unacquainted with the possibility of Common Cause's lobbying on an issue. Since 1975, Common Cause headquarters has greatly increased the amount of information received by its activists about issues of concern to Common Cause. The national staff also gives new issues publicity in its bulletins months, or even years, before an alert is called on a new measure. It is now unlikely that Washington headquarters will issue an alert on a measure that is unfamiliar to the activists.

The eighty or so Washington connection volunteers are supervised by four full-time employees at headquarters. The telephone coordinator at the congressional district level ordinarily calls about seven members, each of whom calls another seven. Many district coordinators have two or more telephone networks, and there have been as many as 550 at one time.

In addition to providing a means to relay information, the new technology of the long-distance telephone is important to Common Cause because it is vital to the maintenance of organizational morale. District coordinators and others at the local level have the opportunity to converse regularly with Washington headquarters, which greatly increases their sense of participating in a national organization that is doing something important. This feeling of being a part of a group increases the activity of the local coordinator, which increases the number of letters sent to Congress. Building such morale would not be possible if communication with the district units was conducted solely through the mails.

Part of the theory of the Washington connection is to avoid calling too many alerts in a short period of time if this means that the *same* activists are called upon to communicate with Congress several times in one month, for example. In 1972 Common Cause discovered that this produced irritation and decreased the number of letters written. Headquarters avoids activating local telephone networks more than once every six weeks. Alerts are not usually sent to the full list of activists more than once a month. On the other hand, some members who are very active complain that they are not asked by headquarters to do enough. For them, conferences of activists provide several days of meetings a year, which may satisfy this desire to do more in Common Cause.

One problem with insider-outsider lobbying is the variation in the need for effort by members in different congressional districts and states. In 1975-76, for example, there was a great need to put pressure on congressmen on the House Judiciary and Government Operations committees, and activists residing in the districts of these congressmen had much more to do than the typical Common Cause activist. At the other extreme, several dozen congressmen can be counted on to support almost all the legislation that is part of the Common

Cause program. Common Cause activists in such districts have much less to do than the typical activist. (They do have the option of devoting their efforts to pressuring one or both senators or working for the Common Cause program at the state government level.)

Another problem for the Washington connection is that state units now activate the same telephone networks to pressure state legislatures on local issues. Simultaneous state and national alerts produce irritation and confusion as members confuse the messages with one another. In most cases, Washington headquarters sets the timing for state and national alerts that occur close together because it is in the interest of both national and state units to avoid confusion.

Clear communication with local Common Cause members is important for reasons other than getting effective letters to Congress. Personal contacts with congressmen are as important a source of members' influence on congressmen as is writing letters. Perhaps half the members of Congress have a friend in their district who is a Common Cause supporter, and who will broach Common Cause issues to the legislator (see chapter 6). In addition, at least a hundred congressional district steering committees regularly meet with their representative to discuss Common Cause issues. When Common Cause members meet with their congressman, it is important that they clearly understand the bills they are supporting, or a reluctant congressman may adroitly avoid committing himself to the Common Cause position.

In sum, Common Cause has evolved the Washington connection to enhance the effectiveness of members' communication to Congress in the face of the complexities of the legislative process. The Washington connection is dependent on the technology of relatively inexpensive long-distance dialing systems. This mode of coordinating insider-outsider lobbying was technologically impossible twenty-five years ago.

State Organizations

A major effect of Common Cause's political activity is the passage of numerous good-government reform bills by state legislatures. These bills require open meetings of legislative and executive institutions, report sources of income of elected officials and top appointed officials in state government (to prevent conflicts of interest), force lobbyists to disclose their expenditures and limit them, and mandate the reporting of contributions to various state campaigns. Common Cause has also lobbied for public funding of state elections on a matching-grant basis.[2] In 1975, with the passage of this basic Common Cause government reform platform (except for funding of elections) by the majority of state legislatures, Common Cause began action on less familiar reforms, generally aimed at public lobbying of state executive agencies. The most popular of such reforms were "sunset laws," which provide for a statutory time limit on the existence of agencies; the agencies would have to apply for renewal every five to seven years.

By 1972, Common Cause had become a nationwide symbol of reform with 200,000 members and a concrete program for institutional change. The theory was that special interests assume too much control over public policy through campaign donations and influence exercised over decisions made in secret. Common Cause maintained that public interests could be advanced by the "open up the system" program of Common Cause, known as the "OUTS program." The methodology for attaining passage of state OUTS programs was expressed in the national headquarters' collection of model state reform bills plus its accumulated knowledge of political tactics gained through innumerable long-distance phone conversations.

Common Cause members, dissatisfied with state government and either politically ambitious or idealistic, were provided with a concrete program of action: form a statewide committee (the "Program Action Committee")* to push Common Cause government reform legislation. If the local civic reformers did not possess tactical sophistication, strategy could be discussed with national headquarters.

In 1973 the Watergate scandal erupted, and people everywhere became more skeptical of government and clamored for reform. The state PACs could ordinarily count on the support of a substantial number of state legislators, eager to show the electorate a dynamic response to governmental decay by sponsoring Common Cause model bills. At that time, legislators were not so critical as they were later about the consequences of Common Cause legislation on their legislative lives, such as embarrassment at taking controversial positions at open committee meetings, the regulation of contributions to campaigns, and the regulation of lobbyists (who are frequently friends of legislators). It was easier for the PACs to get bills passed than it was in subsequent years when the public clamor for institutional reform subsided.

A basic strategy, particularly in western states, for getting a legislature to pass OUTS legislation is the threat of an initiative. (About twenty-two states have initiative provisions.) Common Cause prefers its state organizations to pressure the legislature before using the initiative strategy because sponsoring an initiative consumes a lot of an organization's resources, and if an initiative

*It is important not to confuse these state Program Action Committees with Political Action Committees, although both use the same PAC acronym.

fails, the sponsoring organization looks weak. But if a legislature shows little interest in OUTS reforms, the threat of an initiative usually induces a consideration of some of the reforms. Legislators know that Common Cause is well equipped to form a coalition to get the necessary number of signatures to put an initiative on the ballot and then to campaign for its ratification by a public that is generally disaffected with political institutions. Moreover, if an initiative is passed, a legislature loses the chance to get Common Cause to compromise on portions of the OUTS legislation, and the original reform language may get written into a state's constitution without modifications.

A signal victory for Common Cause was the June 1974 passage of California's Proposition 9, embodying all the OUTS provisions plus an electoral commission to enforce them. Proposition 9 was opposed by business, by labor, *and* by most politicians; but it was backed by a relatively small coalition of public-interest groups and by the media (it got favorable publicity). The measure then passed with 70 percent support. The well-organized California Common Cause organization got credit for the victory, as did the national organization, which contributed $200,000 to the initiative drive and was subsequently described as politically powerful in *Newsweek, Time,* and other national media.[3] Common Cause spearheaded the Proposition 9 drive and probably deserved the credit it got, although a local citizens lobby, The People's Lobby, also worked hard on the measure and claimed that Common Cause took more than its share of the credit. In any event, an adequately financed "clean up government" campaign triumphed over the "save free speech" slogan of the opposition. Winning Proposition 9 subsequently made the threat of a Common Cause initiative something to be seriously considered by politicians.

What accounts for the varying influence of Common Cause state organizations? The field staff has a number of ideas about this. The basic indicator of state strength is membership per capita. The basic incentive to join Common Cause results in a constituency of well-educated, upper-middle-class liberals; such people must live in sufficient numbers in a state. One expects more Common Cause members in Maryland or Connecticut than in Arkansas or West Virginia. A second factor affecting membership is whether the state has a weak tradition of civic reform movements among middle-class groups at the city and state levels. This tradition is weak in the South, which has particularly low membership rates. Even when a strong tradition of civic reform exists, however, we cannot always expect an influential Common Cause organization because in some states with such traditions (Minnesota, Wisconsin), much reform-minded activity is channeled into the state political parties receptive to such ideas.

In chapter 3 we listed Common Cause membership per capita by state (see table 3.10). In the discussion that follows, you may wish to refer back to that listing. In the 1970s, Common Cause state organizations in the highest third of the states were usually more influential in their states than were most organizations in states lower down on the list. But there were exceptions. The highest-ranked District of Columbia organization is respected, but it is not very powerful. The large-membership Connecticut organization once disbanded because of poor leadership and because a local Nader organization was already pre-eminent in public-interest reform in that state; it was revived in the late 1970s. Florida, Michigan, and Montana—midway in the listing—had organizations of comparative influence to higher-ranking states. Florida has developed widespread support for state government reform, which has been advocated by former Governor Reubin Askew and former U.S. Senator Richard Stone (who once removed the door of his senatorial office to symbolize his commitment to open government). Michigan acquired a strong state Common Cause leadership partly due to the confluence of the huge Michigan State University and the state capital in Lansing. Montana fortuitously rewrote its state constitution at the time of the state Common Cause's initial organization. Through its influence at the Montana state constitutional convention, Common Cause made a long-lasting impact on the state's government. The Nebraska and Alabama organizations have achieved success, despite their few members per capita. The Nebraska state Common Cause spearheaded an initiative that passed most of the OUTS program in 1976. Hugh Spitzer, a surgeon in Birmingham in 1973, led a lobbying campaign in Alabama that codified a set of legislative ethics proposals. Spitzer, who later moved to Dallas, was considered by the national staff to be the kind of exceptional leader who energizes an entire state organization.

Thus, level of membership per capita is not directly related to level of Common Cause power at the state level. It is rather an *indicator* of influence. Such variables as state political culture, the size of the Common Cause constituency, and the quality of leadership in a state organization are more important when discussing the influence of a state organization. Most states with a strong tradition of civic reform, a high percentage of upper-middle-class professionals, and one or a few talented leaders field influential Common Cause units.

In establishing local Common Cause organizations, and in establishing the somewhat independent state PACs, the Common Cause national organization runs some risk of what the staff calls "breakaway groups." What if local units act on issues far from the Common Cause platform that would arouse animosity toward Common Cause, such issues as pro- or antiabortion, or pro- or antipornography? What could the national staff do? Or what if a group seceded from the national organization but still used the Common Cause name for its purposes? Gardner and his associates created a symbol, "Common Cause," and they created a reputation to go with that symbol. Most of the 30 percent or so of the population who have heard of Common Cause have a favorable image of the organization.[4] The same is true of the press. But Gardner could not register the name Common Cause as an economic entrepreneur can register the trademark for a successful product, thereby forbidding others from using "the brand name." Of course a Common Cause lawsuit could prevent a breakaway group from using the name, but by the time an injunction could be issued, the damage would be done.

Although a group in Manhattan considered pulling out of the national organization in 1975, few other problems with potential breakaways have occurred. Perhaps this reflects the unusual unity found in Common Cause; almost all members agree that the structure and process reform program is important. The widespread belief that civic balance needs to be restored by balancing the power of special interests has been translated into a political program by Common Cause's program of reforms of governmental structure and process. In the form of OUTS programs, Common Cause's platform is easily understood and readily translated into practical politics. State OUTS reforms are enough to keep activists busy. On the other hand, people who disagree with Common Cause programs can simply quit the organization.

The unity around structure and process values has alleviated any problem with breakaway groups. But national headquarters has another important power to prevent breakaways—the control of organizational finances. In 1982, about two-thirds of the money for state organizations came from national headquarters. National contributions to the states were $991,000 at that time. Of this amount, $185,000 came from contributions from members, who are asked to contribute to their state Common Cause organization in addition to their yearly dues ($20) to the national organization (about 30 percent do so). Under this system, any state organization would have difficulty continuing operations without money from the national group, which would cut off the money if a state started to pursue a platform different from the overall Common Cause program. State PACs do have independent fund-raising efforts, however, and raised about one-third of their operating expenses in 1982.

The basic unit of Common Cause organization is the congressional district steering committee. This is a group of Common Cause members who meet monthly or bimonthly to coordinate the local functions of the organization. Ordinarily a congressional district steering committee has a "coordinator" (chairperson), a telephone network supervisor, a membership director (who keeps membership lists and tries to recruit new members), a public relations director (who contacts local media in behalf of Common Cause), and a speakers' director (who is in charge of getting people to speak to local groups). The district steering committee ordinarily elects one or two delegates to the state committee, the Program Action Committee (PAC). Thus the district steering committee is responsible for conducting Common Cause alerts through its telephone network and for putting forth efforts to get new members and communicate Common Cause's message through the media and by speaking to local groups. In addition, the steering committee sometimes sponsors a yearly Common Cause Day for the entire membership, at which time the Common Cause program is discussed and a new steering committee elected.

Because Common Cause was intended to be primarily a national lobby, the state PACs were not immediately organized. Indeed, the PACs did not begin to flourish until 1973. In Common Cause staff jargon, a few PACs were "organized from the top down," that is, they grew out of the initial four regional offices in Boston, New York City, Denver, and San Francisco. Other PACs were established by the national staff, drawing on activists in preexisting congressional district steering committees set up in 1971-72. The new state PACs were in charge of lobbying tactics for state OUTS campaigns and coordinated communication with the state's U.S. senators.

In 1976 the national staff attempted to mandate that the PACs consist of delegates elected at congressional district Common Cause Days but that from one-third to one-half of the PAC was to consist of persons appointed by other PAC members. Appointees would possess the various skills—lobbying knowledge, relationships with the state media—needed for the realization of the state Common Cause program. In other words, the hard-working telephone network coordinator from Scarsdale might know nothing about how to influence the legislature in Albany. Most state PACs simply ignored this injunction of the national organization, however, and the overwhelming majority of PAC members have consisted of delegates elected from congressional districts.

Clearly, the state PACs could acquire a tendency to ignore the national program in pursuit of a state program. But congressional district steering committees, plugged into the "Washington connection," are typically oriented to national programs. The centrifugal tendencies of state PACs are the Achilles heel of the Common Cause organization. But nothing much can be done about this; the nature of American federalism imposes this organizational problem on Common Cause, which cannot forbid activists from pursuing the structure and process reform program in state capitals. (This problem is discussed at greater length in the next chapter.)

By the mid-1970s, forty-eight state Common Cause committees were organized. Members of state PACs were selected at the local level, as was the state staff, although the national staff maintained a veto over state hiring.[5] At first, national leaders were somewhat nervous at this development—would some state organizations disgrace the national organization? This concern was reflected in the tight set of controls the national group initially exercised over state PACs. Such controls were seen by the PACs as legitimate because the national organization then provided three-fourths of the PACs' budgets and recruited almost all Common Cause members. In 1975 the national governing board ruled that state PACs could lobby only for a limited set of goals that corresponded to Common Cause's basic government reform program. But controls over state PACs loosened with time. By 1977 state organizations were encouraged to act on a list of issues—including tax reform and reapportionment—that were not part of the Washington lobbying program. At that time, the national staff considered the danger of PAC stagnation to be greater than that of PAC rebellion, and state units were encouraged to initiate new lobbying programs. By 1981 restrictions on state lobbying campaigns were further loosened so state PACs could lobby on a wide range of issues, similar to the Washington lobbying program.

The most striking fact is the infrequency with which state PACs sought to depart from Common Cause's basic structure and process reform program. Even though members of state PACs personally support environmentalism, gun control, or restrictions on the construction of nuclear power plants, state PACs almost always define their duty as sticking to lobbying on government reform issues. This is another instance of the near-unanimity of Common Cause members in support of its government reform program. The national organization can exercise a veto over state PAC lobbying on new issues, but conflicts reach the governing board only about once every two years.

State-national conflicts have been mostly over resources and procedures, particularly over budgets of states and the representation of states on the national board. (These issues are discussed in chapter 5.) The national organization not only gives money to the states but is legally responsible for any debts incurred by improvident PACs. The national group exercised detailed control over state budgets and expenditures during the 1970s. A great deal of staff time was used in national-state negotiations over forty-eight or so annual state budgets. Many state activists found this process frustrating and a needless diversion of staff time. Finally, in 1981 Common Cause president Fred Wertheimer "deregulated" state budgets and allowed states to allocate funds according to the choices of the local PACs. National control was limited to maintaining proper accounting procedures and guarding against deficits. The general expectation is that any increases in waste in PAC expenditures will be offset by the release of staff time and better morale among state staff.

Finances

About 90 percent of Common Cause money comes from donations (including dues) of under $100. Common Cause does not accept contributions of more than $100 from corporations or unions. It does not seek grants from foundations, which it could do by establishing a separate legal branch or an "education fund" that would be eligible for grants under the tax laws. It does not seek large contributions from millionaires, although the national staff does look for donations in the $1000 range. Basing financial support on small contributions is a matter of organizational policy. Much of the Common Cause program revolves around criticism of politicians' acceptance of large campaign contributions or other large gifts. To make its position credible, Common Cause must raise funds from small donations, and generally it has done so.

TABLE 4.2
Corporate and Union Contributions Over $500

	Number	Amount
1970	14	$ 42,500
1971	7	35,000
1972	1	500
1973	7	20,000
1974	6	7,000
1975	1	3,000
		$108,000

NOTE: None accepted after 1976.

It was in April 1976 that the Common Cause governing board voted not to accept contributions of over $100 from unions or corporations. In fact, not much money had come from such donors anyway, as table 4.2 indicates. Common Cause also does not receive many donations over $1000. Exact dollar amounts of large gifts are not available after 1975, but it has been possible to compile the gross number of donations of over $500 for 1976-81 (see table 4.3). Large donations increased in 1980 because of a special fund-raising drive to mark the tenth anniversary of Common Cause. Of eight donations amounting to $10,000 or over, the largest was $11,126.

About $75,000 of the $3.2 million received by Common Cause in its first year came from John D. Rockefeller III, Nelson Rockefeller, and board members of the Chase Manhattan Bank or the Rockefeller Foundation. Since that time, gifts from the Rockefeller family have amounted to less than $1000 annually; even the broadest definition of Rockefellerdom could account for only a tiny percentage of contributions. Nevertheless, various polemical writers have

TABLE 4.3
Contributions of $500 or More

	1976	1977	1978	1979	1980	1981
$500 to $999	32	65	77	54	110	113
$1000 to $4999	54	39	46	43	53	45
$5000 to $9999	1	3	2	3	2	0
$10,000 and over	0	1	0	2	1	3
Total	87	108	125	102	166	161

seized on the initial Rockefeller contributions as evidence of some sort of covert control by the millionaire family.

What was the effect of the Rockefeller contributions? John Gardner was a friend of Chase Manhattan Bank president David Rockefeller and was acquainted with other members of the Rockefeller family. The Rockefellers had contributed significant sums to Gardner's Urban Coalition Action Council — in fact, $50,000 in the UCAC's last six months. In late March 1970, when Gardner decided to start a new, mass-financed organization, he knew it would cost at least $300,000 for mailings and newspaper ads. (Gardner did not expect to get more than 100,000 contributors and could have made do with half that number.) Perhaps Gardner expected the Rockefellers and their associates to contribute a substantial fraction of the money needed to ward off organizational disaster. This "ace in the hole" no doubt influenced Gardner's decision to take the big risk of starting a mass-based lobby.

As it turned out, Gardner's founding of Common Cause was one of the most successful political fund-raising efforts in recent American history. Viewers sent $60,000 on the strength of a "Meet the Press" television appearance, even though he did not ask for money and the organization had not yet been started. In Common Cause's first eleven months, $3.2 million was raised; thus the $75,000 in Rockefeller money did not play a pivotal role. Common Cause's major initial stands contradicted many positions held by Rockefeller interests, among them that of limiting campaign donations. And Nelson Rockefeller was at the time a fervent supporter of the Vietnam war effort.

Common Cause's financial activity is similar to that of a collegiate alumni office. Common Cause and alumni offices have a similar task: to raise money, mostly in amounts under $50, from large numbers of well-educated professionals who, on an individual cost-benefit basis, have nothing to gain by their contribution. The income, education, occupation, and geographical demographics of graduates of better private colleges are similar to those of the Common Cause membership. Both Common Cause and alumni offices rely on mailings to get numerous small donations; they provide their constituents with monthly bulletins designed to show that they are continuing to perform good deeds; they circularize their constituents a few times a year to make extra contributions for special projects (the new science laboratory or the new program to lobby the executive branch). No doubt some readers of this book receive more mail from their college and from Common Cause than from any other source.

The pie graph in figure 4.1 illustrates the sources of Common Cause's income in 1982. The "dues" category is self-explanatory. "National contributions" indicates members' contributions to the national organization in addition to the basic $20 annual dues ($15 before late 1980). Common Cause practices fund-raising procedures typical of American voluntary associations. Contributors are requested to give more than their dues when they join or renew (yield — $535,000 in 1982); about three special appeals for funds are sent to most

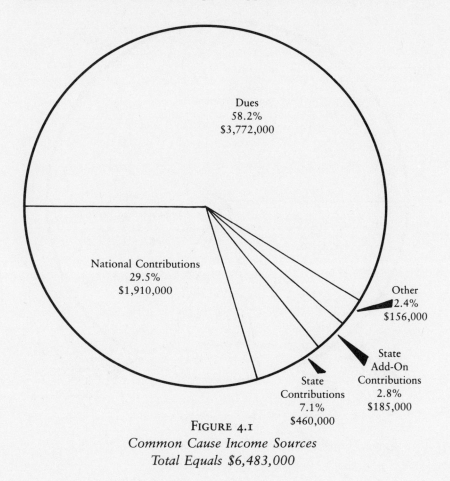

FIGURE 4.1
Common Cause Income Sources
Total Equals $6,483,000

members each year (yield — $550,000); exempted from these three appeals, about 14,000 "special donors" who have at one time given more than $50 are sent more personalized appeals (yield — $450,000 per year); and 1500 "sustaining members" pledge monthly contributions that are much greater than their dues (yield — $250,000 per year).

State PACs raised $460,000 through local fund-raising activities typical of middle-class associations: soliciting contributions directly or by mail; charging for parties, entertainments, and visiting speakers; and holding raffles (if legal in a state) or auctions. State "add-on contributions" refer to funds resulting from an appeal to renewing members to "add on" a contribution to their state Common Cause organization.

The "other" category in the graph, $156,000, came from certificates of deposit ($100,000) and from renting mailing lists of Common Cause members

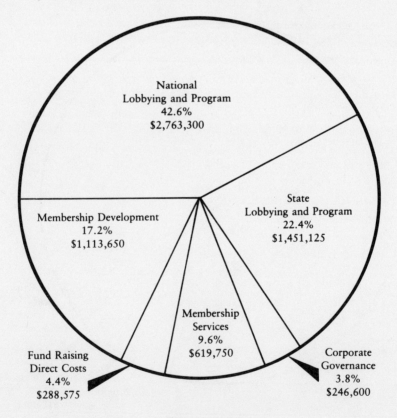

FIGURE 4.2
Common Cause Total Expenditure Budget
Total Equals $6,483,000

($56,000). Common Cause is circumspect in renting its membership list (e.g., stipulating that it can be used only once), but given the low financial return and the resentment against this practice by some people, it seems possible that Common Cause may stop renting its lists in the future. At present a Common Cause member can request that his or her name not be included in the rental lists.

Figure 4.2 is a pie graph of Common Cause's expenditures as budgeted for 1982. As you can see, the organization spends twice as much money on national lobbying as on state lobbying. The single largest national program expense was salaries; rent was budgeted at $250,000; and telephone usage cost $163,500. *Common Cause* magazine and other publications were budgeted for $472,900; litigation costs were $202,500; and issues research spent $226,400.

Note that large sums are spent for recruiting and maintaining members. "Membership development" refers to the costs of recruiting new members by direct mail. In this budget Common Cause planned to send 5 million pieces of direct mail. Each letter would cost 20 cents to produce and mail, accounting for about $1 million. "Membership services" is a data-processing category. The money is spent "putting the members on the computer" and computer printing address labels for membership literature, renewal notices, and monthly lists of residences of members organized by congressional district. This operation is similar to data processing at a medium-size magazine. Indeed, Andrew Heiskell, a national board member for six years, was chairman of Time-Life Inc. for more than a decade and gave Common Cause much useful advice on its membership operations.

"Corporate governance" in the graph refers to costs incurred in holding national board meetings and elections.

Mail, Members, and Money. During the late 1970s, 98 percent of Common Cause money came from member contributions. And most members were recruited by mail. Accordingly, virtually all discussions of income and budgets in Common Cause are linked to discussion of changes in the organization's number of members, changes reflected in the varying number of positive responses to Common Cause's mailings.

Common Cause uses direct mail, and a lot of it. The organization had sent out 82 million solicitations by second-class bulk mail by the end of 1983. (When an Ann Arbor political scientist was informed of this, he remarked, "Eighty-two million? I believe it. I got eight thousand of them myself!") Common Cause is a lobby and thus paid a relatively high postal rate (7.7 cents in 1976 for each direct-mail solicitation) until a change in postal regulations enabled it to mail at the standard rate for nonprofit organizations (2 cents a let-

ter) in the spring of 1977. This saved Common Cause about $228,000 a year.
The rate was increased several times, however, and reached 5.2 cents in 1983.
In recent years Common Cause has mailed about 5 million membership solicitations a year; this number will increase if the percentage of favorable responses
increases, as it did in 1983.

In 1982 each solicitation cost about 20 cents including the cost of postage,
paper, printing, mailing lists, address labels, and of course copywriter's fees.
Direct mail is costly, even though it is often the most inexpensive way for an
interest group to ask for public contributions. But mail is the most efficient
way to get members: 72.16 percent of new members in 1972-75 joined because
of direct mail; in 1981, this figure was 71.2 percent. (All response cards to membership solicitations are coded so that Common Cause knows which methods
of solicitation are the most successful.) In the first year of Common Cause it
was thought that newspaper ads, initially quite successful, might be a continuing source of members; but by 1972 it was apparent that this method no longer
worked, and it was dropped. An attempt to recruit members in 1971 by producing a television show featuring John Gardner proved a financial failure. In
1982-83 Common Cause experimented with 30-second television "spots," featuring well-known television personalities, as a means of attracting new members.
The television time was free because the "spots" were defined as public service
messages; the actors donated their time. This technique was not particularly
successful.

During 1971 about 70,000 people simply wrote to Common Cause asking to join without the prompting of solicitation by mail. A similar phenomenon happened during the Watergate period of 1973-74. But in times of politics
as usual, unsolicited memberships dropped to 4000 a year.

Common Cause sends mail solicitations to people on lists traded with or
rented from other organizations or rented from direct-mail specialists. The most
productive lists for Common Cause are those that indicate "public-contributor
households"—contributors to Nader's Public Citizen, the ACLU, public television and radio stations, and so forth. Common Cause also rents lists of subscribers to such magazines as *Harper's* and *Saturday Review.* Lists of academicians were productive before 1975, but after that were of marginal usefulness.
In its first years, Common Cause mailed solicitations to a broader constituency than it does at present, but such broad mailings have proven financially ir-
rational.

In the 1970s, Common Cause direct mailings were written by Jack Shelton
and Jack Newhouse of the Shelton firm of direct-mailing consultants in Sausa-
lito, California, in collaboration with John Gardner. There is a skill to writing
effective mail solicitations, and it is not easy. Except for the first Common

Cause mailing in 1970, mailings written solely by John Gardner, a skilled publicist, did not work well. Like almost all public-interest groups, Common Cause must resort to professional copywriters. The Shelton firm had a specialized knowledge of public-interest mailings and claimed credit for the mailing that launched Friends of the Earth in 1969 and for Sierra Club mailings.

Contrary to what one would assume, Common Cause loses money for a year on each new member it recruits. The organization makes money only when the first-year member renews for a second year. Let us examine some hypothetical figures that are not very different from the actual numbers of the early 1980s. Suppose Common Cause mails 7000 solicitations; these cost $1680 at 24 cents per letter. A typical response may be an average of $25 from .7 percent of the total solicited, or about 50 persons, contributing $1250. For the first year, Common Cause loses $430 on this mailing. The organization then spends $1.50 each on the 50 persons, or $75.00 to get them to renew. About 28 members (56 percent) renew, contributing on the average $28, for a total of $784. Common Cause is now ahead $279. After the second year, the profit grows still larger as Common Cause spends $42 on renewal messages for the 28 members, successfully recruiting 17 of them (62 percent), who each contribute $30, for a total of $510, or a second-year profit of $468. A similar pattern holds for environmentalist organizations and probably for the great majority of political groups that recruit members by mail.[6]

After 1975, faced with the prospect of a large decline in membership, Common Cause devoted considerable organizational effort to experimenting with ways of getting members other than by mail. The basic problem is that members of Common Cause are very reluctant to persuade others to join the organization. In American political society, it is not the current practice for contributors to public-interest groups to try to get others to contribute, except at the level of elite fund-raisers. The national staff did have some success, however, with a plan to get congressional district steering committees to persuade current members to renew by rewarding the treasuries of such steering committees.

Relationships with the Press

Common Cause had a very favorable press in the 1970s. This was true both at the level of nationally influential newspapers and among small local papers. Getting favorable treatment in the press is important for two reasons. First, it provides good impressions of Common Cause to people who might be inclined to become members. Second, favorable press treatment of the Common Cause program increases the chance of its passage by Congress or state legislatures.

Favorable coverage in the press does not necessarily imply mentioning the name of Common Cause. It is vital to Common Cause to have its program considered seriously by congressmen and other policy makers. The organization is very happy to see the publication of editorials or articles supportive of the Common Cause program, even if such articles do not mention Common Cause. Getting press coverage for its reform proposals is a major goal of the organization.

The major national newspapers and television networks have a concept of the government reform agenda that is similar to the Common Cause definition. Items such as the public financing of elections, reforming the congressional seniority system, permitting public attendance at almost all legislative committee meetings, and requiring top government officials to disclose financial holdings get mentioned repeatedly in the press. This favorable coverage of the Common Cause agenda is the result of many factors, but Common Cause's public relations work is one of the more significant ones.

John Gardner did not try to exploit his success as a best-selling author to get press coverage for himself. However, his appointment as HEW Secretary meant a *Newsweek* cover story and, inevitably, a certain degree of attention in the national press. Press treatment was overwhelmingly favorable. Gardner's basic image combined the attributes of minister, professor, and businessman. In fact, Gardner actually is a charming, articulate, and intelligent idealist who maintains a concern for practical action.

Gardner impressed national political reporters with his personality and with the newsworthy fact that he was different from other leading Washington policy makers. Gardner's favorable press carried over to the summer of 1970 when his announcement of a new citizens' lobby got a great deal of publicity and editorial approval, which was later cited in Common Cause's direct-mail solicitations.

Tom Mathews, press relations director for Gardner's Urban Coalition, performed ably in setting up Common Cause's press relations. Mathews had a wide variety of contacts among the nationally known reporters and columnists and was able to encourage a great deal of coverage of Common Cause. In its first year the press emphasized the newsworthy aspects of the appearance of an unusual phenomenon—a citizens' lobby with 200,000 members. During the second year, Mathews gained publicity for Common Cause as Gardner traveled about the country, speaking in conjunction with the Common Cause effort to found congressional district units and inject Common Cause issues into the 1972 campaign. When such gambits were no longer newsworthy, Tom Mathews and John Gardner had to set up a more institutionalized mode for dealing with the press.

The two men designed two innovations. The first was to begin a Common Cause citizens' press network by encouraging each congressional district to appoint a member as the local Common Cause press liaison. The second innovation was to send out Common Cause "editorial memoranda," which consisted of three to eight pages of papers on some problem of government reform. The memoranda relied on the research of the Common Cause issues staff. These memoranda were easily converted into editorials by relating the factual material and then writing an opinion at the end. This approach has been very successful in getting favorable editorials in small newspapers, largely because it carries more credibility with editors than sending out "canned" editorials, the approach used by most Washington pressure groups. A typical editorial memoranda was "More Taxpayers Earmark Dollars for Presidential Campaign Fund" sent in March 1975, which cited IRS statistics to that effect, explained the presidential campaigning provisions of the recently passed 1974 act, and was suitable for the beginning of an editorial urging taxpayers to check off the relevant box on their income tax return. Editors have confidence in Common Cause's figures and information; they are invariably correct, although, of course, the interpretation of such material varies with the opinions of its readers.

If Common Cause fields minimally active units in 300 congressional districts, perhaps 250 of these have a press coordinator on the steering committee, and maybe 125 of the 250 are good at the job. But 125 local press liaisons are enough to get large amounts of publicity, as Common Cause has done. In addition, about 30 state PACs have someone responsible for press relations. The local Common Cause press liaisons try to develop friendly relationships with the media in order to place stories about local units and statewide activities, including those that are part of nationally coordinated drives. Talented press coordinators can rewrite national stories with a local angle ("Congressman McClean Supports John Gardner's Call for Immediate Action on Reform of Lobbying").

By early 1975, Common Cause's clipping service was sending it 2000 clippings a month, and this did not include copies of all the reprints of wire-service stories. This was three times the clippings gained by the Jackson-for-President drive at the time, and Jackson was then viewed as the leading declared presidential candidate. This period was a high point of favorable publicity for Common Cause; the amount of coverage has since declined.

Common Cause sends most of its news releases to a national list of 1600 who have expressed interest in receiving Common Cause publicity. Of course, Common Cause strives to maintain active contact with Washington's political reporters. In addition, it sends its editorial memoranda to the 1700 daily newspapers in the country.

Common Cause tries to be reliable and factual in its relationships with Washington's political reporters. In particular, Common Cause attempts to be reliable on matters concerning government reform issues. For example, Common Cause maintains a very useful collection of campaign finance data that includes a list of contributions over $100 to federal elections campaigns, indexed by donor, and a list of such contributions indexed by campaign. Reporters trust Common Cause to give them correct information, and they reward the organization by citations in published articles. In the first months of 1975, when discussion of institutional reforms was at a high point, Fred Wertheimer of Common Cause was cited so frequently in newspaper stories that Senator William Proxmire reportedly joked: "I used to be quoted in the press more often than anyone else in Washington, but now it's Fred Wertheimer!"

The Policy Research Group

Common Cause's policy research group, which they call the "issues development division," in 1982 had a budget of about $226,400 and consisted of seven researchers, a secretary, twelve volunteers, and about twenty-five student interns, who typically worked part time for several months, thereby providing the equivalent of about five full-time assistants. This group has at least four functions. Its major function is "to develop issues" for Common Cause, which implies understanding issues in which Common Cause might become involved and developing a stance on such issues. A second function is to explain and defend Common Cause positions and provide technical assistance for legislative strategy, such as assistance in writing bills. A third function is the coordination of information and tactics concerning state-level government reform. A fourth function is routine service, such as providing answers to members' questions about issues, writing speeches for Common Cause's top officers, and collating issue positions of presidential candidates.

Common Cause does not do "original research"; but it does handle "Washington research," in the terminology of the staff. Such Washington research has three basic steps: (1) library research in reviewing the existing policy research in an area; (2) interviews with experts and interest-group spokesmen in Washington; and (3) position development.

Thus, a researcher turns to government studies and testimony, foundation studies, the work of policy institutes, and academic work to get an initial understanding of some issue area. He supplements this by clipping the *Washington Post* and *New York Times* and by reviewing magazines and journals. Washington research means seeking to understand what is "going on" in some area. Of course, first there is the technical aspect to a policy area; a researcher may have experience with the area, or may simply be a "quick study." But beyond the technical background, Washington research means asking: What are the political issues? Who is for and who is against which alternatives, and why? Later it means talking to people, seeking out those with technical expertise who seem to have similar values to one's own. A researcher must strive to understand these positions, as they are likely to be similar to those he develops. Washington research also means talking to interest-group spokespersons on all sides of the question to make sure that something important is not being missed, and conversing with congressional staff about issue development. A few key problems and policy choices gradually emerge from such discussions.

Then, Washington research means developing a position. Such a position may not be, in many respects, the ideal policy choice, but it is the stance that seems to make sense in the context of the current political situation. Further, the policy researcher may be constrained by his superiors, who may have made up their minds in advance.

The Common Cause policy researcher develops positions that will be, first, acceptable to leaders of the staff, and second, acceptable to an overwhelming majority of the national governing board. If 20 percent of the board is expected to object to a suggested position, it will not be adopted. The Common Cause policy research group has sometimes chafed at this rule of thumb—that the anticipation of one-fifth in opposition defeats a proposed position—but it has remained in effect. This informal one-fifth veto, plus polls of the membership, pretty well guarantees that positions will not be offensive to a large fraction of the membership. In addition, Common Cause will consider the feelings of its lobbying allies in developing a position. Thus, Common Cause will not take a stance offensive to its allies unless organization leaders decide that there are strong grounds for doing so. For example, Common Cause was hesitant to publicly advocate the deregulation of natural gas, which would have offended many of its usual allies.[7] Still, Common Cause in 1975 advocated controls on lobbyists that were so strict that virtually all other public-interest lobbies objected to the bill, and Common Cause certainly lost a lot of its political "credit" with those lobbies. But controlling lobbyists was an issue that the Common Cause leadership considered to be of preeminent importance for their organization, and they were willing to lose politically valuable goodwill.

In Washington research, the primary skill is the political interpretation of technical data. Common Cause can claim superior knowledge about good government. Some of its policy analysts are experts in the area and now and then publish short articles.[8] Common Cause has accumulated expertise in state government reforms, problems of conflict of interest in public administration, and electoral campaign reform.

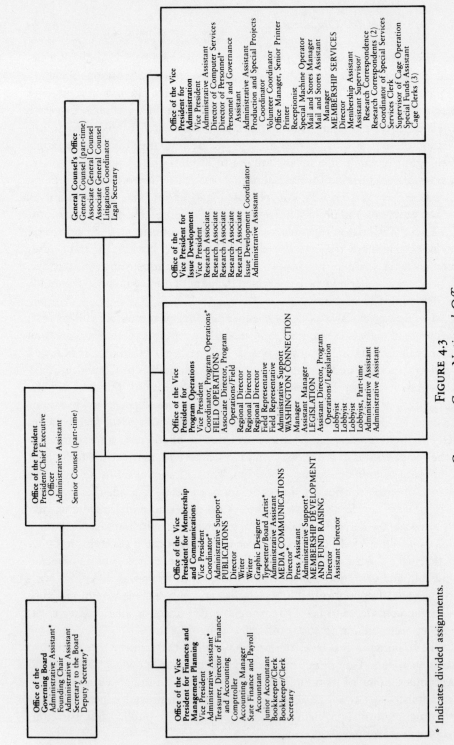

FIGURE 4.3

Common Cause National Office

* Indicates divided assignments.

The National Staff

An idea of the various Common Cause jobs can be gotten by looking at the Common Cause organizational chart shown in figure 4.3. Common Cause tends to be reorganized every few years, and so the exact structure of the national headquarters will vary somewhat. The people who have staffed the organization are described in the discussion that follows.

Common Cause has had four staff managers, or "presidents": Lowell Beck (1970-71), Jack Conway (1971-75), David Cohen (1975-81), and Fred Wertheimer (since 1981). Beck worked for the American Bar Association from 1960 to 1968, then left to become the chief lobbyist for the Urban Coalition Action Council. Aside from John Gardner, Beck and publicist Tom Mathews were the two most influential people in the decisions that led to the establishment of Common Cause in 1970. Beck returned to the American Bar Association in 1971; he left Common Cause on amicable terms.

Jack Conway, who left his imprint on Common Cause's basic organizational pattern, started his career as a sociology instructor, became a United Auto Workers organizer, and then worked for fifteen years as Walter Reuther's chief assistant. Conway organized the UAW's research, lobbying, public relations, and worker organizing staff. Conway served in the Kennedy administraton as the developer of the community action program of the war on poverty (the OEO). After heading the AFL-CIO's Industrial Union Division's Washington office, in 1968 Conway formed the Center for Community Change, an organization funded by the Ford Foundation and aimed at organizing poor people. Like Gardner's Urban Coalition, the Center did not achieve satisfying results, and the Tax Reform Act of 1969 cut off most of its money by forbidding foundation grants to political organizing groups.

With Conway came David Cohen, who, after working as a lobbyist for the upholsterer's union and the Americans for Democratic Action, worked for Conway as a lobbyist for the Industrial Union Division and Center for Community Change. Conway groomed Cohen to be his successor as president of Common Cause, a job for which Cohen was well suited. When Conway left Common Cause in 1975, Cohen received the president's job from the governing board by acclamation. Similarly, Cohen groomed as his own successor Fred Wertheimer, who rose through the Common Cause national organization from lobbyist to head lobbyist to political director to president.

As might be expected, many of the top- and medium-level Common Cause staffers were acquaintances or friends of Gardner, Conway, and Cohen. In particular, most of Gardner's immediate circle at UCAC continued to work for him at Common Cause. But staff appointments were not limited to friends of the three leaders. Many Common Cause staffers started as volunteers; after they performed capably on an unpaid basis, they were hired to work full-time for compensation. Many Common Cause employees have, in effect, greatly facilitated the task of hiring capable people by volunteering their services for several months in what amounts to a period of unpaid trial employment. Common Cause also hires a few people who previously worked for other public-interest organizations.

Because of the publicity given to the minimal salaries of "Nader's Raiders" in the 1960s, some readers may imagine that the Common Cause staff lived in penury. But John Gardner never wanted to pay minimal salaries. Before inflation went over 10 percent a year in 1978, Common Cause generally paid its staff the equivalent of the federal government salary for their work. After 1978, however, Common Cause's funding fell behind the rate of inflation, and salaries fell behind government salaries. Even so, Common Cause received many applications for open staff positions from younger persons without dependents.

Common Cause employees work a forty-hour week except during unusual situations such as meeting political deadlines or traveling to inspect district and state operations. In this respect, Common Cause staffers resemble John Gardner, just as "Nader's Raiders" are expected to put in extraordinarily long working hours similar to those of Ralph Nader. Gardner, on the other hand, preferred to work a nine-to-five day when possible and then to go home and read.

Working for Common Cause in Washington is not a sinecure. Older employees lose the option of early federal retirement (in Washington, jobs are always compared to government working conditions). Younger employees worry that working for Common Cause might be a "dead end" and that they might lose their jobs in a future budget cut. For example, the first head of Common Cause's policy research division left in 1974, not out of dissatisfaction with Common Cause, but because he was offered a good federal job and was worried about the future of his three children.

The Common Cause staff tends to be rather young. Today two of the high-ranking staff are over fifty years of age, but most of the Common Cause management are under forty, and division directors tend to be thirty to thirty-five. Fred Wertheimer, the president of Common Cause, is in his early forties.

The impression exists in some quarters that Common Causers are WASP (White Anglo-Saxon Protestants). There are two reasons for this impression. First, good-government reformers, particularly before World War II, were disproportionately of Anglo-Saxon stock. A second reason for associating Common Cause with WASPs was John Gardner's public image.

Gardner seemed to be one of those blue-blooded reform intellectuals, descended from the Pilgrims, who spring from the Ivy League to hobnob with the elite of New York City and who write morally uplifting books about the future of America. The truth is somewhat different. Although he has resided in Scarsdale or Chevy Chase for the last thirty-five years, Gardner was raised in California and likes to go West whenever he can. Gardner attended Fairfax High School in the West Los Angeles area, where his mother was a successful real estate developer. He received a B.A. and M.A. from Stanford, and a Ph.D. in psychology from Berkeley. Before his senior year at Stanford, he married a Guatemalan exchange student, Aida Marroquin. Thus, while John Gardner is undoubtedly a WASP, he resembles middle-class Californians as much as he resembles "the Cabots and the Lodges."

The national staff of Common Cause is not notably WASP or Ivy League. There has been no ethnic census of the national staff, but there are many Catholics and Jews working for Common Cause. As for education, about half of the staffers attended one of "the good schools," but the other half attended ordinary public universities or not-so-exclusive colleges. No one cares who went where. One should not force Common Cause into Anglo-Saxon or Protestant categories without considering Jewish liberalism, Catholic social reform after Pope John XXIII, and West Coast Progressivism. Today's public-interest reformers are multiethnic.

Headquarters Volunteers

Both Gardner and Cohen have stated that "Common Cause could not function without its volunteers at headquarters." Most of the organizational work at congressional district and state levels, and all the letters to Congress, are the product of voluntary work. But Washington headquarters has the largest concentration of volunteers within Common Cause. In the late 1970s, an average of 166 persons volunteered each month in Washington. The typical volunteer works for three afternoons (or mornings) a week for about a year, after which he or she takes up a new avocation or job or simply loses interest in volunteering. Common Cause has never had a problem getting enough volunteers for its headquarters. Indeed, at times of high publicity for Common Cause, it has to turn people away.

About eighty of the headquarters volunteers work in the Washington connection. As noted, each is in charge of liaison with four or five congressional districts. This is particularly interesting volunteer work. It involves regular phone calls to the same people, and enjoyable relationships are formed via long distance.

About twenty volunteers participate in "Congress watch."[9] They go to committee meetings in Congress that are of interest to Common Cause. The volunteers are broken into groups by subject matter—open government, energy, tax-ing and spending, for instance—and attend hearings in their field and report on them to Common Cause. Thus the volunteer becomes an expert at policy making in a particular issue area, while the lobbyists gain valuable intelligence as to the positions and concerns of various congressmen.

From fifteen to thirty volunteers collect and tabulate data for Common Cause volumes chronicling campaign donations in an election year. During the election period, volunteers check the campaign reports filed with the Federal Election Commission to see if they are done correctly. After the election, vol-unteers copy the campaign reports and code them for the computer. It is a trib-ute to the high quality of the efforts of these volunteers that practically no er-rors have been discovered in the compendia of electoral finance that Common Cause publishes.

About twelve volunteers work as research assistants for the policy divi-sion. Others do typing. Volunteers also do some routine work of the "envelope stuffing" variety, but paid staff is assigned to do most of the routine labor. In general, volunteer work at Common Cause is interesting for people concerned about politics, and thus the national headquarters has never suffered from a lack of volunteers.

The Washington volunteers come from the same well-educated, profession-al class as the membership. However, there is a greater variety of age among the volunteers than among the members. Thus there are considerable numbers of volunteers in all age ranges of both sexes between seventeen and seventy-five years, except for men between twenty-five and fifty-five. In other words, many volunteers are high school and college students. Others are housewives whose children have reached school age. Still others are retired people; Com-mon Cause provides an attractive form of political participation for older peo-ple. A type of volunteer particularly valuable to Common Cause is the retired federal executive, many of whom are only in their late fifties. Such executives are often encyclopedias of knowledge about federal policy. For example, one volunteer was a retired Defense Department official with twenty-five years of experience in preparing the defense budget. Such a volunteer can explain to Common Cause leaders "what is really happening on the inside."

Because national headquarters volunteers are so important to Common Cause, the organization has been active in lobbying Congress for extending self-government for Washington, D.C. Common Cause has been active in the lobbying effort to get state legislatures to ratify the "D.C. Statehood Amend-ment" to the Constitution. But even though Common Cause headquarters is only a mile from one of the largest conglomerations of urban blacks in the world, and though Common Cause has a generally favorable reputation among middle-class blacks in Washington, there are hardly any black volunteers at national headquarters. While blacks may prefer to work for their own institutions (political campaigns, churches, etc.), the conspicuous lack of black volunteers indicates that even educated blacks feel distant from the whites of Common Cause.

Common Cause is a complex organization. It has 250,000 contributors, 300 active congressional district branches, 48 state units, 115 full-time employees at its national and state offices, an annual budget of $8 million, and the capacity to send about 225,000 individually written letters to Congress each year. Common Cause operations are further complicated by the realities of American federalism; state and national lobbying campaigns must be coordinated in respect to financial support and the expenditure of members' efforts. Directing such an operation requires exceptional technical and managerial skills, which the Common Cause national staff possess.

NOTES

1. These alerts are inclusive in the sense that if all members are requested to write Congress, then the telephone networks will be activated, and the networks include all activists.
2. By March 1977, Michigan, New Jersey, Montana, and Minnesota provided public funds to candidates in some statewide elections. Common Cause state units were important in getting such laws in Michigan, Montana, and New Jersey. Several other states had laws that provided for transferring public funds to state political parties when individual taxpayers indicated on a state income tax return the desire to transfer a dollar or two for the support of a party. See Ruth S. Jones, "State Public Financing and the State Parties," in *Parties, Interest Groups, and Campaign Finance,* ed. Michael J. Malbin (Washington, D.C.: American Enterprise Institute, 1980), 283-303.
3. *New York Times,* 6 June 1974, 1; *Newsweek,* 17 June 1974, 35, 38; *Time,* 17 June 1974, 18.
4. Common Cause has a pollster check on its image in a nationwide poll about once a year.
5. There are no definitive data on state staff. I have met Common Cause staff from ten states and have the following impressions: Many are recent college graduates who want to work for a good cause for a few years. Others are married women who are returning to the job market because their children are attending school. In the better-financed states, the Common Cause lobbyist may be a professional who has been a paid lobbyist for other liberal or reform causes.
6. See Robert Cameron Mitchell, "National Environmental Lobbies and the Apparent Illogic of Collective Action," in *Collective Decision Making: Applications from Public Choice Theory,* ed. Clifford S. Russell (Baltimore: Johns Hopkins University Press, 1979), 102.

7. Andrew S. McFarland, *Public Interest Lobbies: Decision Making on Energy* (Washington, D.C.: American Enterprise Institute, 1976), 59, 66.

8. For example, Thomas S. Belford and Bruce Adams, "Conflict of Interest Legislation and the Common Cause Model Act," *The Municipal Year Book, 1975* (Washington, D.C.: International City Management Association, 1975), 170-79; David Cohen and Andrew Kneier, "Agency Reform and the Public Interest," *Federal Bar Journal* 34 (Fall 1975): 357-62; Andrew Kneier, "Ethics in Government Service: A Critical Look at Federal Conflict of Interest Regulation," in *The Ethical Basis of Economic Freedom,* ed. Ivan Hill (Chapel Hill, N.C.: American Viewpoint, 1976), 215-32; Lawrence Gilson, *Money and Secrecy: A Citizen's Guide to Reforming State and Federal Practices* (New York: Praeger, 1972); Bruce Adams, "A Model State Reapportionment Process: The Continuing Quest for 'Fair and Effective Representation,' " *Harvard Journal on Legislation* 14 (June 1977): 825-904; Bruce Adams and Betsy Sherman, "Sunset Implementaton: A Positive Partnership to Make Government Work," *Public Administration Review* 38 (January-February 1978): 78-81; Bruce Adams, "The Unfinished Revolution: Beyond 'One Person, One Vote,' " *National Civic Review* 67 (January 1978): 19-25; Bruce Adams and Kathryn Kavanagh-Baran, *Promise and Performance: Carter Builds a New Administration* (Lexington, Mass.: Lexington Books, 1979); Bruce Adams, "The Limitations of Muddling Through: Does Anyone in Washington Really Think Anymore?" *Public Administration Review* 39 (November-December 1979): 545-52; and David Cohen and Wendy Wolff, "Freeing Congress from the Special Interest State: A Public Interest Agenda for the 1980s," *Harvard Journal on Legislation* 17 (1980): 253-93.

9. "Congress Watch" happens to be the name of Nader's lobbying organization. The use of this term by Common Cause to describe its volunteer observation of Congress is coincidence. There is no special link between the Nader effort and the Common Cause effort having the same title.

5. Who Controls Common Cause?

Is Common Cause itself a democratic organization? Do the national leaders represent the interests of the organization's members, or is the organization ruled by a self-perpetuating oligarchy?

The main difficulty in treating such questions is that we have to clearly understand such terms as "democracy" or "representing interests." These terms can have several different meanings, meanings that are valid both to participants in politics and observers of politics. To deal with this problem, I use the approach of Hanna Pitkin, a political philosopher, as outlined in her pathbreaking works, *The Concept of Representation* and *Wittgenstein and Justice*.[1] Pitkin showed that valid concepts of representation have been discussed for centuries. Rather than pick one such concept as *the* concept of "representation," following the style of thought of modern philosophy of language Pitkin enjoined us to treat with respect the several conceptions of representation that participants in a political situation may find valid in understanding that situation. Our understanding is enhanced, according to Pitkin, if we understand the concepts of representation applied by the participants and then go on to analyze the relationships among these ideas. Pitkin's approach has been applied with success by several empirical writers about American political institutions.[2]

Accordingly, to understand the dynamics of power and governance within Common Cause, we shall consider five concepts and the relationships among them.

1. One concept of democracy is the *exchange model*. The exchange model refers to followers controlling leaders by giving or withdrawing support in terms of political resources, such as votes. Political scientist Robert A. Dahl developed this idea in terms of votes, political contributions, and campaign work. Political economist Albert Hirschman generalized the exchange model to include "the exit option," the withdrawal from an organization by a member or a unit.[3] The exchange model is applied to Common Cause in terms of the election of its national governing board, issue referenda among members, and acts of support or withdrawal such as joining or quitting and volunteering or not volunteering.

2. A second concept of democracy might be termed the *participation model*. This model emphasizes the importance of widespread, face-to-face participation of equal citizens in jointly discussing and resolving political issues that affect the future of the community (or organization) as a whole.[4] Since a citizen or organization member may vote but not discuss issues nor resolve them as part of a community-wide (organization-wide) process, this idea of democracy does not jibe with the exchange model. The participation model is applied to Common Cause in noting a rather low level of discussion of organizational issues among the membership.

3. A third idea is not on the same level of generality, but it is important in discussions of democracy in America. This is the idea of *descriptive representation*—if an institution is to be considered democratic, its governing elite should correspond proportionally to certain demographic characteristics of its constituency.[5] In other words, there ought to be a certain number of blacks, women, youth, or some other group on the governing board of an organization such as Common Cause.

4. A fourth issue about representation is the issue of *federalism*. What should be the relationship between the central unit of Common Cause and its state units? Common Cause was founded to be an organization to lobby in Washington, D.C., on national policy issues. But the logic of its structure and process program—its good-government program—implied the establishment of state units to pursue the Common Cause platform at the level of state government. By the mid-1970s the question of the relative division of resources between the national lobbying effort and state lobbying efforts became the greatest conflict within the organization. The question of the division of resources became overlaid with the question of the proper decision-making structure for Common Cause: should state units be empowered to appoint or elect delegates to the national governing board?

5. A final idea is the *consensus* of Common Cause leaders and members about the importance of action on governmental process reform issues—public funding for campaigns, sunshine laws, and the others. People who do not think these issues are important do not join Common Cause. Common Cause thus has an agenda of issues that produces little disagreement among its members and unifies the organization. The consensus on the importance of "structure and process" issues limits the incidence of disagreements among members and reduces the amount of conflict about decision making within Common Cause because the most important decision has already been made and is expressed in the nearly unanimous support for the government reform agenda.

Let us examine the five ideas and then briefly consider the relationships among them in the governance of Common Cause.

The Political Exchange Model

John Gardner founded Common Cause as a "people's lobby"; consequently, he had to give attention to the question of the role of the membership in internal decision making. Gardner set up a system of participation through an elected national governing board, a body similar to those found in other voluntary associations. The board now consists of sixty people, twenty of whom are elected by the total membership each year for a three-year term. After serving two three-year terms, a member must withdraw from the board but can run for the board again after a one-year hiatus. The chairman and president of Common Cause sit on the board ex officio.

The governing board has an elections committee, which each year slates thirty candidates for the twenty open positions on the board. Members can nominate themselves for the board by submitting a petition signed by only twenty members. Ordinarily, perhaps three such petition candidates are elected; perhaps seventeen of the thirty board-slated candidates are successful.

Common Cause's official responses to questions about its internal democracy usually emphasize that Common Cause is directed by a governing board elected by the membership and that anyone can run for that board. Such official responses also point out that the membership is polled yearly about which issues Common Cause should pursue and that Common Cause is guided by these polls.

Political scientists, journalists, and active participants in politics are likely to be skeptical of the official answer to the question of democracy within Common Cause. Both research by social scientists and practical experience seem to show that voluntary organizations are ordinarily controlled by a small group of leaders, variously described as an "oligarchy" or an "active minority."[6] Accordingly, one may well wonder whether the governing board and national staff leaders constitute a sort of an elite that is not controlled by Common Cause members. A second conjecture is that Common Cause is really controlled by the staff, while the board serves only as the trappings of democracy.

It is true that the Common Cause governing board has some power over the national staff. About once a year, a majority on the board defeats a significant proposal backed by the national staff. In 1973, for instance, the board vetoed a staff proposal for Common Cause to be a member of the Coalition for Human Needs, a lobbying coalition that acted on social welfare issues. The board expected this coalition to take stands on issues that could not be supported by an overwhelming majority of Common Cause members. In November 1974 the board refused to endorse a staff proposal that Common Cause launch a lobbying campaign against "tax loopholes." Several board members argued that there were good reasons for some federal subsidies and that the staff had not shown that the membership would back such a lobbying campaign.

On other occasions, the governing board (rather than the staff) has taken the initiative to launch some significant actions. For example, in 1976 most of the push to get Common Cause active on the ratification of the Equal Rights Amendment came from the board; in 1978, board members took the lead in deciding that lobbyists should play a major role in working for the congressional passage of a three-year extension for the ratification of ERA. In the summer of 1981, the board again took the initiative to press Common Cause to become more active on issues involving the nuclear arms race and increases in the defense budget.

The fact that the governing board occasionally vetoes staff proposals has the effect that the staff must anticipate board opinion in designing proposals. The board exercises power through such "anticipated reactions," which are, however, particularly difficult for an observer to identify.

Since the governing board seems to have some power, it is worth asking whether the annual elections make the board responsive to members' opinions. The answer seems to be that the board elections have a little impact on the organization's policies, but not too large an impact.

Board elections are low-information elections in which only 20 to 25 percent of the members participate. At the time of the election, each member receives a first-class letter, which contains the 150-word platform statements of the candidates, together with the list of those endorsed by the elections committee (30 endorsees for 20 slots). Only a tiny percentage of members is in a position to have independent knowledge about many of the candidates, and thus the voting in board elections is heavily influenced by demographic and regional criteria (members have opinions as to how many women, minorities, and so forth should serve on the board). Almost all those elected are committee-endorsed candidates, but the board cannot control which seventeen (or so) of the list of thirty are to be ratified by the members. Thus, board members popular with other board members have frequently not been reelected.

Ordinarily, such an election is not a significant vehicle for members' control of the governing board because the membership has so little information when they vote. However, even this kind of election has some effect on representation. First, members show by their voting their desire for "descriptive representation" (blacks, women, etc.) on the board, as is discussed below. Second, the existence of petition candidacies provides a means for opponents of the national leadership to express themselves. If a significant number of people intensely oppose the leadership's policies, this will be reflected in a number of petition candidates stating platforms definitely opposed to the established leadership.

Such a phenomenon will be a clear signal for the national leadership to reconsider whatever policies are alienating members.

In reference to the exchange model, its importance in understanding Common Cause lies not so much in governing board elections as in members' capacity "to exit" the organization, in Hirschman's terms. The main control that members exercise over top staff and the board is the implicit threat that large numbers of them will quit volunteering their labor (by writing letters and so forth) or quit the organization altogether. Ninety-five percent or more of the budget of Common Cause comes from membership dues and contributions; if many members quit, programs must be cut back, salary raises must be foregone, and staff must be laid off. No one is more aware of this than the staff and the board, who accordingly are very concerned not to take actions that might prove offensive to large numbers of members. John Gardner stated this point very clearly:

> In the course of our first year we set up a system through which the membership elects members to the board, and we held our first election. . . . Of course, in any voluntary citizens' organization like Common Cause, the most conclusive vote cast by the individual is his decision to join or resign. His joining is in effect a vote for the movement; his resignation or failure to renew membership is a vote against. Thus, collectively, the members hold life-or-death control over the organization. If enough of them fail to renew their memberships, that will be the end of Common Cause.[7]

Common Cause needs more information about its members' preferences than it can get from board elections. Accordingly, the membership is frequently polled. Some of the early polls were mailed with the board ballot and seemed rather perfunctory. Such polls often consisted of picking, say, five issues out of a list of fifteen as worthy of lobbying. However, after the membership went into a decline in 1975, the organization initiated a number of careful, serious polls about member preferences. Occasionally, professional pollsters were hired.

After 1976, Common Cause leaders paid close attention to these polls because of their fear of offending members and hence losing them. Since then, the national leadership never lobbied for a controversial goal that would displease a significant fraction of their membership. In fact, the last time Common Cause lobbied for measures offensive to a significant fraction of its members occurred in 1975 when the organization was active in supporting a 20-cent federal surcharge on gasoline and against building the B-1 bomber.[8] The board adopted an energy platform that contained a provision advocating a moratorium on the construction of new nuclear electric-power plants in 1975, but a year later, after learning that 30 percent of its members opposed this idea, the board reversed its position and took no stand.[9]

Consequently, rather than manipulate members into supporting positions on new issues, the national leadership after 1976 was subjected to a sort of minority veto, expressed in polls, concerning issues on which Common Cause should become active. The leaders' caution was increased by members' perception of the appropriateness of an issue for Common Cause. In other words, x percent of the members might oppose the leadership's position on an issue, but commonly $2x$ percent would find the issue to be an inappropriate matter for Common Cause lobbying. For instance, in regard to the moratorium on the construction of new nuclear electric-power plants, 15 percent of the members thought that more nuclear facilities should be constructed, but 30 percent thought that Common Cause should *not* lobby for the moratorium. In one of its last lobbying efforts not subjected to the minority veto — its opposition to the construction of the B-1 bomber in 1975 — the leadership received many complaints from members that the position might be politically correct but was inappropriate for Common Cause action. By the 1970s, Common Cause had created an organizational identity as the lobbying specialist on issues concerning the reform of governmental processes; many members would object to departures from this sphere of lobbying specialization.

A 30 percent opposition to Common Cause's participation on an issue, as registered in a membership poll, was certainly enough to block activity on the issue; 20 percent opposition was ordinarily enough to cast a minority veto. Even John Gardner could not override a poll of the membership in 1976. Gardner at that time hoped that Common Cause would become active on international issues, such as disarmament negotiations, energy problems, and worldwide imbalances in food production. But most of the members opposed any activity on such issues, and even Gardner could not overturn this opinion.

The minority veto, combined with the idea of issues being inappropriate for Common Cause, was linked to the philosophy of Gardner and other national leaders that Common Cause should not diffuse its political resources among too many issues. From 1976 on, the organization took a number of advanced positions on governmental reform issues (e.g., advocating sunset laws to terminate authorizations for government agencies every seven years), but it took a cautious approach to most issues on the agenda of liberals. Common Cause did *not,* for instance, lobby for handgun control, abortion rights, gay rights, the legalization of marijuana, or against the construction of nuclear plants. Common Cause did not lobby on international issues before 1981, although it would have lobbied for the SALT II treaty in 1979 if the issue had gone to the Senate floor.

The national leaders became adept at suggesting a form of compromise that would appeal to advocates of action on a matter and that would be acceptable to opponents of such action. The compromise suggestion could be activity in lobbying for a governmental process reform in the area of the proposed action. For instance, rather than lobby for a moratorium on new nuclear plants, Common Cause lobbied for the abolition of the Joint Committee on Atomic Energy of the U.S. Congress, a one-sided supporter of nuclear development. Or, rather than lobby for abortion rights, from the standpoint of working to preserve the independence of the judiciary within the separation-of-powers system, Common Cause opposed in 1981 congressional measures to redefine the meaning of "life" in federal law. This tactic was an effective means of reducing conflict by expanding the scope of governmental process reforms amenable to Common Cause.

The leadership of Common Cause is also dependent on its members to contribute small amounts of work to the organization, especially the effort needed to write or phone a member of Congress. A secondary reason why Common Cause began to poll its members carefully was that the membership did not respond with many letters in support of the leadership's positions against the B-1 bomber and for the 20-cent gasoline tax. Many letter-writers did not understand the reasons for Common Cause action on these issues, or considered these issues inappropriate for action and accordingly did not write Congress. From this experience, the leadership concluded that members could not work for new issues unless some months elapsed in a process of explaining the issues to members. Again, the leaders were restrained in the selection of issues by the opinions of the members.

In sum, the national leadership is not limited to a great extent by governing board elections. But since 1976, the national leadership has become very restricted in selecting issues for activity by a process of membership polling and a concern about offending members, who might then quit the organization.

The Participation Model of Democracy

Proponents of the participation model emphasize the role of discussion and political education in democracy, as opposed to those who emphasize the exchange of political resources among leaders and followers. Participation writers tend to be influenced by the humanities; exchange writers are influenced by the economic theory of markets. During the 1960s, leading political scientists Robert A. Dahl and Seymour Martin Lipset emphasized the exchange model, but they were in turn criticized by such participation writers as Peter Bachrach and Carole Pateman.[10]

The participation model sees democracy in terms of widespread participation by citizens (or organization members) in face-to-face discussion to resolve political issues that affect the future of everyone in a community. Some participation writers derive inspiration from descriptions of decision making by citizen assemblies in ancient Greece. Leftist participation writers emphasize the importance of establishing workplace democracy in the factory and regard such hypothetical worker participation as a counter to the alienation of labor described by Marx.

The participation model of democracy can be applied to Common Cause. The chief instance of this was a critical article written by a graduate student in political science in 1974, which was reprinted in the *Washington Star* (and was read by a number of congressmen, thereby damaging Common Cause).[11]

The political scientist, Mary Topolsky, argued that Common Cause was encouraging an alienated, ersatz form of participation in politics that relied on the attractiveness of easy, solitary action; on avoiding other persons; and on discussion of political tactics but not political issues. According to Topolsky, Common Cause members—whom she believed never meet with one another—receive communication from unseen persons in Washington, requesting the initiation of some form of political activity, usually one conducted in solitary fashion, such as writing letters. The members' motivation to support Common Cause is the desire to avoid the conflicts, disappointments, boredom, and failures incurred in direct action in politics. The member thus prefers to pay someone else to do his or her political work, in Topolsky's view. While her criticisms emphasized the dubious value of Common Cause as a model for participation in politics, this implies a criticism of the lack of face-to-face participation within the internal governance of Common Cause.

Common Cause would not receive high marks for democracy in its internal processes, according to the participation model. In its defense, however, practically no effective lobby in Washington, with the exception of the League of Women Voters, would get a high rating according to the participation model. And, in fact, writers in this tradition usually are uninterested in or critical of the prospects of participation in nationally organized interest groups.

In starting Common Cause, John Gardner had in mind forming a lobby—a group of citizens who would support the efforts of Washington lobbyists. He clearly rejected the idea of forming a group that would emphasize educating members about political issues. Gardner and subsequent leaders of Common Cause assumed that members already had formed political opinions. In 1972 it was assumed that almost all members would support the prime lobbying goal of having in the House a full-scale debate on the war in Vietnam. After 1974 it was assumed that almost all members supported the basic governmental reform issues, such as public funding for federal elections and sunshine laws. In 1982 the leaders could assume (backed by their polling efforts) that most members would favor action in support of negotiations to reduce the incidence of nuclear weapons. And because of the minority veto on new issues after 1976, there were not many new Common Cause issues for the members to discuss.

Consequently, there is not much discussion of political issues within the organizational network. On the other hand, the staff is very enthusiastic about teaching members effective political tactics in attaining Common Cause goals. And, of course, those active within Common Cause view it as providing an effective organizational means for lobbying politicians to attain those goals. There is a great deal of discussion among participants about the mechanics of organizing effective lobbying campaigns at the state and national levels. As part of these campaigns, activists are taught how to approach legislators and how to deal with "the media."

Much of the tactical discussion within Common Cause is conducted on a face-to-face basis at regular meetings of the state Program Action Committees. The various committees of the national governing board meet for about four days a year, and this is another source of direct, face-to-face participation. In addition, committees sometimes meet to discuss specific local tactics in conjunction with national or statewide lobbying campaigns. At any one time, however, only about 5 percent of the membership participates in meetings about tactics.

As a result of the recurring conflict among state-level activists and national leaders, Common Cause established in 1978 an annual series of regional meetings between the two groups. These meetings, which usually lasted for a weekend, were direct, personal discussions of all issues confronting Common Cause and thus satisfied the requirements of the participation model of democracy. In 1981 these regional meetings were replaced by a single "state leadership conference" at which 110 state leaders meet with national staff at the national organization's expense. This change seems to have reduced the amount of face-to-face interaction of state leaders and national staff but has increased such interaction among state leaders themselves and may produce a consciousness of their own identity as a group within Common Cause. In addition, state chairpersons recently have been encouraged to attend one national governing board meeting a year at the expense of the board.

Descriptive Representation

One of the several concepts of representation outlined by Pitkin is descriptive representation. This concept refers to the expectation that representatives correspond in certain characteristics proportionally to the incidence of those characteristics in the representatives' constituencies. As applied to Common Cause, descriptive representation means that a certain proportion of the governing board and staff leadership must be women or have minority status or be Republicans (because Common Cause strives for a nonpartisan image). In addition, regional balance among board members is an important consideration; an effort must be made to encourage the election of members from the South and the West to balance the election of interest-group leaders and political celebrities who live on the Eastern Seaboard or in metropolitan Washington, D.C.

What is perhaps most interesting about descriptive representation within Common Cause is that active members nearly unanimously agree on its necessity and think in terms of the same categories of descriptive representation. This is most apparent in board elections. The Common Cause board must contain a significant number of persons in the categories just mentioned (women, Republicans, minorities, the West, the South) or else lobbying will be hindered by criticisms of its "unrepresentative" nature. Everyone seems to believe this, and every year the board election committee recommends thirty candidates balanced according to the important categories. Members who vote in these elections — 80 percent of whom are *not* Republicans, virtually none of whom are minorities, and 60 percent of whom reside in Eastern Seaboard or Pacific Coast states — regularly vote onto the board twenty people who maintain descriptive representation.

Descriptive representation has an impact on Common Cause policies other than protecting the organization from journalistic charges of being "unrepresentative." The substantial number of women on the board ensured a significant amount of activity to gain ratification for the Equal Rights Amendment. The Republicans on the board prevent Common Cause from lobbying for many of the cherished goals of northeastern liberals. The existence of minorities on the board guarantees that Common Cause will be active in lobbying for civil rights issues, such as the extensions of the Voting Rights Act in 1975 and 1982.

Federalism and Representation

One's view of representation within Common Cause can be expressed by the kind of districting one supports for the election of the governing board, the major representative institution authorized by the charter. John Gardner envisioned Common Cause as a centralized organization. Thus the board he established is elected from one nationwide district, all members eligible to vote for representatives from anywhere in the United States. Leaders of state units, on the other hand, have proposed that the board be elected on some sort of federal basis. For instance, state boards might elect delegates to the national board, or some national board members might be elected from districts composed of states or regions. Such electoral districts reflect the view that the state units play a critical role within Common Cause. This might be termed "the federal" view of representation within the organization.

Conflict between the national leadership and state organizations is the Achilles heel of Common Cause. The organization's main goal is to reform governmental processes. Accordingly it is only natural for some of its resources to be directed to reforming state governments, especially as activists residing thousands of miles from Washington, D.C., are sure to want to work for the platform in nearby state capitals. (As a general policy, the national leadership has restricted Common Cause activity at the city or local government level.) In an organization with limited resources, it was inescapable that conflict between the national and the state units would break out. And one can predict that if resources shrink, as a result of inflation or a decrease in membership, such conflict may worsen.

No matter how capable the national management, state-national conflicts will occur every few years. In fact, they have occurred in 1976, 1978, and 1981-82. In 1976, in response to numerous complaints from activists at the state level, the national organization set up a study commission on questions of governance that established annual regional meetings among national staff and state activists during 1978-81. The commission also clarified the formulas by which the national group allocated money to the states (75 percent of the money for state organizations at the time came from the national headquarters) and instituted an appeals process for states that felt they had been slighted in the national budget.

In 1978, because of inflation and a decline in membership, the national leadership proposed that money be saved by consolidating some state organizations (e.g., rather than have one full-time staffer in Missouri and one in Kansas, perhaps one person could serve both states). This suggestion was met by a storm of protest from members of state boards and volunteers in state organizations. At a hectic national board meeting, the national leadership withdrew its proposal to so consolidate state organizations, while state activists agreed to support some cutbacks in the national staff's allocations of funds to state organizations.

In 1981, further protest occurred from state activists who felt ignored by the governing board and the national staff. Furthermore, at this time, the platform of state leaders gained new legitimacy because it seemed clear that a conservative President and U.S. Senate would block the adoption of Common Cause measures at the national level that would stand a much better chance of adoption at the state level. In addition, the country seemed to be heading into a decade in which state governments would become more important in relation to the federal government, and it seemed logical for Common Cause to become more state oriented. Leading state activists called a national meeting of their fellow state activists in September 1981, at which time it was proposed that state units select some of the members of the national governing board.

Unity

It has already been noted that almost everyone at all levels within Common Cause agrees with the basic government reform platform (public funding of elections and so forth). This chapter has carried this observation a step further. With the exception of the issue of federalism within Common Cause, there is not much for members and staff to fight over. Various minorities among the membership are able to veto controversial new positions on issues. But the reaction to this is not one of conflict; perhaps it is more one of boredom. Common Cause does not have much participatory democracy, but there is little reason for the members to participate and discuss issues because almost all the members give top priority to the government reform issues. Virtually everyone within the organization agrees on the principles of descriptive representation as reflected on the national board. Finally, those who have at one time signed on as members, but who do not give the government reform issues top priority among their own preferences for political change, do not renew their memberships and "exit" the organization, which thereby becomes even more unanimous in its opinions.

Relationships among Conceptions of Democracy

Pitkin's theory implies that interesting behavior concerning representation can occur when two or more conceptions of democracy are joined in a situation.[12] A number of these conjunctions have occurred in the history of Common Cause.

In 1976 the Common Cause national staff mandated that participation and exchange be joined in the election of local congressional district steering committees. The national staff considered that face-to-face interaction would improve the quality of personnel selected for the steering committees because mail ballots had a tendency to result in the election of local celebrities, who might not have a grasp of the organization and its tactics, and who might not be especially motivated to work hard for Common Cause. Accordingly, the national unit provided that local steering committees be selected at an annual Common Cause Day, a meeting of all the members in the congressional district. In theory, exchange democracy and participatory democracy can work together to produce a more informed "electorate," although in the case of Common

Cause, there is a danger that attendance at the annual meeting might be very low, thereby leaving the selection of the steering committee in the hands of a self-perpetuating clique.

On the other hand, exchange democracy and participatory democracy are in a contradictory position in the membership polling and minority veto situation. Because the possibility of action on most new issues is quickly vetoed by annual membership polls, Common Cause activists and staff members spend little time in discussing such new possibilities for action. The exchange model works so efficiently that many possible situations for participatory democracy are eliminated.

Within Common Cause, exchange democracy conflicts with descriptive representation in one instance. Every year, about 10 percent of the sixty members of the national governing board resign, usually because they do not have time for Common Cause activities. The charter provides that the other members of the board may appoint new board members to fill such vacancies, but during the 1970s the board was never able to do this. On the one hand, it seemed that such appointees should be selected according to position in the governing board election—with the first runner-up getting the appointment. On the other hand, resignations altered the balance of descriptive representation on the board, and it seemed appropriate to appoint unsuccessful candidates, without regard to order of finishing, to restore descriptive representation. (For instance, if a black board member resigned, it might be fitting to appoint another black, even if he or she was fifth runner-up in the election.) This dilemma was irresolvable for the board, which could not decide between two concepts of democracy. Accordingly, no one was appointed to fill the empty positions.

Finally, there is an important interaction with the exchange model and conflict over federalism within Common Cause. Activists for reform of state governments ordinarily do not have the option of "exiting" from Common Cause, at least if the activists want to continue to pursue the goal of reform of state government. There is no other lobby for procedural reforms in the state capital with the experience and prestige of Common Cause.

Albert Hirschman notes that, besides "exit," organizational members have the option of "voice"—staying within an organization and voicing their objections to organizational policy, thus striving to change such policies in the directions of their opinions.[13] This applies to Common Cause. The state-level activists who disagree with the allocation of resources by the national leaders have a strong incentive to continue to work within Common Cause and continue to raise the issue of the role of federalism within the organization. This is another reason why the issue of federalism is a permanent one for Common Cause.

Who Rules Common Cause?

The national governing board and national staff are closely controlled by the members in respect to the selection of issues for lobbying. But the staff has broad leeway on lobbying tactics, although there is always the possibility of a check from the board. The national staff and the board have so far had their way on the issue of federalism within Common Cause.

Then, is the Common Cause national leadership acting democratically? Following Pitkin's theory of multiple conceptions of democracy and representation, the answer is probably a matter of personal judgment. The leadership is closely constrained on issues by the exit model of exchange; yet the board elections would seem to be more symbolic than substantive. There is little participatory democracy within Common Cause, but except for the issue of federalism, there would be few issues for the members to discuss if they should opt for more participation. Board elections are a model of the operation of descriptive representation. A number of state-level activists feel that Common Cause is less than democratic on the federalism issue, but a judgment on this matter is tied to one's conception of the organizational mission of Common Cause.

One general lesson from this discussion of Common Cause can be applied to other interest-group organizations. The mechanisms of control emanating from the exit option can be subtle but powerful. Even John Gardner, a hero within the organization he founded, was by 1976 controlled by the possibility of members leaving the organization. It is likely that the leaders of many other organizations are similarly controlled. The exit option is an important limit to oligarchical tendencies within interest-group organizations.

NOTES

1. Hanna Fenichel Pitkin, *The Concept of Representation* (Berkeley: University of California Press, 1967); and idem, *Wittgenstein and Justice* (Berkeley: University of California Press, 1972).
2. See, for example, Paul E. Peterson, "Forms of Representation: Participation of the Poor in the Community Action Program," *American Political Science Review* 64 (June 1970): 491-507; Jeane Kirkpatrick, "Representation in the American National Conventions: The Case of 1972," *British Journal of Political Science* 5 (July 1975): 265-322; Austin Ranney, *Curing the Mischiefs of Faction* (Berkeley: University of California Press, 1975), 111-15; and James A. Morone and Theodore R. Marmor, "Representing Consumer Interests: The Case of American Health Planning," *Ethics* 91 (April 1981): 431-50.
3. See Robert Dahl, *Preface to Democratic Theory* (Chicago: University of Chicago Press, 1956); and idem, *Who Governs?* (New Haven: Yale University Press, 1961). Also see Seymour Martin Lipset, *Political Man* (Garden City, N.Y.: Doubleday,

1960), chap. 2; Albert O. Hirschman, *Exit, Voice, and Loyalty* (Cambridge, Mass.: Harvard University Press, 1970).

4. An excellent presentation of the participation model of democracy, therein styled "the theory of democratic citizenship," is found in Dennis F. Thompson, *The Democratic Citizen* (Cambridge, England: Cambridge University Press, 1970). Three critics of Dahl and Lipset from the participatory democracy standpoint who have been widely read in recent years are Peter Bachrach, *The Theory of Democratic Elitism: A Critique* (Boston: Little, Brown, 1967); Carole Pateman, *Participation and Democratic Theory* (Cambridge, England: Cambridge University Press, 1970); and Jack L. Walker, "A Critique of the Elitist Theory of Democracy," *American Political Science Review* 60 (June 1966): 285-95.

5. Pitkin, *Concept of Representation,* chap. 4.

6. See the introduction by Seymour Martin Lipset in Robert Michels, *Political Parties,* trans. Eden and Cedar Paul (New York: Collier, 1962). Also see David B. Truman, *The Governmental Process,* rev. ed. (New York: Knopf, 1971), 139-55. The League of Women Voters is an impressively democratic interest group; see Andrew S. McFarland, *Public Interest Lobbies: Decision Making on Energy* (Washington, D.C.: American Enterprise Institute, 1976): 77-83.

7. John W. Gardner, *In Common Cause* (New York: Norton, 1972), 118-19.

8. McFarland, *Public Interest Lobbies,* 57.

9. Ibid., 121.

10. See notes 3 and 4.

11. Mary Topolsky, "Common Cause?" *Worldview* 17 (April 1974): 35-39, reprinted as "Is the 'Common' in Common Cause an Illusion?" *Washington Star,* 21 April 1974.

12. Pitkin, *Concept of Representation,* 225-40.

13. Hirschman, *Exit, Voice, and Loyalty.*

6. Lobbying: Working to Persuade the Undecided

The structure of Common Cause has been described. The nature of decision making and democracy within this structure has been examined. Now let us consider the most important activity of the organization—lobbying.

The major site of Common Cause's efforts to wield influence is the U.S. Congress, the House of Representatives in particular. But the organization's political activities involve much more than lobbying in the sense of directly contacting congressmen or getting members to write Congress. Especially in the OUTS ("open up the system") reforms, the political strategy of Common Cause is based on a comprehensive coordination, not only of writing letters to congressmen and talking to them, but also of publicity, research, litigation, organizational imperatives, and tactical planning.

Multifaceted activity is needed to pass a law that might rectify a political ill. Publicity is needed to get widespread support for a Common Cause-backed measure. Research makes sure that the remedy seems adequate to the problem in the eyes of the legislators. Litigation is part of an overall lobbying strategy, as, for instance, when Common Cause sued Nixon's Committee to Re-Elect the President to force a disclosure of donations and discredit the system of campaign contributions in order to enact reform. Common Cause managers must be sure that a lobbying strategy does not impose too-heavy tasks on its staff (e.g., requiring impossible amounts of research) or overload the field organization. In addition, political tactics must be coordinated with congressmen and other groups supporting a bill.

Common Cause believes that getting an issue on the "congressional agenda" is the hardest part of the battle in getting a reform enacted. In other words, drafting a measure, lining up congressional supporters, and making sure that the measure is reported from committee constitute greater obstacles to enactment than the subsequent processes of voting by both houses, gaining agreement in conference, and getting presidential approval. The earlier stages of congressional activity, those leading to committee approval of a bill, involve a great amount of research, publicity, possibly litigation to clarify the legal situation, and tactical planning. Hence the Common Cause lobbying strategy goes beyond sending lobbyists to Capitol Hill and stimulating letters to Congress.

The existence of a three-branched government and federalism further complicates political action. Common Cause occasionally institutes lawsuits in the political reform field, both for the sake of getting reform by judicial decree and to help define a legislative issue. In addition, in the 1970s Common Cause tried lobbying the federal executive branch to enact such reform measures as getting top administrators in the energy and environment agencies to log contacts with persons outside their agencies as an attempt to discourage frequent contacts with lobbyists for corporations.[1] And, of course, Common Cause's state units run lobbying campaigns at the state level to enact OUTS legislation, and so there is a need to coordinate national and state political efforts so that the organization does not try to do too much at any one time.

Despite all this activity, the major emphasis of Common Cause's national political strategy has been on getting the U.S. House of Representatives to pass reform measures, such as OUTS bills, the public financing of electoral campaigns, and requiring a withdrawal of troops from Vietnam. In the early 1970s the House proved more of an obstacle to the enactment of Common Cause-backed reforms than the Senate. And even Presidents Nixon and Ford felt constrained to sign most Common Cause-supported measures after their passage by both houses of Congress. Senator Mike Mansfield, the Senate majority leader from 1961 to 1977, was a critic of the Vietnam war and scheduled wide-ranging floor debates on the issue, but the House leadership supported the American effort in Vietnam and permitted no overall discussion of the Vietnam effort until an antiwar coalition forced a series of short debates and votes in 1971 (which they lost).[2] The Senate Government Operations Committee, chaired by Senator Abraham Ribicoff before 1981, was generally favorable to institutional reforms supported by Common Cause. But in the House, bills for campaign reform were referred to the House Administration Committee, which was less friendly to such legislation — especially when led by Representative Wayne Hays, the chairman from 1971 to 1976, and a man who intensely disliked Common Cause and its reforms. Further, bills for regulating lobbyists were referred to the Administrative Law and Government Relations Subcommittee of the House Judiciary Committee. The subcommittee chairman before 1979, Representative Walter Flowers of Alabama (who may be remembered from the televised impeachment hearings), was not initially favorable to Common Cause and was able to stall its lobbyist control bill, for example, by not calling hearings for two years.

Thus, partly because Representatives Hays and Flowers were able to delay Common Cause-sponsored legislation, before 1979 the Senate passed such bills earlier than the House. For example, the Senate passed a bill providing for public financing of congressional elections on a matching-grant basis in 1974; the House has not yet done so.[3] Yet the Senate was not always responsive to Common Cause. For instance, a powerful Senate committee chairman under the Democrats, Russell Long of the Finance Committee, was relatively favorable to giving special tax exemptions to particular businesses or industries, something Common Cause opposed (although it did not adopt a comprehensive position on taxation). On the other hand, the House Ways and Means Committee, particularly since the election of many reform Democrats in 1974, has been more critical of narrowly defined tax exemptions than was Senator Long's committee.

Ways of Influencing Congress

In the 1970s, 150 to 175 members of the House of Representatives were typically in initial agreement with a major Common Cause lobbying position, such as the public financing of presidential and congressional elections, the need for major changes in the seniority system in Congress, the need for the strict regulation of lobbyists, or the need to hold open meetings of congressional committees and regulatory commissions. About 100 members typically were initially undecided on one of these measures. In addition, another large bloc of representatives, perhaps 150 to 175 members, typically was initially opposed in general to a major Common Cause lobbying position. Thus, the lobbying job was usually to work with friendly congressmen to persuade the undecided congressmen to support the position.[4]

Final votes on the House or Senate floor sometimes exaggerated the actual support for a Common Cause-supported measure.[5] In the early 1970s, the major bills for reform of government institutions usually had so much support from outside Congress by the time they reached a floor vote that congressmen evidently were reluctant to go on record in opposition, even if they had opposed them initially.

In the Senate, Common Cause in the 1970s faced a pattern of about 40 senators initially favorable to major lobbying positions, about 30 undecided, and perhaps 30 opposed. Because Senator Ribicoff was generally cooperative in reporting Common Cause-endorsed measures from his Government Operations Committee, the major lobbying concern in the Senate was the anticipation of votes to end filibusters, which before 1975 required a two-thirds vote of those senators present. (A rule adopted in March 1975 permitted ending debate by a three-fifths vote of the entire Senate.) Particularly in the years of the two-thirds rule, Common Cause lobbyists would anticipate, six months to a year before the actual vote on the floor of the Senate, who the critical swing votes on a filibuster might be. Such strategic planning was an important part of the passage of the Federal Election Campaign Amendments of 1974 when lobbyists David Cohen and Fred Wertheimer correctly predicted the critical senatorial votes on a filibuster cloture vote, and pressure by Common Cause provided the major force in getting the last few votes needed for the necessary two-thirds margin.[6]

Common Cause did not invent the idea of reforming Congress and federal election campaigns. The organization of liberal Democrats in the House, the Democratic Study Group, looked to reform of the House's seniority system and procedures as one of its major goals. The group had acquired considerable cohesion and staff expertise by 1970 and was about to push reform when Gardner started Common Cause. In addition, many Republican members of the House, particularly among liberal Republican members of the Wednesday Club, realized by 1970 that Republicans might never attain majority status and hence never attain control of the House. Accordingly, some of the Republicans also supported government reform measures, such as open committee meetings, which would lessen the power of senior Democrats over the House as a whole. Moreover, while Republicans historically raise more money in congressional races than Democrats do, the Republican financial edge began to erode in the late 1960s because Democrats tended to be incumbents, most of them from safe districts, and hence were in a position to do favors for campaign donors. Further, as it became clear that Democrats could be expected to retain control of both houses of Congress, campaign donors realized that only Democrats would be committee or subcommittee chairmen and that other Democrats tended to have the most influence over such leaders of Congress. Accordingly, a reform position became attractive to as many as one-third of the Republicans in Congress by the early 1970s.[7]

Common Cause can generate considerable mail to Congress, but if that was all it did in regard to lobbying, it would be a minor lobby indeed. Congressmen often have a pretty accurate idea of opinion in their districts, and on government reform issues most congressmen in the fifty districts in which Common Cause is strongest already hold a reform position. (This is good politics on the West Coast and in eastern suburban districts.) I do not deny that constituent mail is important, particularly when it is written by individuals and is sent to the right decision maker at the right time, as Common Cause is able to do. But on issues on which Common Cause is active, such as electoral campaign reform and the regulation of lobbyists, congressmen are subject to pressure from their immediate circle of colleagues and friends (some of them lobbyists) that frequently cancels out the effect of mail from constituents. Common Cause must do more than generate letters to Congress to have significant influence.[8]

Mail to Congress.[9] Sending mail to Congress is only one of the political tactics employed by Common Cause, but it is a very important one. Generating 225,000 letters a year is not enough to make Common Cause a major lobby on a range of important bills, yet not to generate those letters would lessen the organization's influence considerably. The letters are a concrete indication that a fair number of people care about how their congressmen vote on government reform and other issues.

There is a great variation in the amount of mail received by members of Congress from Common Cause members. If we presume that about two-thirds of the letters go to the House and one-third to the Senate, the average representative receives 320 letters a year and the average senator about 700 letters a year. The 100 or so members of the House without a functioning Common Cause unit in their district, however, probably receive less than 100 letters a year.[10] On the other hand, several members of the House are likely to receive more than 1000 letters a year. A similar variation would be true of senators; senators from less populous western and southern states will get only a few hundred letters a year, while 2000 or 3000 letters will go to senators from New York and California.

The mail generated by Common Cause in the first two years of its existence was probably more important than the mail generated since then because the mail sent at the beginning of the organization showed that Common Cause had widespread support. At first, almost all Washington observers, including members of Congress, did not believe that Gardner would succeed in establishing a group that could significantly influence Congress. Even after 100,000 persons had joined the new organization in its first six months, this did not imply that its lobbying would be fruitful. But Common Cause managed to generate large amounts of mail on Vietnam and the SST. This demonstrated that Common Cause could reach voters across the nation and induce them to act in politics. This initial mail indicated, at least to some northeastern, West Coast, suburban, and reform-oriented congressmen, that the Common Cause Washington lobbyists ought to be listened to as representatives of a significant force in public opinion. (Most southern or rural congressmen did not feel this way.[11])

Mail was important initially in establishing Common Cause's potential for exercising political power. But today the impact of mail is largely routinized — it is hypothesized that about 150 members of the House expect that, as a matter of routine, Common Cause can generate a significant amount of mail. Most of these congressmen have long since decided how much political weight to give to the lobbying positions of Common Cause. They are impressed only by an unusual number of letters, such as occurred in December 1976 over the issue of removing Florida congressman Robert L.F. Sikes from the chair of the military construction subcommittee of the House Appropriations Committee after Sikes had been reprimanded by the House for unethical conduct.

On the other hand, congressmen will notice if they do not get mail from Common Cause. Also, if Common Cause were to achieve organizational success in a congressional district where they do not generate much mail, the receipt of that mail for the first time would impress a member of Congress. These same considerations hold for the Senate.

Common Cause members write their own letters, using information that is gleaned from special "alert" messages from Washington headquarters, from monthly bulletins to the membership, or from phoned messages from the congressional district steering committee. This is important because congressmen often discount letters that are not individually written but are merely provided by some interest group.[12] And congressmen cannot be sure how many of the letters they receive are initiated by a Common Cause alert. In addition, congressmen with reform-oriented constituencies cannot discount Common Cause-sponsored letters because such congressmen frequently see the letter-writer as an opinion maker, as an educated professional who may influence the voters among his or her circle of friends.

Meetings with Common Cause Members. Interviews with congressmen have indicated that meeting with a congressman, formally or informally, is a more effective way of influencing congressmen than writing letters to congressional offices. The members of Congress that are interviewed usually did not have a clear idea of how much mail they got from Common Cause on recent issues, but they did recall personal encounters with Common Cause members or Washington lobbyists. (Nevertheless, Common Cause must generate a significant amount of mail on a continuing basis to seem important in the eyes of congressmen.)

The better-organized congressional district units arrange meetings with their representatives from one to six times a year. Frequently the district steering committee is the group that meets with the congressman. At such meetings Common Cause members try to get the representative to commit himself to Common Cause-endorsed measures. If a member of Congress has already endorsed a sponsored bill, his constituents may try to persuade him to become active in passing the measure. For example, the representative could write the House Judiciary chairman to urge him to get the subcommittee chairman to hold hearings on a bill.

Such meetings also enable the congressman and local Common Cause leaders to get acquainted, which enhances communication between the members and their representative. A district leader who knows his congressman will be sufficiently confident to write or telephone him on a number of occasions. And the representative will pay attention to the message because he knows that the district leader will discuss his views at their next meeting.

Such meetings need to be monitored by national headquarters. This is an important job for the Washington connection. Washington volunteers encourage the congressional district organizations to meet with their congressmen. In the great majority of cases, Common Cause members need to be encouraged to make appointments with their representatives and press a sponsored issue on them. Even members with high social status feel some anxiety at the prospect of taking the initiative and stating their views to a member of Congress.

Washington volunteers also tell local members what issues ought to be discussed with congressmen, although this is not a last-minute, ad hoc decision but a reminder to the members as to which issues are at the top of the list of priorities. In addition, headquarters volunteers must be sure that steering committee members understand the issues they discuss with their representative. While local leaders are intelligent, Common Cause-sponsored measures can be complicated, and they are not easy to discuss. Most people find it difficult to remember the various rules of the Federal Election Campaign Amendments of 1974 or the sponsored lobbying regulation measure.

After two years of experience in arranging meetings of members with congressmen, the national staff realized such meetings were often unsuccessful in producing commitments to back a sponsored bill because congressmen frequently engaged in abstruse discussions of technical details to avoid stating a commitment. Thus, Washington volunteers now inform local members about three to five essential principles involved in some proposed legislation, and local members then concentrate on getting congressmen to discuss these principles.

Common Cause headquarters also must monitor local members in their dealings with congressmen to avoid blunders. Some local leaders may be offensively moralistic in lobbying for backed measures, or they may threaten to oppose a congressman in a forthcoming election campaign if he does not agree with a Common Cause position. Both moralism and threats are likely to be counterproductive.[13] Common Cause has a problem in that many of its activists, particularly those who have not previously dealt with politicians, regard the sponsored reforms as morally sacrosanct measures that should not be criticized or compromised. Moralistic activists must be instructed by headquarters volunteers to be soft-spoken and pragmatic; such cautions have been extremely valuable in the political education of well-meaning political moralists.

One example of a member counterproductively threatening a congressman was told by the political assistant to a moderately liberal representative from the Chicago area. The Common Cause member announced himself as the head of the local Common Cause chapter and told the assistant that if his boss did not vote for the clean-air bill, he would oppose the congressman in his next election (the representative had won by only 53 percent). The congressional aide related: "I was so furious that I felt like physically throwing him out of my office." Somewhat later, the aide mentioned the threat to Robert Meier, the budget director of Common Cause, whom he happened to meet at a party. Meier assured the aide that such threats were not a matter of Common Cause policy, and he was satisfied with the explanation. Still, this incident indicates a problem in managing a reform lobby that involves members meeting with their congressmen. Unless the members are counseled on how to deal with congressmen, and unless headquarters communicates with local units frequently by telephone, such meetings may move congressmen away from a lobbying position rather than toward it.

Being a member of Congress today is hard work. Moreover, since the mid-1970s the congressional job has become less enjoyable because members of Congress have been less respected by the general public. Legislators who are ordinarily either indifferent or opposed to Common Cause bills sometimes resent numerous requests from members for meetings and votes. For example, the irascible former Congresswoman Edith Green regarded her mail from vigorous Oregon organizations of Common Cause as an unnecessary irritation, an attitude that presumably also would be applied to requests for meetings.

> Rep. Edith Green (D-Ore.), who is retiring at 66 after 20 years in the House . . . thinks no representative can keep up with all the matters that now come before Congress. . . . Mrs. Green and some of the other retiring representatives are also bothered by the growth of public-interest lobbying operations like Ralph Nader's groups and John Gardner's Common Cause.
>
> Says Mrs. Green: "In my judgment these groups are very undemocratic in terms of their organization. A few people back in Washington make the decisions and then they spread the word and tell their members to write their congressmen to support this or that legislation. This is like the reflex action of Pavlov's dog, and you wonder how much it represents the opinions of the people who have a good thing going for them back here. They give the impression that if they can generate 100,000 letters that per se good government is going to result. I have about reached the conclusion that the impact of such a tremendous amount of mail is in inverse ratio to good government. If I have to spend 80 to 100 percent of my time in just answering letters — and to survive politically you have to respond to your mail — then I have just that much less time to give to studying legislation." [14]

This comment is somewhat disingenuous as Mrs. Green had sixteen staff em-

ployees to help her with her duties. Nevertheless, her remarks reflect the feelings of a substantial number of members of Congress, particularly senior members from districts having numerous public-interest group members. In dealing with such members, Common Cause has learned to avoid approaching them
with their full lobbying potential from members and to rely, instead, on lobbying from other members of Congress, who are friendly both to Common Cause
and the irritated representative.

But Mrs. Green's criticism of Common Cause can be extended in a different direction. By encouraging its members to write and meet with their representative, Common Cause is increasing the workload of the members of Congress. Beyond that, the overall effect of the Common Cause legislative program
is to cause more work for members of Congress. For example, open committee meetings may have the effect of increasing the amount of explaining about
votes and actions a congressman has to do.[15]

In the late 1970s, perhaps 125 representatives met regularly with Common
Cause members from their districts.[16] Groups from Common Cause seldom
met with U.S. senators because senators are even busier than representatives,
and because Common Cause used to receive more support for its program from
the Senate than from the House.

Friendship, Lobbying, and Influence. A Common Cause state leader told
me: "One thing we learned was that when we criticized lobbyists at the state
legislature, we were criticizing the friends of the legislators." Indeed, it is difficult
to draw a line between lobbying and friendship. The most effective lobbyists
become friends with various congressmen and members of the congressional
staff. Congressmen and their aides do not normally think of such lobbyists
as outsiders putting "pressure" on the congressman in behalf of some interest.[17]
Such lobbyist-friends ordinarily agree with the positions, at least in the policy
area of the lobbyist's employment, taken by the congressional friend. The lobbyist-friend often does research for the member of Congress in areas of mutual
concern, and will work with the legislator in getting the support of other legislators for bills of mutual interest. Such a lobbyist will also have friendly relations with workers in a congressman's office. Since the lobbyist may have many
years of experience on the Hill, he is in a position to give useful advice to legislative aides and press assistants. He may help a congressman's staff do research.
Thus the lobbyist-friend becomes viewed as a useful adjunct to a congressman's
office. He may even spend quite a bit of time there doing his own work, which
is nevertheless work in behalf of the congressman when they support the same
measure. Such a lobbyist may buy refreshments for a congressional office small
gathering to celebrate a wedding or say good-bye to a resigning aide.

Nevertheless, personal friends of a congressman may "lobby" him in the sense of speaking to the congressman about issues that concern both of them. Such conversations may not be overtly political; they may consist of communicating, for instance, worries about government controls on medicine or about the difficulties of finding adequate child-care facilities. But the congressman will think of his friend when it comes time to consider legislation relevant to the matter of the friend's concern.

Communication from friends to congressmen may focus more on legislation. Thus a friend may tell a congressman that he hopes that Congress will pass some bill supported by an interest group to which the friend belongs. Accordingly, interest groups, who number among their members personal friends of numerous congressmen, have an important lobbying resource, although the friendships may not be ordinarily viewed that way. Common Cause is one such interest group, as is the American Medical Association, the National Education Association, the AFL-CIO, the National Rifle Association, the U.S. Chamber of Commerce, and a few other groups.

Thus, when I asked twenty members of Congress what they thought of Common Cause, they commonly answered the question partly in terms of their relationships with friends who are members of Common Cause. Three congressional allies of Common Cause said that Common Cause leaders in their districts were friends of theirs, people who would also work on the electoral campaigns of the congressmen. Another ally of Common Cause mentioned that the steering committee leader in his district was his Methodist minister and that the minister who had preceded him also had been a coordinator for Common Cause. Still another congressman recalled that a friend of his had been a founder of Common Cause in his state and that the present executive director was also a friend of his. One Democrat, critical of Common Cause for "self-righteousness," even though he always voted with Common Cause, mentioned that the leader in his district was a retired schoolteacher he had known for twenty years. Still other members of Congress spoke of friendships with Washington lobbyists David Cohen and Fred Wertheimer. In the course of ordinary social relationships—after church or at parties back in the districts—many congressmen hear about the Common Cause point of view from active members. If such members of Congress deviate from Common Cause lobbying positions, they will have to explain their action to their aggrieved friend, who will learn about the deviation from bulletins from Washington or from the Washington connection. (The Washington volunteer, even though he or she has probably never set foot in the congressman's district, will be incensed that "his man" in Congress let him down.) Thus, judging from the salience of such friendships with members in my interviews with congressmen, personal friends of congressmen are probably as important a source of influence as letters from the district or meetings with district steering committees.

From 1970 to 1973, Common Cause had among its lobbyists five persons who had considerable experience as lobbyists or congressional staffers: David Cohen (fourteen years as a lobbyist), Jack Moskowitz (fifteen years), John Lagomarsino (five years), Lowell Beck (more than ten years), and Fred Wertheimer (five years as a congressional aide). Each man numbered among his friends a few congressmen as well as a number of congressional aides. It may be presumed that, in its early period, Common Cause's lobbying in the House followed the ordinary practice of forming friendships with congressmen and then attempting to get the friend (the congressman) to lobby some of his friends (i.e., other congressmen).

Evidently David Cohen and other leaders of Common Cause recognized the problem posed by the frequent transformation of an interest group into a "service bureau"[18] for its congressional friends. Thus, if Common Cause became tied to its congressional friends in the way that other lobbies sometimes are, congressional reformers might pressure Common Cause to back the legislators' pet reform schemes.

In recent years lobbyists for Common Cause have become more distant in their relationships with congressmen. This was summed up in chief lobbyist David Cohen's aphorism: "Common Cause has no permanent friends and no permanent enemies." This is an overstatement, but Common Cause frequently criticizes someone who has aided it in the past if such a congressman is not currently a supporter. Common Cause does not try to make excuses for its friends when congressmen appear on lists of legislators who seem to have conflicts of interest or lists of those who have accepted large campaign donations from special-interest groups.

Institutional reform measures, unlike other technical legislation, are subjects about which intelligent legislators all have relevant personal experiences and opinions. There are a considerable number of reform congressmen who would draw up their own measures and then get Common Cause to do research on the proposals and lobby for them, if Common Cause was not careful. Then Common Cause would lose its organizational autonomy; friendly congressmen would set its lobbying agenda. In addition, such congressmen might force Common Cause to take on too many reform bills at once.

The policy of "no permanent friends" enhances the reputation of Common Cause for independence. This is important because its congressional reputation, as well as its reputation among journalists, would suffer if it became known as a tool of specific congressional leaders. Nevertheless, Common Cause had a few friends in Congress who were so well liked and respected as to be essentially immune from public criticism by Common Cause. In the House during the mid-1970s these friends of Common Cause included Democrats Morris Udall (Ariz.), Dante Fascell (Fla.), Joseph Fisher, (Va.), Andrew Maguire (N.J.), Richard Bolling (Mo.), and Norman Mineta (Calif.) and Republicans John Anderson (Ill.), Alan Steelman (Tex.), and William Frenzel (Minn.). Bolling and Steelman served on the governing board after leaving the House.

Campaigns to Get Public Commitments. In the 1972 and 1974 elections Common Cause put great effort into national campaigns to get public commitments from all of the major-party candidates for Congress to support the Common Cause position on its high-priority issues. Congressional candidates were asked by members of Common Cause in their districts to support the organization's position on seniority system reform in Congress, the public financing of federal election campaigns, the regulation of conflicts of interest among persons holding congressional and executive positions, new laws regulating lobbying in Washington, and open meetings of congressional and executive decision-making bodies. Common Cause organized a similar campaign in 1976, but that year it emphasized getting candidates for the Presidency to agree to conduct their campaigns according to principles suggested by Common Cause. The "Campaign '76" program was applied to congressional candidates only fitfully because suggesting standards for political campaigning was a new effort. Trying to influence numerous campaigns would have been too difficult, given the lack of experience Common Cause had with this kind of program.

In August 1974, Common Cause mailed a 22-page booklet to its then 325,000 members. The booklet described an "action plan—we call it Open Up the System." The member was asked to "speak out":

> First, become familiar with the issues outlined here [the familiar list of Common Cause reform priorities—campaign finance reform, conflict of interest rules, and so forth].
>
> Second, write a letter to each candidate for Congress in your area, saying in your own words why these issues of open and accountable government are important to you as a voter. The names and addresses of candidates in your state accompany this report.
>
> Please write your letters right away. They will pique the candidates' interest and start them thinking about our issues. Then small groups of Common Cause members will follow up by interviewing the candidates to get their answers on a questionnaire.
>
> You need not ask questions of the candidates you write to—they are busy campaigning and have little time to reply to letters. Their eyes and ears are open for issues that concern their constituents, and letters are a good way to catch their attention. The mail can influence the issues candidates talk about and the promises they make to the voters.

Third, raise these issues in letters to the editors of your local papers, particularly the small dailies and the weeklies that don't cover political issues in depth.

Fourth, when you attend candidates' meetings and panel discussions, or if there's a question period on the air, raise Open Up the System issues and ask for clear answers. Questions you might ask appear at the end of each chapter in this report.

Later on, the candidates will be interviewed by Common Cause members who will put specific questions to them. These, we hope, will produce commitments on which we can follow through when the elections are over.[19]

This message was followed by: "Our first and most important job is to make Open Up the System issues a key part of every election campaign—visible and important to every citizen." This is an important aspect of what Common Cause means by putting issues "on the agenda."

This tactic was interesting in that it combined a number of separate activities to produce the integrated effect of persuading candidates to support the Common Cause position on reform issues. First, the Washington connection was able to phone local steering committee members and make sure they understood the issues and encourage them to run an active "OUTS campaign" in their district. Given the fact that in 1974 there were perhaps 15,000 members willing to write letters to candidates, and a few thousand were eager to be more active than that, a significant amount of activity was guaranteed. Second, the campaign combined the techniques of writing letters, candidates meeting with district leaders, and friendship, since many congressional candidates were contacted by friends who lobbied them on the OUTS reforms. Third, these other techniques of persuasion were used: members were urged to get local newspapers, radio, and television to mention the reforms sponsored by Common Cause; the suggestion was made that members raise the reform issues at public campaign meetings; and experienced candidates realized they would be "rated" by Common Cause when they filled out the issues questionnaire. In other words, many candidates realized that, if elected, their responses would be published in Common Cause bulletins from Washington, along with the responses of other congressmen. Since most senators then had several thousand members of Common Cause in their state, and the typical representative had 700 Common Cause members in his district, the publication of responses could be embarrassing in case of disagreements with Common Cause.

There are three major effects of such public campaigns. First, given the level of organization of Common Cause (especially after 1974 when the Washington connection was established and steering committees were active in the majority of congressional districts), the sponsored reforms were a matter of some discussion in the congressional campaigns of perhaps two hundred districts.

Second, when a candidate agreed to support the Common Cause position on some or all of the OUTS issues, he would be reminded of this promise if he got elected to Congress. His promises would be published in Common Cause's *Bulletin from Washington*. More important, the Washington lobbyists would remind him of his promises. And given what David Cohen calls "insider-outsider lobbying," that is, combining the insider lobbyist on the Hill with the organization in the individual congressional district, if a congressman reneged on his promises, this breach of promise would be communicated back to his district via the Washington connection. The summary chart of the promises made during the OUTS campaign was submitted to the *Congressional Record* by a congressman friendly to Common Cause, and thus a congressman's campaign promises to Common Cause could be easily located.

A third major effect of the OUTS campaigns was that they raised the morale of Common Cause. Many members were interested in electoral politics, but such people might become less interested in participation in Common Cause activities unless the activities were related to elections. Moreover, campaigns to get commitments from candidates raised the morale of the staff and volunteers, who saw activities related to elections as especially meaningful. Also, such campaigns gave local units something interesting to do, and there was a continuing problem of boredom among local units because of the necessarily sporadic nature of letter-writing campaigns to Congress.

Campaigns to get commitments from congressmen, combined with the insider-outsider technique of Common Cause lobbying, serve to create a bandwagon effect. Thus Common Cause may get a majority of Congress, or a majority of the Democratic Caucus, to support a proposed reform during the fall congressional campaign. After the election, the Washington lobbyists may announce that a majority already supports some reform, and the lobbyists, together with their allies among congressional reformers, can emphasize this point in conversations with legislators undecided about a reform. The reform lobbyists' announcement of a reform majority on some question is particularly persuasive because they can point to an actual list of supporters compiled by Common Cause. An undecided congressman may conclude that Common Cause is sure to win on the issue and may decide to join the winning side and get credit in his district for being a reformer.

The most striking example of this bandwagon effect occurred in December 1974 when the Democratic Caucus in the House voted to take away the appointing power to committees from Democrats on the Ways and Means Committee and give the power to the Steering and Policy Committee of the caucus, a more reform-oriented group. Common Cause had gathered 146 promises to support this shift during the fall campaign, and this constituted a majority of the Dem-

ocrats in the House. When this fact became known in November 1974, the reaction among House Democrats was one of surprise—few had thought that
it would be possible to accomplish the change at that time. But the shift in
the committee appointment power was accomplished at a meeting of the caucus on 3 December 1974 by a vote of 146 to 122. While the Democratic Study
Group, the caucus of liberal Democrats in the House, spearheaded the campaign to adopt this reform, Common Cause played an important part in its
adoption because of its gathering of commitments from candidates.

A later experience with legislative delay of a Common Cause-sponsored
reform indicates that campaigns to get congressional commitments are more
effective in getting reforms adopted by the caucus of the majority party than
they are in getting measures passed by the entire Congress. Thus, even though
316 members of the House backed Common Cause on the need for legislation
to get legislators and top executive officials to file lists of their financial holdings, this measure was pigeonholed for two years in Walter Flowers's subcommittee of the House Judiciary Committee. Even though a majority of the House
agreed, in the abstract, on the need for disclosure of financial holdings by federal officials, the prospect of detailing their own investments and sources of
income irritated many congressmen, some of whom publicly stated support
for such a bill but privately hoped that a disclosure measure would be blocked
in subcommittee. As it turned out, a strict disclosure provision was part of
the House ethics code passed in March 1977, in the wake of the Hays scandal,
the Carter election, and an upsurge in concern for "morality in government."[20]

Similarly, while three-fourths of the members of the House were willing
to announce public support for the more stringent regulation of lobbyists, such
measures were, naturally enough, opposed by virtually all lobbyists, including
most public-interest lobbyists.[21] Since most congressmen have friends who are
lobbyists, the Common Cause-sponsored regulation put most congressmen in
a conflict between their public support for the measure and their friendship
for lobbyists. Again, many congressmen were happy to see the lobbyist regulation bill bottled up in Flowers's subcommittee.

This stalemate lasted for years. In 1975-76 a majority of the House would
have voted for the regulation of lobbyists and the financial disclosure measure
if votes had been scheduled on the floor. But according to a five-term member
of the House, Congressman Flowers received covert encouragement from many
colleagues in his refusal to consider the two bills in subcommittee.

Walter Flowers was a Democrat who represented the 7th District in Alabama, which included part of suburban Birmingham and various rural coun-
ties and small cities (Bessemer, Tuscaloosa, Selma) in west-central Alabama.
Flowers did not ordinarily receive strong competition in elections. Further, the

reform-oriented Alabamians were impressed by his performance in the televised impeachment hearing of the Judiciary Committee. Flowers came out against Nixon.

It was difficult for Common Cause to put pressure on Flowers, who had only 104 members in his district and who ordinarily had little opposition in elections. One Birmingham newspaper was friendly to Common Cause, and thus Common Cause was able to get unfavorable publicity about Flowers's actions into the Birmingham media in the summer of 1975. At the same time, a group of reformers in the House circulated a petition among the members urging Flowers to consider the two bills. The petition received no public mention, to avoid angering Flowers, but Common Cause lobbyists may have helped draft the petition. Flowers expressed outrage at Common Cause for pressuring him and held perfunctory hearing on the lobbyist regulation measure. But he continued his stalling tactics.

In June 1976 Common Cause tried the tactic of getting its members to write representatives on the Judiciary Committee to urge the importance of the committee's seriously considering the two measures bottled up in its subcommittee. This was followed by a full-scale letter-writing campaign in July 1976 in which members wrote their congressman, urging him to ask the chairman of the Judiciary Committee, Peter Rodino, to act on the two bills. Finally, Flowers's subcommittee and the full committee reported both the disclosure and lobbyist regulation bills in August 1976. By this time, however, it was too late to get passage in the legislative logjam at the end of the session. In any case, the fate of the two measures during the 94th Congress (1975-76) illustrates that the tactic of getting public commitments is not enough to get a bill passed, even if a majority in the House states its intention of voting for a bill.

A political tactic that is a part of the effort to get commitments is to get large numbers of co-sponsors for a bill in the House. This indicates a great deal of interest in the measure and provides one indication that it will pass a floor vote. Thus the Common Cause-sponsored financial disclosure measure had 168 co-sponsors, while the lobbyist regulation bill had 155 co-sponsors. Even so, Flowers bottled up the measures. A congressman who was a leader in circulating the petition to Flowers said that the petition was circulated chiefly among the 155 co-sponsors of the lobbyist regulation measure, to make it obvious to Flowers that the co-sponsors really wanted the measure to pass and were not sponsoring it merely to please constituents.[22]

Common Cause and its reform allies in the Democratic Study Group are able to put on a great deal of pressure to get a reform measure through the House. But if many congressmen privately do not want a measure to pass, and if it gets sent for consideration to a committee or subcommittee chaired by a representative hostile to the reform, the pressure can be effectively counter-manded for a couple of years. This indicates that outsider lobbying tactics of organizing public pressure must be supplemented with "insider lobbying" con-ducted by people with a great deal of understanding of the House.

Common Cause ranks with the most effective lobbies, such as the Nation-al Rifle Association and the American Medical Association, in its ability to manage a campaign to extract public commitments from congressional candi-dates. Among reformers working at the national level of government, Com-mon Cause ranks second only to the Anti-Saloon League of the early twenti-eth century in this capacity.[23]

Publicizing Positions. In my interviews with congressmen, they several times mentioned that they were concerned about their Common Cause "rating." By this they were referring to the chart of congressional positions included with the membership bulletin once a year, which typically lists the stands of con-gressmen on about ten issues that most concern Common Cause. Evidently many congressmen think of Common Cause as having a "rating" similar to those of the Americans for Democratic Action or Americans for Constitutional Action. This would surprise the Common Cause staff, who never refer to "rat-ing" congressmen in their discussions. Common Cause does not call its an-nual chart of congressional positions a rating system. The chart uses conven-tional adjectives to describe a congressman's attitude toward Common Cause: "good," "bad," "neutral," and so forth. The idea of an interest group "rating" congressmen implies that the group releases a set of summary numbers, usual-ly from 0 to 100, by which congressmen are ranked. Common Cause merely publishes a listing of positions. These positions are *not* aggregated into a sum-mary number and then used in Common Cause publicity.

Congressional sensitivity to the annual charting of positions suggests that publishing such charts is probably an effective political tactic. Members of Con-gress from districts in which reformers are numerous do not want to look bad on the Common Cause charts. Publishing such charts is an inducement to con-gressmen to adopt the Common Cause position on any issue on which Com-mon Cause might publicize congressional positions. When Common Cause did not publish a chart of congressional positions in 1975, several congressmen telephoned national headquarters to inquire when the next "ratings" would appear. These members of Congress thought that having a good Common Cause "rating" was politically helpful to them.

Common Cause's charts of congressional positions are different from most charts or rating systems in that Common Cause is able to include legislators' positions on issues that have never been voted on. Common Cause can do this because of its extensive network of active members, who are able to get congressional candidates to respond to questions about their stands on government reform issues, including those that have never been the subject of a congressional vote. Combining recent congressional votes with public positions on issues not yet considered in a full vote gives a more accurate picture of a congressman's current stance toward an interest group than just listing recent votes. This was particularly true for Common Cause in the 1970s because many of its sponsored measures faced their main opposition in committee, before voting by an entire house of Congress.

Common Cause indicates that it does not issue ratings because it would be hard to be fair to the members of Congress in such ratings. How many issues should be used in a rating, and which issues should be used? A Common Cause series of ratings might be greatly altered if environmental issues were included, for example. If Common Cause publicly issued numerical ratings of congressmen, many legislators would be very irritated at receiving a low rating. By not issuing numerical ratings, Common Cause indicates a desire to avoid irritating congressmen unnecessarily.

Public Questioning. The Common Cause "Campaign '74" booklet asked members to go to election campaign meetings of candidates and ask them publicly about their positions on Common Cause-sponsored reforms. (Sample questions appeared in the booklet.) This is a tactic of some significance, for in a district in which Common Cause is well organized, a candidate for public office, if he does not have strong feelings about a measure, may simply accede to the Common Cause point of view rather than face the prospect of repeatedly trying to explain some other position at his campaign rallies. Because most Common Cause members are substantial citizens in their communities, a candidate must treat their questions with respect, even if he does not like Common Cause and has answered the same question twenty times previously in his election campaign.

The technique of asking questions at political rallies obviously can be used to pressure or harass a candidate. A political candidate sometimes plants supporters to ask embarrassing questions at opponents' rallies. Common Cause has used this technique sparingly. Thus, in May 1974, when William Fulbright left Washington to campaign for reelection in the Democratic primary in Arkansas against Governor Dale Bumpers (who eventually won), Common Cause was trying to collect every possible senatorial vote to get the necessary two-thirds to shut off a filibuster against its Federal Campaign Amendments. Common Cause sent a member to all of Fulbright's campaign meetings to ask: "Senator Fulbright, we know that you support cleaning up elections in this time of Watergate. Your vote may be vital to shut off the filibuster in the Senate against the bill to clean up election campaigns. Will you go back to Washington to cast your vote if it is needed?" Fulbright had to say that he would vote his convictions, and thus he had to take a day out of his campaign to go back to vote against the filibuster when his vote proved to be vital.

Common Cause lobbyist David Cohen was too sagacious to dog a senator's footsteps unless it was absolutely necessary. Fulbright's Washington office was in daily touch with Cohen to see if the senator's vote was needed. What Cohen called his "sense of professionalism" prevented him from distorting the truth to get an insurance vote when Fulbright was in deep trouble in his campaign. Thus Fulbright's staff trusted Cohen and believed the lobbyist when he said that Fulbright had to return to Washington. A good lobbyist tries to cultivate a sense of trust in his word.

But public questions can be unfair to members of Congress for the same reason that ratings can be unfair. Representative David Obey (Dem-Wisc.), who is regarded as a leader among reform-minded liberal Democrats in the House, complained to me that he was tired of answering critical Common Cause questions at public meetings. Congressman Obey argued that his reform credentials are bona fide, that he was a reformer before Common Cause came into existence, and that he sometimes voted against a Common Cause position for complicated tactical reasons that he could not explain to constituents. The Wisconsin congressman felt it unfair of Common Cause to decide what the reform position is on a matter.

Some other liberals in Congress also have become irritated with Common Cause for this reason. They think of themselves as reformers, but they disagree with a Common Cause interpretation of reform. Still, it is a tribute to the tactical effectiveness of Common Cause that some congressional reformers regard the organization as an important force in determining the reform agenda to the extent that their constituents accept the Common Cause definition of reform rather than the congressman's definition.

Working with the Press. Common Cause has no difficulty getting its major reform ideas into influential newspapers: the *Washington Post, New York Times,* and *Wall Street Journal,* for example. Leading columnists and reporters for these papers know the leaders of Common Cause, and thus a major proposal automatically gets some treatment from them. Editorials about Common Cause-sponsored reforms often do not mention the organization's name, however.[24] Further, other articles and columns in these newspapers may appear to be criticizing Common Cause measures, such as the public financing of elections or strict regulation of lobbyists.[25]

Common Cause is unusually successful in placing articles and editorials in small-town newspapers. An estimate is that a major Common Cause reform, on which one must presume four years between initial advocacy and final passage, will be the subject of about 2000 favorable articles and editorials, mostly in papers of small circulation.[26] (This does *not* include the distribution of nationally syndicated columns favorable to a Common Cause idea.) Common Cause distributes editorial memoranda that are easily convertible into good-government editorials in agreement with the Common Cause point of view. Many of these memoranda are published by local newspaper editors, some of whom are members of Common Cause. Small-town editors are frequently well educated, concerned about the functioning of governmental institutions, and receptive to the idea of nonpartisan political reform — the kind of people most attracted to Common Cause.

The great majority of Senate and House members employ a full-time press aide, who follows the local press, among other duties. Thus, favorable mentions of Common Cause-sponsored reforms in the local press are likely to be known to a member of Congress and to be regarded as significant. If a congressman votes against a reform that some local newspapers like, the member of Congress may be criticized in the local press, which is something to be avoided. A congressman who is undecided on a bill often can assume that he will be criticized by the local Common Cause unit if he does not vote for the measure. Adding that criticism to criticism by hometown newspapers may be enough to sway his vote.

The national staff does *not* try to pressure members of Congress through explicit tactics, such as calling up the hometown newspaper and asking for an editorial criticizing the local representative, unless circumstances are extreme, as was the case with Flowers's delaying tactics. Trying to turn a hometown newspaper against the local congressman is viewed as "dirty pool" by most congressmen and journalists. But local Common Cause leaders frequently write letters to the editor, which may be published because of the prestige of the signatories, criticizing the local congressman. The letters-to-the-editor section of a newspaper is widely read, and a critical letter from a local leader hurts a congressman politically.[27]

Professionalism in Lobbying. Common Cause lobbyists in Washington know the legislative process, thoroughly understand the issues with which they are concerned, and make a good personal impression. The lobbyists are assigned to particular issues, which they follow for years; this makes them familiar with the details and with all arguments connected with a bill. Common Cause lobbyists are well liked by congressmen sympathetic to their platform.

David Cohen was well liked even by members of Congress who did not like Common Cause. Cohen wanted Common Cause lobbyists to be regarded as "professionals." He wanted them to understand the overall political situation of a congressman and not make unreasonable demands on him. In return, Cohen wanted members of Congress to regard the lobbyists as people with a job to do, as representatives of a group with members who want to change the political institutions of society and have the right to employ lobbyists to work for these goals.

Some members of Congress view Common Cause as *less legitimate* in its lobbying than many of the more traditional lobbies, such as economic groups. These congressmen think that it is arrogant to form a lobby that purports to speak for public interests, good government, and the reform of Congress. Such critics view the efforts of Common Cause as hypocritical; they would prefer to deal with old-fashioned lobbyists who are seeking money for a particular group. Cohen tried to get congressmen with these attitudes to view Common Cause lobbyists as legitimate professionals. And he discouraged the "holier-than-thou" tone that reform lobbyists often take, and that greatly offends legislators.

The lobbyists for Common Cause in Washington are professional in their relationships with congressmen, but this frequently was not true of state lobbyists, particularly in the early days. Some state lobbyists were too moralistic. On the other hand, one lobbyist in Albany boasted that he had arranged for female Common Cause volunteers to date legislative aides to extract information from them (he must have been reading *All the President's Men*) and had to be censured for his conduct by the legislature.[28] Common Cause has tried to upgrade its lobbying, but distance and the power of the state committees to hire their own lobbyists make mistakes inevitable.

Exchanging Information. The existence of full-time lobbyists in Washington, a WATS line, and local units who meet with their congressmen provide Common Cause with an unusual capacity to relay information about a congressman's attitudes from the district to Washington, then back to the district. This is especially valuable in lobbying members of Congress who are genuinely undecided about a Common Cause-sponsored bill. Thus a local steering committee may meet with its undecided congressman and then telephone Washington and report to a headquarters lobbyist the arguments that appeal to the legislator and those that annoy him. The Washington lobbyist's pitch can then be much more effective. Or the reverse can hold. A Washington lobbyist can report back to the local members about which arguments are most persuasive to the congressman.

Washington can also tell the local leadership about a congressman's maneuvers to defeat a measure he claims to support, such as voting for obscure amendments designed to sabotage a reform bill or voting to send the bill back to committee. Or a congressman may be strongly supportive of a Common Cause bill, and thus there is no need for local members to talk to him about it. In fact, such redundant action can annoy a congressman. Washington can tell the district steering committee simply to thank the congressman for his support and not bother him.

Lobbying. Common Cause's basic lobbying maneuver is to work with its congressional friends to persuade undecided legislators; known opponents to a bill are let alone.[29] Common Cause will work with its friends on a committee in designing a bill and formulating the strategy to get it passed. Allies of Common Cause on the committee will lobby other members of Congress on the committee. Common Cause will supplement the work of friendly congressmen with visits from its Washington lobbyists to other members of the committee, combined with communication from a committee member's district. If a committee or subcommittee chairman refuses to consider a Common Cause bill, the organization and its congressional allies will organize congressmen who are *not* on the committee to ask the stalling chairman to consider the bill. If this does not work, Common Cause will organize more constituent pressure — more communication from voters to committee members, and to congressmen not on the committee to ask the committee chairman to consider the bill.

The House Administration Committee, particularly during the chairmanship of Wayne Hays (1971-76), was not especially friendly to Common Cause bills.[30] Nevertheless, the committee acceded to the public financing of presidential elections provisions of the Federal Election Campaign Amendments of 1974 because a majority of the House members felt strongly about the matter during the Watergate years. During the Hays chairmanship, Common Cause's two best friends on the committee were two senior members: Frank Thompson (Dem-N.J.) and John Brademas (Dem-Ind.).[31]

As noted, House Judiciary subcommittee chairman Flowers was able to bottle up lobbyist regulation and financial disclosure legislation. In addition, the House Government Operations Committee, which considers open meeting bills, was slow to act on such legislation under its traditionalist chairman Chet Holifield (Dem-Calif.) and his successor, Jack Brooks (Dem-Tex.).

In the first years of Common Cause, the Washington connection was not sufficiently developed to be able to lobby individual congressmen on committees concerning committee agendas by generating communication from their constituents. Common Cause put most of its lobbying effort into influencing floor votes. But with the increasing sophistication of its organization, Common Cause shifted much of its effort to lobbying committees (particularly House committees) so that, by 1975, more effort was directed toward influencing committees than was directed toward influencing floor votes. Much of the reason for this was that in the late 1970s, open meeting bills, lobbyist regulation, and financial disclosure were virtually sure of winning House floor votes, and most of the political effort had to be devoted to getting the bills past committees that were covertly collaborating with congressmen who privately did not want such legislation to pass.[32] On the public financing of congressional elections, however, floor votes were held in the House in 1974, 1976, and 1978. Each time, this Common Cause-supported idea was voted down.[33]

On floor votes, Common Cause continues its basic strategy of working with friends to persuade the undecided, while not wasting resources on those known to be in opposition. Again, it is better strategy to let congressmen who agree with Common Cause try to persuade the undecided congressmen. Here it is important for the lobbying operation to keep a "head count," that is, a running tally of expected congressional voting on some matter.[34] Then Common Cause can inform friendly members of Congress about which undecideds have recently switched to the Common Cause side of a bill, and so the time of the friendly congressmen can be better used by trying to persuade the truly undecided. Common Cause supplements the work of its congressional allies with communication and visits from its Washington lobbyists, plus communication from the districts of the undecideds.

A secondary maneuver on a floor vote is to visit congressmen known to be friendly to Common Cause and generate some communication from their constituents. It is a good idea to reinforce the favorable stand of congressmen, but it is counterproductive to bother members of Congress with more than one visit from a Washington lobbyist or with a storm of constituent pressure. A congressman who feels that Common Cause is wasting his time may be biased against its lobbying on some other measure.

Common Cause frequently asks a local unit to write a member of Congress in behalf of a measure to which the congressman is known to be opposed. This indicates to a congressman that some of his constituents disagree with him, which may increase his chances of voting with Common Cause on a measure to which he objects less strongly. But Common Cause does not bother "opposed" congressmen with personal visits, and it certainly does not send people to argue with them.

Cohen's maxim "Common Cause has no permanent enemies" led to effective lobbying by finding support among conservatives. Some conservatives, particularly in the Senate, supported Common Cause occasionally, or even frequently. Thus, former House Republican leader John Rhodes (who had a 1974 ADA rating of 6 percent) told a delegation from Arizona Common Cause that "I have been surprised at how often I agree with Common Cause." (Rhodes agreed twice, disagreed three times, and abstained twice in the 1974 Common Cause chart on congressional positions.) Senator Barry Goldwater (ADA rating −6) had a record of 5 "agrees," 2 "disagrees," and 1 abstention on the 1974 Common Cause chart.

Lobbying Coalitions. One aspect of congressional politics that is frequently overlooked is the existence of lobbying coalitions.[35] On many proposed bills of general import, there will be anywhere from a few to several dozen organized interest groups on the same side of the issue. Obviously it would be poor strategy for them to send their lobbyists to the Hill without coordination. Thus lobbying coalitions are formed by interest groups with common goals on a particular bill. The lobbyists of the various groups meet regularly, share information about the politics of the bill, coordinate their tactics, and discuss strategy. Such lobbying coalitions often have a leader; that is, an interest group that is particularly identified with some position takes the lead in coordinating lobbying on that measure. Occasionally, more permanent coalitions are formed, financed by donations from the member groups, which thereby provide for a few staff workers. The most famous of these is the Leadership Conference on Civil Rights, which coordinates lobbying for civil rights bills.

Common Cause participates in temporary lobbying coalitions on those issues that make up its secondary priorities (e.g., environmental issues or the coalition to stop the B-1 bomber). On these matters the Common Cause lobbyist usually follows the lead of a group that has specialized on the issue. Thus, Common Cause followed Ralph Nader's lead in lobbying to establish a Consumer Protection Agency; it followed the lead of the Environmental Policy Center in working for stricter regulation of strip-mining. Common Cause usually does not join permanent lobbying coalitions. In 1973 the staff wanted to join the Coalition for Human Needs, a church, union, and black group to get legislation to help the poor. But after initially agreeing with the staff, the governing board decided that Common Cause could not be a participant in a coalition that might take positions with which many Common Cause members would disagree.

In its field of lobbying for good-government reforms at the national level, Common Cause's resources and experience have become so great relative to those of other groups that Common Cause makes important decisions virtually by itself. On some government reform issues, few lobbies will take a stand. Perhaps once a year, Common Cause lobbies for a measure supported by the

League of Women Voters and nobody else. For instance, Common Cause lobbied for the Bolling-Martin bill to redraw the jurisdictions of congressional
committees in 1974; the bill was otherwise supported only by the League. (The
measure lost).[36]

Washington lobbyists recognize one another's "turf."[37] An interest group
is expected to take the lead in lobbying for an issue on which it has specialized
and has considerable experience. In this respect, the relationship between Common Cause and Ralph Nader is interesting. Such ideas as the Consumer Protection Agency or legislating the chartering of large corporations (which could
lose their charters for malfeasance) are "Nader's babies." Common Cause would
not lobby independently for such ideas. Similarly, such measures as the public
financing of elections, regulation of lobbyists, open meeting laws, financial disclosure rules, and sunset laws are regarded as Common Cause's "babies." Other
groups will not become active in lobbying for such legislation without direction from Common Cause.

Providing Expertise. Lobbyists help friendly members of Congress by providing the legislators with research about technical matters related to public
policy.[38] They provide information about how the members of an interest group
regard a public policy. They play a more direct role in congressional decision
making by writing speeches for congressmen and even by drafting bills.

Like other well-organized lobbies, Common Cause does all these things.
From 1974 to 1978, Common Cause was one of two centers that compiled and
analyzed available data about the financing of presidential and congressional
campaigns, before the Federal Election Commission assumed this function in
1978.[39] Volunteers laboriously copied the campaign finance reports filed with
the Federal Election Commission onto a form for a computer, which collated
the information and printed the data—organized both by campaign and by
donor (persons, unions, committees). It is noteworthy that while Congress col-
lected these data in 1972, 1974, and 1976, pursuant to electoral reform laws,
it did not index the data for the public. This meant that most discussions of
public financing of elections during that time relied on the Common Cause
compilations of data. Presidential primary and congressional financing reports
were filed every two or three months during an election year. Only Common
Cause had the resources (volunteer work) to compile these reports, and it issued press releases about campaign financing abuses that could not be count-
ered by others. Common Cause gave congressmen who supported public financing of elections the best data available for use in congressional debate.

Common Cause still releases brief reports about group contributions to
campaigns as part of its argument for reform. For example, banks are giving

so much this year, or unions so much. Common Cause frequently provides congressmen with research reports that are more simple and direct than its multivolume presentation of the financing of federal elections. For example, in 1976 Common Cause issued a report on career overlaps between top ERDA (Energy Research and Development Authority) executives and oil, gas, coal, and other energy-related corporations. The report presented a persuasive argument for conflict-of-interest legislation.

Perhaps the most successful document of this kind was the "Report on House Committee Chairmen," which played a major role in unseating three incumbent House chairmen in January 1975 (Representatives Hebert, Poage, and Patman). Committee chairmen are elected by the Democratic Caucus, when Democrats have a majority, and the 1974 elections sent to the House 75 new Democrats (out of a total of 290). The newly elected Democrats held the balance of power in the election of committee chairmen for the 94th Congress, and most of them were open to persuasion as to the competence of various incumbent chairmen. The Common Cause document analyzed which committee chairmen had abused their prerogatives. The document was not written in propagandistic style; it resembled a legal brief, and contained technical passages, such as: "The Committee Rules give the full committee the power to waive subcommittee consideration of legislation, in violation of the Caucus Rule (Addendum #13c/M III 3) vesting such authority with the majority of the Democrats on the committee."[40] The Common Cause analysis proved very persuasive to the new Democrats.

Research reports have limited value in persuading congressmen, however. The document on House committee chairmen was influential because it persuaded those 75 freshmen Democrats. But on most of the government reform issues of high priority to Common Cause, congressmen regard themselves as experts because they have personal experience with the issues. This is particularly true of campaign reform and ideas about reorganizing Congress. All members of Congress have run for public office, and most of them have strong opinions about what is good and bad about the process.

Common Cause has provided expertise to other interest groups, particularly women's groups that are seeking to ratify the Equal Rights Amendment in state legislatures. Because of the Washington connection and the existence of local lobbyists, it was relatively easy for Common Cause to compile data on the opinions of legislators about ERA in states that were the focus of efforts to ratify the amendment. Such information could then be phoned over the WATS lines to state-level lobbyists for the various women's groups. These data were also useful to the pro-ERA coalition of groups in Washington in planning strategy.

Observing Committee Meetings. Common Cause regularly sends volunteers to meetings of congressional committees and subcommittees that deal with Common Cause-sponsored legislation or related issues. The volunteers report to the lobbyists if anything unusual happens in committee discussion. Congressmen now expect a Common Cause presence at such meetings, which acts as a deterrent to extraordinary congressional tactics to kill legislation, such as amending in committee to change the nature of a bill and then rushing the new bill to the floor. If such tactics were tried when a Common Cause volunteer was present, the maneuver would be reported to headquarters, and lobbyists would be present within the hour.

Sending volunteers to committee meetings also provides useful information about the attitudes of committee members toward Common Cause-sponsored legislation.

Early Advocacy of Reform. In 1974 and 1975 the staff of Common Cause pressed for a thoroughgoing law for the public financing of federal elections and also tried to get a strict law regulating lobbyists. It was felt that during the Watergate era, the chances of getting far-reaching reform might be better than at any subsequent time. Political scientists will see here a conflict between good political strategy—pressing to get as much as possible at a particularly opportune time—and the injunctions of Lindblom's theory of incremental policy making—better policy is made in step-by-step fashion because that is how policy makers learn to deal with complex situations.[41] For example, some would say that by the fall of 1974, the need for public financing of presidential elections had been amply demonstrated by the Watergate scandal and the rapidly rising amount of donations needed for presidential campaigning. Others would say that in 1974 the need for federal grants to help finance the campaigns of congressional candidates had not been clearly demonstrated and that it is best not to enact such a measure until we have more knowledge of the effects of the regulation of congressional campaign contributions.

But a prudent strategy of delay is inconsistent with the reform outlook and organizational needs of Common Cause. On particularly complicated reform measures, such as the public financing of congressional campaigns, the staff does not spend years studying the complexities of what might happen, given the adoption of the reform, if such reforms have great appeal to the membership. Instead, Common Cause advocates the popular reform rather early in the game. The staff argues that unanticipated adverse consequences of the reform can be dealt with by later legislation, after the reform has been passed.

One reason for the early advocacy of reforms that may have complex consequences is competition among public-interest lobbies. For example, if Common Cause had in 1974 eschewed the advocacy of public financing of congressional campaigns and had followed the political scientists' advice to analyze the changes other reforms produced in the 1976 elections, Ralph Nader probably would have taken over the issue in 1975. If Common Cause had followed the prudent strategy of incremental analysis and then decided in 1978 that public financing of congressional elections was a good thing, it would have found that the issue had become "Nader's baby." Common Cause would have had to defer to him or initiate a conflict that would have hurt the organization image. In addition, some supporters of Common Cause would have become disgusted if the organization had acted so cautiously on such an appealing reform issue. Therefore, when an appealing structure and process reform comes to the attention of the staff, it must decide within a year whether to advocate the measure.[42]

How Enemies Help One Another. Common Cause had a well-publicized feud with House Administration Committee chairman Hays until he left Congress in 1976. Hays took a traditional view of Congress. He thought things worked well enough in the House without the various reforms proposed by Common Cause. He saw no need to form pressure groups to work for good-government reforms in the public interest. To him, good government meant good relationships between a congressman and his constituency. If constituents had problems with the federal bureaucracy, they were entitled to enlist the aid of their congressman. In return for the privilege of serving in Congress, the representative should spend as much time as possible in his district, as Hays did, going back to southeastern Ohio almost every weekend.

In Hays's opinion, the leaders of Common Cause were lobbyists drumming up public support so that they could ply their trade at a good salary. "They are not in it for eleemosynary motives," he said caustically to me. Hays resented Common Cause's badgering him as the Administration Committee chairman. (Communication between Common Cause and Hays ceased in 1973.) As a personality Hays was mercurial, aggressive, and by his own admission, "mean."

In 1972 Hays tried to charge Common Cause $1 a page for copying reports filed by congressional candidates, which were under Hays's jurisdiction as Administration Committee chairman. Common Cause had the charge dismissed by a lawsuit.[43] Hays coined the term "Common Curse" in congressional debate, much to the amusement of many of his colleagues. In 1973, Hays held a $1000-a-plate dinner in Washington to raise money for the House Democratic Campaign Fund, of which he was chairman. Common Cause bought a full-page ad in the *Washington Post* criticizing the dinner as an invitation to special-

interest influence. Hays furiously retorted, "John Gardner is a common crook."
Hays denounced Common Cause at the dinner, and the story was well reported
in the *Post*.[44] At one time, while denouncing Common Cause, Hays began
pounding a lectern and hit a microphone, breaking it. In the spring of 1974,
Common Cause called a press conference in Columbus to announce that Hays
was late in filing his first campaign report, a true charge but one that angered
Hays further. He asked the Justice Department to investigate Common Cause
for not filing a report listing those contributors who gave more than $100, which
was required of all political campaign committees. A few months later, the in-
vestigators concluded that Common Cause was not a group formed to give
money to political candidates.

In 1973 John Gardner realized that it was impossible for Common Cause
to influence the powerful committee chairman, who had jurisdiction over election reform legislation. After this time, Common Cause delighted in recount-
ing Hays's furious assaults in its bulletins. The Common Cause staff enjoyed
repeating Wayne Hays stories, including stories about how much Hays hated
Common Cause. In general, the organization called attention to Hays as a mean-
minded opponent. This indicated to the members that Common Cause was
engaging in important work; it was fighting an arrogant legislator who was
interfering with the cause of reform.

In turn, Hays's attacks on Common Cause increased his popularity in the
House. Many legislators had become annoyed at the Common Cause pressure,
but the organization had too much power for them to openly express their resentment. These legislators liked Hays for saying things about Common Cause
that they themselves wished they could say. Thus the feud helped both pro-
tagonists. Common Cause's morale was enhanced; and Hays's popularity, a
resource for political power, was increased.

Actually Hays was disliked by most of his colleagues. But they respected
him because he controlled such simple but useful prerogatives as office and
parking space, and he signed the paychecks of their staffs. Everyone knew that
Hays would not hesitate to use his power against a congressman he disliked.
His threat to give Morris Udall a parking space in Maryland was a standard
congressional joke.

Action Teams. A new concept of constituent lobbying is the action team,
which was developed by the Common Cause field staff in 1981-82. The previous
strategies we have been discussing were standard activities for Common Cause
throughout the middle and late 1970s. The addition of a new strategy may fore-
shadow the development by Common Cause of a second generation of lobbying tactics.

An action team involves twelve to fifteen Common Cause constituents that lobby their senator or representative in a personal, continual, informed, and lengthy fashion. The Common Cause Washington staff is still experimenting with this concept, but it implies selecting about a dozen key congressmen to be lobbied in that manner. The members of congress are selected on the basis of their power in regard to Common Cause bills and on their being persuadable, "swing" votes.

The members of an action team are given a considerable amount of information about their "target" congressman by the Common Cause national staff. Special attention is paid to the congressman's positions on Common Cause issues; changes in these positions are noted in "update" memos, which are sent to the citizen lobbyists of the action team. The members of the team are encouraged to write their congressman frequently, to visit the member when he or she is home in the district, and to contact local media about the congressman's positions on issues. Members who participate in this activity are encouraged to view it as a two-year commitment. Participation in an action team is interesting, involving, and demanding.

The action team technique is promising because it motivates the Common Cause participant. It also gives the member of Congress a sense of being watched by Common Cause, and the congressman is likely to get to know action team participants personally, which means that Common Cause will seem less like an abstraction and more like an organization of constituents with a perspective that needs to be considered.

The action team concept may be an effective way to lobby senators, who are usually harder to reach than members of the House. In medium or large states, action teams can be broken into five or six groups in various regions of a state. The senator will thus receive communication from Common Cause members in different parts of his state. The members can also communicate with local newspapers and television stations in different regions of the state. At present, Common Cause has a problem in some states of being overconcentrated in the state capital. If a majority of the communication to a senator comes from a specific geographical area, Common Cause loses effectiveness. It presents an image to a senator of being a hyperactive committee of reformers in a particular place, rather than a grass-roots organization of diverse citizens throughout the state.

The action team concept seems to be successful, but it is resource demanding. The national staff must spend time researching and writing memoranda about a congressman's recent activities and must monitor the activities of the team. Accordingly, the staff expects that the number of action teams will be limited.

Common Cause and Congressional Incentives for Self-Regulation

Common Cause has a special problem in achieving its reform program that most interest groups do not have. Many of the reforms proposed by Common Cause are regulations of political activity, including the activity of members of Congress. This is bound to make some congressmen feel hostile toward Common Cause, particularly as that organization is capable of effectively pressuring congressmen. For example, campaign reform rules affect a very important part of a congressman's life. He and his assistants must follow the rules regulating donations and must file correct reports at the right times. If they do not, they may face moral obloquy, court fines, or even jail.

Laws that force a congressman to make public his financial situation irritate many legislators. And attempts to regulate lobbyists are attempts to regulate friends of congressmen. In addition, some members of Congress believe they have the right to hold closed committee meetings; Common Cause backs legislation mandating public meetings.

As noted, Common Cause also annoys some congressmen because it is not a traditional lobby, although it uses some traditional political tactics. Some members of Congress, especially those from the South, Midwest, and rural areas, have had little experience in dealing with good-government interest groups. They find Common Cause too aggressive and moralistic, and without legitimate justification in asserting its program to regulate Congress. Numerous visits from Washington lobbyists and Common Cause supporters from the district also annoy these congressmen. One indication of the resentment of many congressmen toward Common Cause occurred in 1975 when mentions of Common Cause were greeted with booing at meetings of both the Democratic and Republican caucuses in the House. Yet the fact that some congressmen boo the name of Common Cause and like to repeat jokes such as "Common Cause is an expensive way to teach John Gardner about politics" does not prove that organization is ineffective in dealing with Congress.

In one instance, however, a congressman friendly to Common Cause told the organization not to lobby for a measure because it would be counterproductive. In the spring of 1975 Congressman Morris Udall told Common Cause to "lay low" in lobbying for a congressional override of President Ford's veto of Udall's strip-mining regulation measure. Evidently Udall calculated that the key votes needed for the two-thirds majority to override the veto contained a large number of House conservatives, who tend to be hostile to Common Cause.

Common Cause support for measures that regulate members of Congress is also a source of friendship with some of them. A large number of congressmen believe in the basic elements of the Common Cause government reform platform. These congressmen tend to be liberal Democrats, Republicans dissatisfied with Democratic-controlled institutions, new members, and those who come from districts with strong traditions of civic reform. They regard Common Cause as an ally. Such congressmen can be critical of Common Cause on specific points, but they finish their discourses with comments such as: "Don't get me wrong. I'm glad they're here."

Indeed, Common Cause's aggressive lobbying for institutional reform does its congressional allies the favor of diverting resentment of traditionally minded congressmen from their reformer colleagues to the "pressure" of Common Cause. A rather extreme example of this occurred when Representative F. Edward Hebert (Dem-La.) blamed his removal from the Armed Forces Committee chairmanship more on Common Cause than on his Democratic colleagues.

> [Hebert] said yesterday his downfall was part of a "vicious and reprehensible" campaign started five years ago by Common Cause. . . . Although critical of the new power invested in the Democratic caucus, Hebert saved most of his criticism for Common Cause, in an interview on the NBC "Today" show.
>
> "Common Cause started this thing in 1969 and they have conducted one of the most vicious and reprehensible campaigns that I've ever seen in my life," Hebert said. He further charged Common Cause with "misrepresentation, downright lies, downright distortions. The American people better wake up to what this outfit's doing because they can destroy this country," he said. "The new Congressmen are not running Congress," he said. "Common Cause is running Congress. Who elected them?"[45]

After voting for a reform they personally favor, congressmen sometimes explain their vote to other congressmen by saying they were pressured by Common Cause. This invites their colleagues to be hostile to that organization, rather than to them.

Congressional Incentives for Reform

Reform rules may irritate Congressmen, but there are several reasons why a member of Congress might support Common Cause legislation on reform. First, the congressman may believe the change is right in and of itself, such as believing in the right of the public to attend congressional committee meetings. Second, the legislator may see procedural changes as helping to achieve substantive goals he favors. For example, liberals usually think that reform rules will decrease the power of a congressional "establishment" or decrease the power of economic special interests. Third, open meetings and other reforms may protect the minority party against arbitrary actions by a majority. Fourth, individual congressmen sometimes think that reforms will increase their power in-

side Congress. New members of Congress may feel that their favored legislation will stand a better chance in a reformed committee system. Members near
the top of committees may hope that new rules will bring more pressure on
superannuated chairmen and top-ranking members, leading to retirements or
the removal of the chairman and thereby opening up top committee positions.

But the most important incentive for supporting reform is a congressman's
concern about his reelection.[46] This is particularly true during periods of widespread disaffection with governmental institutions, as has been the case during the life of Common Cause. Judging from the overwhelming support some
reform measures received on floor votes, during the 1970s most congressmen
believed their constituents supported the regulation of lobbyists, the disclosure
of financial holdings by high government officials, sunshine and sunset bills,
and so forth. These reform positions apparently favorably impress constituents
and are opposed by few voters.[47] Such reform stands are a good countermeasure
to a challenger's most frequent criticism of an incumbent: that he has forgot-
ten the district in Washington, he has "Potomac fever," he is part of "the Washington buddy system."

Common Cause does not endorse candidates, but it can give a congressman favorable publicity when it publishes charts of congressional positions
on measures supported by Common Cause. A member is likely to glance at
his congressman's voting record even if he or she reads nothing else in the Common Cause bulletins. Common Cause members are regarded as opinion leaders
and as persons almost certain to vote in congressional elections. Thus it is helpful for a congressman to look good in the Common Cause charts.

Common Cause is sometimes criticized for giving itself more credit for
passing some reform than is its due. There is some truth to this; Common
Cause has every incentive to stretch the truth a bit in its self-evaluation of the
effectiveness of its Washington lobbying operation. Because of a sensitivity to
this criticism, and because it is good politics to reward congressmen who have
played a leading part in the passage of Common Cause-sponsored legislation,
the organization's bulletins and magazines have given an increasing amount
of mention and praise to the congressmen who have worked especially hard
for the passage of such legislation. Perhaps fifty members of Congress a year
are singled out for praise in Common Cause publications, and such praise can
be cited in a congressman's reelection campaign. In this way, Common Cause
can "give a little help to its friends."

Major Common Cause-sponsored reforms will have about 150 co-sponsors
in the House and numerous co-sponsors in the Senate. Common Cause frequently publishes lists of co-sponsors and requests constituents to write their
congressmen and thank them for co-sponsoring the bill.

Reforming the Executive Branch

The Watergate scandal called attention to abuses of executive agency power in the Department of Justice, the Federal Bureau of Investigation, the Internal Revenue Service, the Central Intelligence Agency, and others. In addition, conservatives, liberals, and public-interest group spokesmen such as Ralph Nader have become increasingly critical of the federal regulation of business. Since its founding, Common Cause has become increasingly concerned with the power of interest groups over government agencies legally charged with regulating such groups. This is a major source of "special-interest power," according to the leaders of Common Cause.

In 1974 Common Cause began developing a program to lobby executive agencies and support reform of the executive branch and independent regulatory agencies. Much of the program Common Cause adopted in respect to reforming the federal executive branch was similar to the programs of good-government reformers of other times. Common Cause began research on questions of public administration; it supported carefully drawn laws to delimit the powers of agencies such as the FBI and the CIA; it asked for measures restricting the number of political appointees in the executive branch and improving their quality. In addition, it called for the creation of ombudsmen: "Common Cause believes that every executive department and agency of substantial size or importance should establish a Citizen Advocate or Ombudsman unit. . . . The office would continually appraise the agency's procedures for handling complaints and must be empowered to make explicit recommendations for change."[48]

Common Cause also developed three new kinds of reforms to be applied to the executive branch: the logging of nongovernmental contacts, getting public commitments from agency heads, and "sunset" proposals to periodically review government agencies (see chapter 8).

John Sawhill, the first administrator of the Federal Energy Agency,[49] agreed in 1974 to order top officials in the agency to log all contacts with nongovernmental persons, a proposal made to him by John Gardner. The logging of contacts yields the interesting fact that top FEA officials talked to energy industry officials 91 percent of the time; and talked to officials of consumer, public-interest, and research groups only 6 percent of the time.

Common Cause sought to extend such logging of nongovernmental contacts to other government agencies. It petitioned the White House in 1975 to issue an Executive Order establishing logging regulations and new conflict-of-interest regulations throughout the executive branch. The Ford administration received Common Cause's request with polite interest, but took no action.

In the spring of 1975 Common Cause first used the technique of getting public commitments from a proposed head of an executive agency. During the senatorial confirmation hearings for Interior Secretary-designate Stanley Hathaway, Common Cause submitted a list of questions to the nominee regarding his policies on conflict-of-interest matters, the logging of outside contacts, leasing, and the opening of department decision making to public observation. Senator Henry Jackson, chairman of the Senate Interior Committee, liked the Common Cause list and directed the nominee to answer the questions. Hathaway did so, although sometimes in terms so general as to preclude commitment. But Common Cause and Senator Jackson did get a greater commitment from Hathaway than if they had not used this procedure. Hathaway's responses were inserted in the Interior Committee's confirmation report, and thus constituted a public commitment on his part.[50] Unfortunately, Hathaway served for only six weeks at Interior because his lengthy and controversial confirmation process induced a state of mental depression that forced him to resign. (Hathaway was opposed by environmentalist groups.) The Senate confirmed the next Interior Secretary-designate, Thomas Kleppe, so rapidly that Common Cause could not secure a detailed response to its list of questions.

Litigation and Political Action

Because the Common Cause organization specializes in structure and process issues to attain accountability in government, it is natural that its litigation division (which has three lawyers) specializes in lawsuits involving the regulation of political campaigns. The control of donations to candidates for office has become a central issue of accountability in government because it is widely assumed that large campaign donations are the primary source of special-interest power over legislators. In recent years, complex lawsuits involving regulation of political campaigns have used up most of the resources that Common Cause budgeted for litigation.

Common Cause gets the maximum effect from these lawsuits by coordinating them with its lobbying for public regulation and financing of political campaigns. Common Cause sued the Democratic and Republican National Committees in 1971 to force them to obey a 1940 statute that limited the expenditures of a candidate's campaign committee in a presidential election to $3 million a year.[51] The prospect of being legally enjoined to obey other seldom-enforced election laws was a powerful incentive for congressional action to revise the regulations on federal elections. Thus a lawsuit was a major factor in undermining the status quo in respect to the regulation of political campaigns. The Common Cause suit to force the Committee to Re-Elect the President (CREEP) to disclose donations given to the Nixon campaign before 7 April 1972 played a part in discrediting a system of financing presidential elections in which, essentially, any person or interest group was free to give as much money as desired to a presidential candidate.[52] This led to the Federal Election Campaign Amendments of 1974, which established a system of public funding for presidential candidates, a limit on how much an individual or a group could give to a candidate for federal office, and an enforcement agency (the Federal Election Commission) to administer the new regulations.

After Common Cause played a leading part in getting the 1974 act, its legal division was central to the defense of the new law by serving as an intervenor when Senator James Buckley (Rep-N.Y.), Eugene McCarthy, and the American Civil Liberties Union attempted to prove the new law unconstitutional (see chapter 7).[53] In turn, Common Cause's lobbying division assisted the intervention in the *Buckley* v. *Valeo* suit on the campaign reform act by providing the lawyers with the best information available on the financing of the 1972 and 1974 elections, information obtained by collating the thousands of separate campaign donation reports filed by candidates. Common Cause made this information available to the public, and the Buckley et al. side of the case was forced to use the Common Cause information to challenge the law. The arguments of Common Cause lawyers, representing an organization that provided important technical information in the case and that was strongly in favor of the law, were much more credible because of this research. In addition, the Common Cause staff, concerned about the details of election reform since 1971, had years of experience in dealing with issues arising out of federal regulation of campaigns and could give useful advice to lawyers defending the 1974 statute.

Common Cause has attempted to undermine by litigation the status quo regarding congressional refusal to legislate public funding for congressional elections. Congressmen are allowed free use of the mails, and in recent years they have used this privilege to send barrages of essentially political self-advertisements through the mails in election years. Common Cause sued to restrict this practice, but lost in court after ten years of litigation.[54]

The political tactics of Common Cause require a coordination of the content and timing of messages to Congress from its Washington lobbyists and members in congressional districts. In addition, lobbying the national Congress is coordinated with efforts to influence state legislatures and the federal executive branch and with lawsuits initiated in the federal courts.

NOTES

1. Bruce Adams, Philip Clapp, et al., *With Only One Ear: A Common Cause Study of Industry and Consumer Representation Before Federal Regulatory Commissions* (Washington, D.C.: Common Cause, 1977).

2. In 1970 there was floor debate on a demand by Representative Ogden Reid of New York (then a Republican, later a Democrat) to bar the use of funds in the military procurement bill from being used to finance the introduction of American ground troops in Laos, Thailand, or Cambodia. See *Congressional Quarterly Almanac, 1970* (Washington, D.C.: Congressional Quarterly, 1971), 26: 388. In addition, there were three voice votes and one standing vote on antiwar amendments to the military procurement and defense appropriations bills in 1970, but these votes were taken without a debate on the merits of the American war effort. See *Congressional Quarterly Almanac, 1970,* 26: 388, 416.

   In April 1971 there were four votes on antiwar amendments attached to the draft extension bill, including a significant amount of debate on an amendment by Donald M. Fraser to prohibit the service of anyone drafted after 31 December 1971 in Indochina. The Fraser amendment lost 122-260. See *Congressional Quarterly Almanac, 1971* (Washington, D.C.: Congressional Quarterly, 1972), 27: 266. There was significant debate on the Nedzi-Whalen amendment to the defense procurement authorization bill in June 1971. The Nedzi-Whalen amendment would have cut off the use of certain defense appropriations in Indochina after 31 December 1971. It lost 158-254. See *Congressional Quarterly Almanac, 1971,* 27: 310-12.

3. In 1977 the Senate became more resistant to passing legislation providing for public financing for congressional elections because Howard Baker and other Republican leaders decided that such legislation would adversely affect the interests of the Republican party. See *Congressional Quarterly Almanac, 1977* (Washington, D.C.: Congressional Quarterly, 1977), 33: 798-810.

4. In the 94th and 95th Congresses, Common Cause was able to get from 125 to 150 co-sponsors in the House for basic OUTS measures. The figure of 150 to 175 members is based on the supposition that among those initially in favor of a measure, about 25 members did not co-sponsor it for various political reasons or because they were not contacted by Common Cause. In these Congresses, about half the Republicans (70 members) and perhaps 80 to 100 Democrats (mostly conservatives) consistently opposed OUTS reforms.

5. Three examples stand out. The Sunshine Act passed the Senate 94-0 in 1975 and the House 390-5 in 1976. See Ted Vaden, "Government in the Sunshine Approved, 390-5," *Congressional Quarterly* (31 July 1976): 2067; and *Congressional Quarterly Almanac, 1975* (Washington, D.C.: Congressional Quarterly, 1976), 31: 725. The lobbying regulation bill of 1976 passed the House 307-34 and the Senate 82-9, but was not finally passed because there was no time to resolve the differences between the House and the Senate bills. See *Congressional Quarterly Almanac, 1976* (Washington, D.C.: Congressional Quarterly, 1977), 32: 484; and *Congressional Quarterly* (19 June 1976): 1575. The Obey Commission ethics proposals passed the House 402-22 in 1977. That year a new ethics code passed the Senate 86-9.

6. See chap. 4 and below, p. 157.

7. In the fall of 1974, 59 of 144 Republicans elected to the House agreed with Common Cause at least five out of seven times on a list of Common Cause proposals. This

agreement was stated in response to a Common Cause questionnaire.

8. Much of the material in this chapter is derived from 20 interviews with members of the House of Representatives. The goal was to get a general impression of congressional reactions to Common Cause rather than a detailed picture of these reactions. Congressmen are extremely busy and to interview an adequate random sample of them would take at least six months of work. In my judgment, the additional specificity and reliability gained by interviewing perhaps another 45 members of Congress was not necessary at this stage of research about Common Cause.

The interviews were basically open-ended, that is, I tried to get the congressman to converse freely about his impressions of Common Cause. However, three questions were asked in each interview: "What do you think of Common Cause?" "Have you got any mail recently from Common Cause members in your district?" "Do you think that Common Cause is politically effective?" I did not tape-record or make notes during the interviews. I transcribed them from memory immediately after they ended.

I interviewed 10 congressmen who were generally supportive of Common Cause, 5 known to be critical of it, and 5 who were not clearly classifiable in this respect. I was able to supplement these interviews with comments about Common Cause by members of Congress that appeared in the *Washington Post* and with anecdotes told by congressional staff at informal social gatherings.

9. For discussions of mail to Congress, see Raymond A. Bauer, Ithiel de Sola Pool, and Lewis Anthony Dexter, *American Business and Public Policy* (New York: Atherton, 1963), 438-40, and numerous other passages indexed under "Letters to Congress"; Donald R. Matthews, *U.S. Senators and Their World* (Chapel Hill: University of North Carolina Press, 1960), 219-28, and other passages indexed under "Mail"; John W. Kingdon, *Congressmen's Voting Decisions* (New York: Harper & Row, 1973), 53-59 and 207-9.

10. Even in districts with an active steering committee, only about 10 percent of the members actually write a member of Congress each year in behalf of a Common Cause-supported issue. Without a steering committee to call members to stimulate letters, perhaps 4 percent of the members would write to Congress. During the late 1970s, almost all congressional districts without a Common Cause organization had less than 200 members. In such a district, it seems likely that only about eight members would write to Congress each year on a Common Cause issue.

11. By 1972, Senators Edward Kennedy, Charles Mathias, and Hugh Scott had made statements praising the effectiveness of Common Cause in stimulating mail from constituents. These statements were featured in recruitment literature. The late San Francisco Congressman, Phillip Burton, made a similar statement in 1972, which is quoted on p. 189.

I interviewed four members of Congress from southern states about Common Cause. One was from a Florida district and was enthusiastic. Another was also enthusiastic, but perhaps was not reflective of the widespread opinion in his district because he resigned from the House after serving two terms and now lives in the Washington area. A third, from a Black Belt district, exhibited little interest in Common Cause. A fourth was interested in discussing Common Cause, but knew little about the organization. Two other congressmen, from Deep South districts, refused to be interviewed about Common Cause.

12. See Matthews, *U.S. Senators and Their World,* 184-86; Jeffrey M. Berry, *Lobbying for the People* (Princeton: Princeton University Press, 1977), 233-37.

13. In three instances, Common Cause staff or activists referred to moralistic lobbyists as constituting a problem in their state.

14. "The Fun Is Gone," *Washington Post,* 15 September 1974, B5. Probably the work-load of congressmen should not be increased beyond the present point, as more work would interfere with studying legislative issues and controlling the bureaucra-cy. It seems incumbent upon Common Cause to consider how the congressional workload could be managed without decreasing the representativeness of govern-ment.

15. Kingdon, *Congressmen's Voting Decisions,* 46-53.

16. This is an estimate, based on conversations with supervisors of the Washington con-nection.

17. Bauer, Pool, and Dexter, *American Business and Public Policy,* 350-57, 433-36.

18. Ibid.

19. "Open and Accountable Government: An Action Program for Citizens in the 1974 Elections," *Common Cause: Report from Washington* 4 (August 1974): 3-4.

20. Thomas P. Southwick, "House Adopts Tough Ethics Code," *Congressional Quarterly* 35 (5 March 1977): 387.

21. See, for example, *Congressional Quarterly Almanac, 1976* (Washington, D.C.: Con-gressional Quarterly, 1977), 32: 480.

22. Cf. Matthews, *U.S. Senators and Their World,* 279.

23. Peter Odegaard, *Pressure Politics: The Story of the Anti-Saloon League* (New York: Columbia University Press, 1928).

24. Common Cause subscribes to a newspaper clipping service. In addition, activists send the national headquarters local newspaper stories that involve Common Cause. This observation is based on my reading of about 500 clippings from 1975 and 1976.

25. For instance, during the 1970s, the influential political columnist David Broder of the *Washington Post* wrote occasional columns criticizing proposals for public finan-cing of presidential and congressional elections. On 24 August 1980 a full-length article criticizing the reforms supported by Common Cause appeared in the *New York Times Magazine.*

26. The figure of 2000 articles and editorials is based on an estimate of an average of 10 favorable articles a week in the country's newspapers over a period of 200 weeks. However, in about half the cases, two or more reforms are discussed in the same article or editorial. See note 24.

27. Advertising Research Foundation, Inc., *Quantitative and Qualitative Aspects of Daily Newspaper Reading: A National Study* (New York: Newspaper Advertising Bureau, 1973), 12:16, 18, 20.

28. *New York Times,* 19 February 1974, 30, and 4 March 1974, 27.

29. This account of lobbying closely approximates the model set forth by Kingdon, *Congressmen's Voting Decisions,* 146-50. It differs somewhat from Dexter's account in that Common Cause is more concerned to get its congressional allies to per-suade undecided congressmen than the groups described by Dexter. See Bauer, Pool, and Dexter, *American Business and Public Policy,* 350-57. My view is that the two basic treatises on lobbying by Dexter and Matthews generally apply to

the case of Common Cause. But modifications are needed. Common Cause is more autonomous and less controlled by its congressional allies than the pressure groups described by Dexter. Second, Common Cause is more aggressive in criticizing opponents and even friends in Congress than the groups studied by Dexter and Matthews. These two points are in agreement with Berry's modification of Dexter's work in regard to public interest groups. (See Berry, *Lobbying for the People,* 216-33.) Berry goes too far, however, in describing Common Cause as extremely aggressive in its lobbying tactics. He describes an instance of Common Cause's antiwar lobbying, an instance that indeed is typical of hundreds of cases of Common Cause lobbying, as extreme aggressiveness. But I read Berry's case to be an example of only mild aggressiveness, directed toward the actions of only one member of Congress, who might have played the deciding role on an important antiwar vote.

30. *Congressional Quarterly Almanac, 1974* (Washington, D.C.: Congressional Quarterly, 1975), 30: 611, 625.

31. In 1978 Common Cause came into conflict with Representatives Thompson and Brademas, who introduced a public financing of House elections bill that would have lowered the admissible contributions from all party committees from $30,000 to $10,000 per candidate. Because Republican party committees had recently given more money to House candidates than Democratic committees, this was seen by Common Cause as a measure slanted to benefit Democrats. Consequently, Common Cause opposed the measure. The Thompson-Brademas measure failed on a key parliamentary vote in March 1978, by 198-209. See *Congressional Quarterly Almanac, 1978* (Washington, D.C.: Congressional Quarterly, 1979), 34: 769-73.

32. See note 5.

33. On 8 August 1974 the Anderson-Udall amendment to provide matching grants for congressional general election campaigns was voted down 187-228. On 1 April 1976 a similar measure, sponsored by Phillip Burton (Dem-Calif.), was voted down 274 to 121. However, the 121 votes somewhat understated the actual support for the concept of matching grants for congressional campaigning because some congressmen feared that insertion of such a provision would increase the possibility of a veto by President Ford of the overall campaign regulation act of 1976. In July 1978 the House voted 196-213 against a rules change that would have allowed it to consider a Common Cause-backed public financing measure.

34. Kingdon, *Congressmen's Voting Decisions,* 154-57.

35. Matthews, *U.S. Senators and Their World,* 186-88; Donald R. Hall, *Cooperative Lobbying: The Power of Pressure* (Tucson: University of Arizona Press, 1969); Berry, *Lobbying for the People,* 254-61; James Q. Wilson, *Political Organizations* (New York: Basic Books, 1973), chap. 13; Anne N. Costain, "The Struggle for a National Women's Lobby: Organizing a Diffuse Interest," *Western Political Quarterly* 33 (December 1980): 476-91.

36. *Congressional Quarterly Almanac, 1974* (Washington, D.C.: Congressional Quarterly, 1975), 30: 634-41.

37. My impression is that one of James Q. Wilson's observations holds true for Washington lobbyists in general and Common Cause in particular: "Associations, seeking to maintain themselves, are highly averse to risk and thus to active rivalry except under special circumstances. The easiest and most prudent maintenance strategy is to develop *autonomy*—that is, a distinctive area of competence, a clear-

ly demarcated and exclusively served clientele or membership, and undisputed jurisdiction over a function, service, goal, or cause. Just as executives seek to minimize
strain in managing the internal affairs of the association, so also they seek to minimize it in their relations with other organizations." Wilson, *Political Organizations,* 263.

38. See Bauer, Pool, and Dexter, *American Business and Public Policy,* 323-25, 350-57;
Matthews, *U.S. Senators and Their World,* 183-84.

39. The other center is the Citizens' Research Foundation directed by Herbert E. Alexander. This research group has published about 25 monographs; in addition, Dr.
Alexander has authored, co-authored, and edited several books.

40. "Report on House Committee Chairmen," Common Cause, Washington, D.C., 13
January 1975, 14.

41. See David Braybrooke and Charles E. Lindblom, *A Strategy of Decision* (New York:
Free Press, 1963).

42. The fact that public interest groups are in competition to advocate an appealing
new idea is an instance of Robert Salisbury's "entrepreneurial theory" of interest-
group activity, which is contrasted by Berry to David Truman's "disturbance theory."
In other words, the leadership of interest groups is seen as searching for new issues
to bring new resources to their groups, as contrasted to the idea that issues are
closely linked to major disturbances in "the social system." Sociologists refer to
the entrepreneurial theory as "the resource mobilization theory of social movements." See Robert H. Salisbury, "An Exchange Theory of Interest Groups," *Midwest Journal of Political Science* 13 (February 1969): 1-32; Jeffrey M. Berry, "On
the Origins of Public Interest Groups: A Test of Two Theories," *Polity* 10 (Spring
1978): 379-97; Berry, *Lobbying for the People,* 18-27; John D. McCarthy and Mayer
N. Zald, "Resource Mobilization and Social Movements," *American Journal of
Sociology* 82 (May 1977): 1212-41. This perspective overlaps with James Q. Wilson's
argument that the goal of resource maintenance is central for the understanding
of interest groups. See Wilson's *Political Organizations.*

43. *Common Cause et al.* v. *Jennings,* C.A. 848-72 (D.D.C.).

44. See *Washington Post,* 21 and 22 March 1974; *New York Times,* 22 March 1974,
24, and 25 March 1974, 22.

45. *Washington Post,* 6 February 1975; United Press International wire service story.

46. The generic statement of the argument that concern for reelection determines a congressman's actions is David R. Mayhew's *Congress: The Electoral Connection* (New
Haven: Yale University Press, 1974).

47. It is difficult to demonstrate with hard data that taking a position in favor of a reform measure sponsored by Common Cause tended in the 1970s to impress
favorably many more voters than it repelled. Perhaps it is more precise to say that
opposing a measure such as the regulation of lobbyists or an ethics code for high
government officials would be a vote difficult to explain to voters in many congressional districts. My hypothesis is that on some measures advocated by Common
Cause, a member of Congress would fear to go on public record in opposition
because such a vote might be criticized by electoral opponents in forthcoming campaigns.

Such a hypothesis is needed to explain the behavior of members of Congress
in regard to the bill to regulate lobbyists, for example. Versions of this legislation

passed both the House and the Senate in nearly unanimous floor votes in 1976, although the legislation failed when a conference committee was unable to agree on a joint version of the legislation before the 94th Congress adjourned. From the floor votes, one might suppose that regulation of lobbyists was a measure enthusiastically supported by members of both Houses. In fact, one prominent member of the House told me that many representatives did not want the legislation to pass. And this group got their way. Accordingly, one can observe a difference between the public behavior of some members of Congress (voting for the measure) and their private behavior (hoping that the measure would fail). My inference is that such members are (1) concerned about their reelection and (2) believe that a vote against certain reform measures will hurt their electoral chances. This inference is congruent with the view of Congress put forth in such works as Mayhew's *Congress: The Electoral Connection* and Richard Fenno's *Home Style: House Members in Their Districts* (Boston: Little, Brown, 1978).

48. "Challenge for a President: Making Government Work," *In Common* 7 (Winter 1976): 22.

49. The Federal Energy Agency was established in May 1974 as the successor agency to the Federal Energy Office. The FEA was succeeded in 1975 by ERDA (Energy Research and Development Administration), which was in turn succeeded by the Department of Energy in 1977.

50. Andrew McFarland, *Public Interest Lobbies: Decision Making on Energy* (Washington, D.C.: American Enterprise Institute, 1976), 62, 113-16.

51. *Common Cause et al.* v. *Democratic National Committee et al.*, 333 F. Supp. 803 D.D.C. (1971).

52. *Common Cause et al.* v. *Finance Committee to Re-Elect the President et al.*, C.A. 1780-72 (D.D.C.)

53. *Buckley et al.* v. *Valeo et al.*, 424 U.S. 1 (1976) *per curiam*.

54. *Common Cause* v. *Bolger*, Civil No. 1887-73 (D.D.C. 7 September 1982), appeal dismissed, 1983. Common Cause's litigation deserves a more extensive treatment by legal scholars. Some of this work has been done by Joel L. Fleishman and Carol S. Greenwald, "Public Interest Litigation and Political Finance Reform," *Annals of the American Academy of Political and Social Science* 425 (May 1976): 114-23; and Carol S. Greenwald, "The Use of Litigation by Common Cause: A Study of the Development of Campaign Finance Reform Legislation" (a paper delivered at the 1975 annual meeting of the American Political Science Association at San Francisco). Copies of Greenwald's thorough treatment of this topic up to 1975 may be obtained from the American Political Science Association's microfilms of the papers given at its 1975 convention.

7. The Program: Campaign Reform

A plausible case has been constructed that Common Cause is effective in lobbying for its program. That program has gotten a significant amount of attention in Congress and in most state legislatures. But the question remains: Common Cause may be effective, but is it effective at doing something significant? Does it make that much difference whether Common Cause measures are enacted or not? Readers are surely aware of laws "on the books" that are generally ignored and that make little difference.

In this chapter and in the next, I present the basic elements of the Common Cause program for government reform. I argue that the program is significant because it will make a significant difference if enacted. Readers may judge for themselves whether the program is a positive contribution to American society.

There is not enough space to offer a full discussion of the Common Cause program, but I try to present the most important program items. Of these, public financing and other reforms of electoral campaigns have first priority. Accordingly, I emphasize campaign reform by setting it apart in this chapter.

Do Good-Government Reforms Matter?

Good-government reformers have been called naive for supposing that passing laws and redrawing organization charts will solve the problems of special-interest rule. And probably some Common Cause activists have such naive beliefs. But John Gardner and the Washington staff never suffered from this illusion. Anyone with a few years of experience in Washington is familiar with the phenomenon, described by Murray Edelman, of reform laws enacted with good intentions and then not enforced.[1] One of Common Cause's first acts was to institute a suit to enforce laws regulating donations to federal elections adopted in the 1920s, 1930s, and 1940s, but not enforced in the 1960s.[2] Similarly, Common Cause was aware that only one successful prosecution had been instituted under a law regulating lobbyists passed in 1946.[3] By the 1970s this law was a Washington joke.[4] The American Telephone and Telegraph Company reported no lobbying expenses under the rules of the 1946 act, but on demand from the Federal Communications Commission, AT&T reported spending $1,040,009 in one three-month period. In 1972, only $6227 was reported as lobbying expenses for the El Paso Natural Gas Company, which admitted to the Federal Power Commission that it had indeed spent $893,862 for lobbying.[5] Because they witnessed the wreckage of earlier reform efforts, John Gardner and other founders of Common Cause realized that reform legislation would not work unless there was a politically organized constituency demanding enforcement.

Even when a group is organized to support a body of enacted political reform laws, it is not obvious that such legislation will change the course of politics. Some observers have argued that political outcomes are determined by economic imperatives (Karl Marx), by power elites (C. Wright Mills), or by widely shared ideas about what is good and bad in politics (Alexis de Tocqueville).[6] From such perspectives, regulating lobbyists, passing conflict-of-interest legislation, and the like will not affect public policy to an important extent. According to such positions, enacting the Common Cause program will not change political outcomes because changing political institutions does not affect the substance of governmental policies.

This point of view is somewhat mistaken when applied to Common Cause. The nature of regulations concerning presidential campaign finances may have altered the course of political events in 1968 and 1972 (see below). True, one assessment is that the effect of some other major reforms recently enacted in Washington — such as conflict-of-interest legislation and open meeting laws — is less than was assumed by the Common Cause staff. Yet the cumulative effect of policy changes may be significant in the years to come.

The Common Cause structure and process reforms are significant for another reason. Even if they do not alter political outcomes, they can be regarded as ends in themselves; they represent the views of many Americans about how government ought to be conducted. This is especially important in an era of increasing mass dissatisfaction with government institutions. For instance, requiring lobbyists to register and to file a log of contacts with congressmen may prove to have no effect on political outcomes. But if citizens feel an increasing trust for a government that so regulates lobbyists, then that regulation becomes a significant political measure.

Campaign finances seem to have been a major factor in deciding the outcome of the contest between Richard Nixon and Hubert Humphrey in 1968.[7] That year of the disastrous Democratic convention in Chicago caused many people to think that the Democrats were so disunited that Humphrey could not win. The convention was scheduled late in the summer and did not nominate Humphrey until 29 August. Candidate Humphrey was confronted with an extraordinarily difficult situation. He was more than 20 percentage points behind Nixon in the polls. The Democratic party was divided and dispirited. Humphrey's campaign desperately needed to raise money, while Nixon was assured of adequate financing from business interests. It is a political maxim that "early money" is more useful than "late money"; money in hand early in a campaign can be spent more effectively than if the same amount of money is contributed at the end of a campaign, when it is often spent hastily and without sufficient planning.

The Humphrey campaign exerted considerable effort to get enough money to compete with Nixon. By early October Humphrey's campaign caught fire, and he almost caught up to Nixon by election day.[8] Assurance of adequate financing on 1 September would have meant a more carefully planned campaign for Humphrey and perhaps a victory.

Changing some presidential election procedures can change the course of American politics. Granting major-party candidates assured public funding can permit the type of planning and forethought that a good campaign needs. But public opinion was not very concerned about inequities in financing presidential campaigns until after Humphrey lost, Nixon won, and the Watergate scandal discredited the system of financing presidential elections.

Campaign Reform

Two of the major accomplishments of Common Cause were in the area of campaign reform—the Federal Election Campaign Amendments of 1974 and the successful suit against the Committee to Re-Elect the President to force the disclosure of donations to the Nixon campaign before 7 April 1972.[9] The 1974 act provided for federal matching grants to presidential contenders (including primary candidates), established limits on total campaign spending by presidential primary contenders, established limits on total campaign spending by party nominees for the Presidency, set limits on donations by individuals or campaign committees to a presidential or congressional race with an overall ceiling of $25,000 for donations to all federal campaigns, and established a Federal Election Commission to enforce the law.

John Gardner was strongly convinced that Common Cause should act on controlling the flow of money in election campaigns. The leaders and members of Common Cause were in agreement with Gardner about the uses of money in politics. During the early 1970s, there was increasing public discussion of the role of money in political campaigns.[10] The cost of running a major political campaign had become widely known. In 1970 a contested race for the

House of Representatives required $75,000 for adequate financing, and a campaign for the Senate needed $1 million in the larger states. About $37 million was spent in the general election for President in 1968. By 1972 this figure had risen to $90 million.[11] Additionally, many people became increasingly concerned about the large amount of television advertising by politicians. These political commercials, written and staged by advertising agencies, violated widely shared conceptions about how candidates should communicate with voters in a democracy.[12]

Gardner stressed the ideas that campaign contributions were the central means whereby special interests bought favors at the expense of public interests and that large contributions bought the wealthy more access to politicians than the average voter could get. In his book *In Common Cause,* Gardner stated that "the game" of politics "includes activities that range from outright criminality to legitimate (although foxy) political deals. We must not be patronizing about the latter. Politics is, among other things, a trading out of conflicting interests. . . . A society that does not want conflicting interests resolved by the edict of a tyrant, and does not want opposing elements to draw guns, will honor its professional conciliators—chief among them, its politicians."[13]

> Unfortunately, however, the game of barter and purchase has gone far, far beyond acceptable limits; the public-interest is sacrificed far too readily and far too often; and the citizen must understand better than he does now the multiplicity of ways in which his interests are compromised. He knows that politics has its seamy side; but he doesn't know that a high percentage of his tax dollar goes to support it.[14]

He noted the kinds of favors politicians give to their financial supporters: interest-free government accounts in banks, buying insurance for government activities; government purchasing contracts; urban renewal contracts; purchases of land; architectural and construction contracts; patronage appointments such as judges, receivers, guardians, trustees, referees, appraisers, U.S. attorneys, assistant U.S. attorneys, and marshals; local government control of business permits, zoning variances, and tax abatements; and the power to "forego prosecution of those who are close to the reigning political powers."[15] It is interesting that many examples in this list pertain to special favors granted by *state* and *local* governments. The list can be cited by Common Cause activists who believe that state and local government needs more attention from Common Cause.

Gardner described special-interest power at the national level, a subject he elaborated at various places in the book.

> The President's capacity to reward his friends is immeasurable. Simply by the level at which he sets an item in the budget he can alter the outlook for an entire industry. By resisting or endorsing regulatory legislation, he can transform the environment in which thousands of firms do business. He can rescue an airline from the

edge of bankruptcy with a favorable route award. He can delay or quash antitrust action where it affects his friends.

Of all the favors government can bestow, none is more succulent than the tax break. . . .[16]

At this point Gardner cited the oil depletion allowance, which Congress rescinded four years later for the larger oil companies, an action that had strong Common Cause support. He related other examples of objectionable tax breaks: "The capital gains tax, the many avenues of escape from the estate tax, the abuse of farm tax losses, accelerated depreciation, and innumerable other devices enable the high-income taxpayer to bring his tax rate far below that of citizens in the middle- and lower-income ranges."[17]

After discussing the political favors that politicians can give, Gardner asked: "With all that flood of favors pouring out from the politicians, what flows in the other direction? The answer is 'money.' "[18]

When the campaign begins the party money-raisers go down their list of "friends"—the architect who received a commission for the new customs house, the bank that benefited heavily from government deposits, the insurance company that profits from a huge policy, the wealthy developer who was tapped for the urban renewal program, the industry that received a tax break involving billions. And the "friends" pay off.

Thus is the public interest bought and sold.[19]

Gardner also expressed concern about the role of corporate money in politics:

But the gravest danger in the concentration of economic power is the increased capacity to influence the public process through the power of money. As that capacity increases, the forms and ceremonies of democracy become a mockery . . . existing antitrust legislation should be more vigorously enforced, and measures should be taken to curb the political influence of corporate giants (through campaign-spending controls, lobbying disclosure and conflict of interest statutes).[20]

A somewhat different argument for campaign finance reform was that large donations create an inequality of access to political decision makers:

The most serious obstacle the citizen faces when he sets out to participate is that someone with a lot of money got there first and bought the public address system. The full-throated voice of money drowns him out. It isn't just that money talks. It talks louder and longer and drowns out the citizen's hoarse whisper.

All citizens should have equal access to decision-making processes of government, but money makes some citizens more equal than others. Harold Geneen, whose company committed $400,000 to help finance the Republican National Convention in San Diego [before Nixon and Mitchell moved the site to Miami Beach], had no difficulty in discussing his antitrust problems with three cabinet members, three White House aides, five senators, five representatives, and the chairman of the Federal Reserve Board. That is *access*. And any ordinary citizen who tries to set up a comparable schedule of appointments will learn all he needs to know about the influence of money in politics.

If we wish to diminish the power of money to corrupt the public process, we must pass laws to control campaign financing, to control lobbies, and to require full disclosure of conflict of interest on the part of all public officials.[21]

Still another argument was a direct appeal to morality:

Only very impatient or stupid men give or take cash bribes anymore. It is dreadfully old-fashioned. The preferred mode of corruption today is either the campaign gift or circuitous and hard-to-trace business favors. . . . It is all very civilized. And low-keyed. And polite. So much so that people raise their eyebrows when one calls it corruption. But some of us are just simple-minded enough to believe that when public policy is bent in a particular direction as a result of financial favors done to the policy-maker, that is corruption, embroider it how you will.

The potentialities for corruption based on campaign spending have increased greatly due to the soaring costs of the political campaign. . . . There are people who give to political campaigns out of honest conviction, and honest politicians who receive campaign gifts. But most political giving is done with the intent to buy influence.[22]

In conclusion: "We must pass laws to control campaign financing, to control lobbies, and to require full disclosure of conflict of interest on the part of all public officials."[23]

It is difficult to emphasize strongly enough how central such measures are to any improvement in our situation. . . . Our system is being corrupted and compromised by the power of money to dictate political outcomes. The capacity or willingness of the government to find solutions to any of the problems that plague us—inflation, inequitable taxes, unemployment, housing, urban chaos, dirty air and water—is complicated by the commanding power of monied interests to define the problem and set limits to public action.[24]

Of course, Gardner's statements appeared in a book intended to increase enthusiasm for Common Cause, and their tone erred on the side of ardor. But Gardner left no doubt about his opinion that political campaign financing practices had to be changed. And his opinion was shared by the great majority of the Common Cause constituency, as well as by many congressmen.

In 1970 the Democratic Congress passed a law limiting television and radio expenditures in federal elections, but this was vetoed by President Nixon on the grounds that "the problem with campaign spending is not radio and television; the problem is spending. This bill plugs only one hole in a sieve."[25] In January 1972 Congress passed another campaign reform act, which Nixon then signed. This Federal Election Campaign Act of 1972 provided for limitations on expenditures in both broadcast and print media and for disclosure of all campaign donations over $100 (the operative date for this disclosure provision

was the subject of the Common Cause suit against the Nixon campaign committee).

The Common Cause lobbying was mainly conducted later, in 1972-74,
aimed at the passage of the campaign reform act of 1974. By fall 1972, the
local organization of steering committees and telephone networks was established in the majority of districts for the House of Representatives. Common
Cause was thus in a better position to pressure congressmen than it was in
fights for campaign reform bills from 1970 until January 1972.

During the summer and fall of 1972, 1300 Common Cause volunteers engaged in a systematic project to issue citizen complaints against congressional
candidates who did not file statements disclosing donations of more than $100
to their campaigns at the March, June, and September dates, as stipulated in
the campaign regulation act of 1972. This legislation states that complaints
could be filed with the local secretary of state. Common Cause filed complaints
against 286 congressional candidates, thereby providing 286 interesting news
stories for local media and embarrassing the candidates. This action provided
an important precedent for the 1974 election when congressional candidates
regularly filed such reports (filing became an established part of the routine
of running for office).

Unfortunately, no one has written a detailed account of the passage of
the Campaign Act of 1974. The staff of Common Cause claims that it was an
important factor in shaping this legislation and getting it passed. Many congressmen agree with this claim. And political scientists David Adamany and
George Agree reported:

> . . . an effective lobby for campaign finance reform, especially public financing,
> emerged for the first time. The spearhead was Common Cause, which brought
> to the fray substantial resources—a relatively large, well-educated, and attentive
> membership; ample funds; a skilled Washington staff; and a genius for winning
> media attention. In addition to the usual techniques of legislative lobbying, Com-
> mon Cause used meticulous research and relentless litigation to good advantage.
> Its 1972 Congressional campaign finance monitoring project revealed the amounts
> spent, the size of gifts, the special interest contributions, and the money edge of
> incumbents in every Congressional race in the country.
>   Joined with Common Cause were the Center for Public Financing of Elec-
> tions, union labor, the National Committee for an Effective Congress, the League
> of Women Voters, the National Women's Political Caucus, and others. The Center
> reported in December 1973 that eighteen groups were coordinating legislative strat-
> egy to enact public financing. . . .[26]

The substance of the Federal Election Campaign Amendments of 1974 had been
the main priority for Common Cause for two years. Almost all the tactics mentioned in chapter 6 had been used.

David Cohen claimed credit for providing the crucial margin on the most critical vote on the reform act—a cloture vote, requiring two-thirds of those present in the Senate, to shut off a filibuster led by Senator James Allen (Dem-Ala.). According to Cohen, the success of the vote reflected intense lobbying of three senators by Common Cause. (This was when Common Cause succeeded in bringing back Senator Fulbright from his Arkansas primary camaign.[27]) The staff of Common Cause was very active in meeting with the staff of many of the congressional backers of the act, and Common Cause helped shape some important provisions of the bill.[28] In particular Common Cause was concerned that the enforcement of the act be given to a newly established agency rather than to the Justice Department, which had not enforced earlier campaign reform legislation. Common Cause was also concerned that ceilings on congressional campaign expenditures (a provision later ruled unconstitutional[29]) not be set at such a low level as to give an advantage to incumbents, since challengers need more money to get themselves known.

Common Cause got most of what it wanted in the reform act. A Federal Election Commission was established to enforce the legislation, and it proceeded to carry out its task adequately. The spending ceilings for House candidates were low, but were still acceptable to Common Cause. However, the ceiling provision was rescinded by the Supreme Court before the 1976 elections.

Common Cause achieved two other important goals with the passage of the Campaign Amendments of 1974: public funding for presidential elections and limits on contributions by individuals and organizations to candidates for federal office. The public funding provision provided for matching grants to major primary contenders and full payment for major-party general election contenders with a spending limit of $20 million in 1974 dollars. The money was to come from a Presidential Election Campaign Fund established in a little-noticed rider to the Revenue Act of 1971. Checking a box on one's income tax form granted one dollar of taxes to the fund. During the first year this provision was operative, it was necessary to file a separate form rather than check a box on the regular form, and the public response was inadequate for financing a presidential election. A suit by Common Cause forced the Internal Revenue Service to drop the separate form and place the check-off box on the main page of the income tax form.[30]

The limits on contributions established by the 1974 act were $1000 for each individual for each primary, runoff, and general election for federal office; each person was limited to an aggregate $25,000 in contributions to all federal elections. The limit for organizations—including union and business political committees and political party committees—was $5000 for each election but with no overall limit on total contributions to federal elections. Both the presidential election funding provisions and the contribution limits were still in force during presidential and congressional elections in 1980 and 1982.

Common Cause was defeated on one important provision it wanted included in the campaign reform act. Common Cause wanted to establish public funding for congressional elections; such a provision was part of the Senate's bill, which provided for matching grants for all federal candidates, including candidates in congressional primary elections.[31] But the provision was not part of the bill reported to the House by Wayne Hays's Administration Committee because Chairman Hays strongly opposed it. An attempt to insert an amendment providing for one-third public funding of general elections only was defeated by a vote of 187-228.[32] The failure of this Anderson-Udall Amendment, named for its sponsors, Republican John Anderson of Illinois and Democrat Morris Udall of Arizona, is one more illustration of the Common Cause program faring better in the Senate than in the House in the 1970s.

An indication of Common Cause's concern for campaign reform is that most of the effort of its legal division after 1972 has been directed to suits in the campaign funding area (see chapter 6). One estimate is that Common Cause spent $1.8 million from 1972 to 1982 in lawsuits regarding campaign funding.[33] The most important such effort was Common Cause's work as an intervenor in *Buckley* v. *Valeo,* which challenged the Campaign Amendments of 1974. The Court, in its 30 January 1976 decision, affirmed most of the 1974 act as constitutional, but it did cancel several provisions as unconstitutional abridgments of free speech. In particular, a provision limiting the amount one could spend for one's own election was seen as contrary to constitutionally protected free speech. It was found that the reform act could not limit the expenditures of independent committees, which might buy advertisements or otherwise spend money on a candidate's behalf without coordinating the effort with the candidate's campaign. This potentially important loophole in the 1974 law did not, however, undermine the law in the 1976 or 1980 elections.[34]

The presidential election years of 1976 and 1980 were less marred by controversies about funding than were the elections of 1968 and of 1972. In the later years there was no impression of unfairness due to a preponderance of contributions to one candidate. Nor were these presidential elections marred by the sense that special-interest contributions had debased the electoral process. Further, there was little reason to allege that "fat cats" were hidden forces in the presidential campaign because of the new $1000 limit on contributions to primary candidates and the complete funding of general elections. Similarly, because of the new ceilings on contributions, there was less reason to allege that congressmen were "bought" by campaign contributions. All these considerations helped maintain respect for the political system.

After the election of 1976, there was widespread agreement that the 1974 act had two flaws.[35] First, many thought that the $21.8 million ($20 million plus an inflation factor) ceiling for the two major candidates was too low. Both Ford and Carter had to severely cut back expenditures for such campaign paraphernalia as buttons and bumper stickers, which were missed by people active in politics. Another mistake was that state political party contributions to Ford or Carter were limited to $5000, the ceiling for interest groups. In addition to the $21.8 million, the national Republican and Democratic committees were allowed to give about $3.2 million to their candidate, but the 1974 act contained no similar provision for state parties.

Neither Common Cause nor any of the principal congressional backers of the 1974 campaign reform legislation had intended to diminish the functions of state political parties. Accordingly, among a package of amendments to the basic Federal Election Campaign Amendments passed unanimously by Congress in 1979, there were provisions to allow state and local political parties to be much more active in the general election for the Presidency than was the case in 1976. Under the 1979 amendments, state and local party organizations are permitted to buy unlimited numbers of bumper stickers, handbills, brochures, and posters; and they are allowed to conduct voter registration and get-out-the-vote drives for presidential candidates without financial limits.[36] Common Cause supported these amendments.

A controversial part of the campaign reform regulations concerns the role of third parties. At present, even small parties must disclose contributions of more than $200. Many believe that parties that get under 5 percent of the presidential vote should not be required to disclose their contributors. Small parties, such as the Trotskyite Socialist Workers party, reflect very unpopular viewpoints, and their contributors may be subject to retribution. The $5000 limit on organizational contributions plus the talents of investigatory journalists should prevent the possibility of a small party's becoming a front for a major party. (This is the main argument for regulating small parties.)

Sometimes people argue that the 1974 act is so grossly unfair to third parties that the law should be repealed.[37] Independent presidential candidate Eugene McCarthy pointed out that major-party candidates received public funds in 1976, while he did not, which might seem unfair on the surface. But a law providing public funds for presidential candidates must draw the line somewhere against giving money to frivolous or hopeless candidacies. In the 1974 act, major parties are defined as those who received more than 25 percent of the vote in the last presidential election, and minor parties are defined as those receiving from 5 percent to 25 percent in the previous election. A minor-party candidate is entitled to public funds according to its fraction of the average major-party vote in an election. Thus, if the average vote for the Republican and Democratic candidates was 42 percent, and an independent received 6 percent, his candidacy would be entitled to one-seventh of the general election funds allocated to the major-party candidates. Such an amount would be refunded to a new party candidate after the election, which is not as helpful as giving money before an election but does help to perpetuate a third party that reaches the 5 percent threshold in a presidential election. In the next election, the new party, having previously reached 5 percent of the vote, would be entitled to its share of public funding during the time the election campaign was conducted. Thus the reform legislation is somewhat unfair to small parties that never get 5 percent of the vote, but it helps maintain minor parties that have reached that threshold. If one accepts the case for public funding of presidential candidates, the problem of funding minor parties becomes an assessment of whether the 5 percent threshold is fair or whether it should be lowered (or abolished altogether). Such a judgment depends on how one weighs the obvious criterion of fairness (funds should be allocated to small parties according to their percentage of the average major-party vote) against one's assessment of the vices of encouraging the formation of a large number of tiny parties. Furthermore, granting public funds of $25,000 or so to small revolutionary or racist parties would undermine public support for the overall program.

Some politically active citizens might have been less interested in recent elections for President than they would have been if they had been permitted by the reform act to contribute to the general election campaign. It would not contradict the purposes of the act to permit the general public to make small contributions (perhaps $25 or less) to candidates in general elections. Allowing small contributions would also alleviate some of the problems that resulted from the rather sparing amounts allocated to candidates from public funds. This argument was accepted in early 1977 by some of the leading congressional advocates of public financing of elections, and Common Cause was willing to back such a change if the revision would not amount to a new system of funding through private donations. However, such a revision of the federal election regulations has not yet been adopted.

Funding of Congressional Elections

Common Cause makes four arguments for the public funding of congressional elections: (1) special interests unduly influence congressional votes through campaign contributions; (2) such special-interest contributions are rapidly increasing; (3) congressional incumbents receive much more in campaign contributions than do challengers; and (4) the present system of campaign contributions fosters disrespect for government. In a discussion of this issue, John Gardner wrote:

> Speaking of the recent presidential election [1976], a nationally respected journalist called campaign finance reform "one of the few genuinely revolutionary changes in American politics in modern times." Today, with the election more than a month behind us, the overwhelming verdict is that the reforms at the presidential level worked exceptionally well. . . .
>
> On the Congressional level, the reforms went only halfway and the consequences were deeply disturbing. In 1974, Congress took the presidency off the auction block, but rejected public financing for itself because the reform would have done too much to even up the relative positions of incumbents and challengers. Incumbents have an enormous advantage, and a majority of the House of Representatives had no intention of diminishing that advantage further by putting public funds in the hands of their challengers. Result: A lot of Congressmen were bought and sold in 1976, just like the good old days except that the going rates were higher. In 1976 special-interest groups poured well over $20 million [actually $22.6 million] into Congressional campaigns, as compared with $12.5 million in 1974. That's an enormous increase in just two years. The money-heavy special interests couldn't buy themselves a President so they tried to buy as many members of Congress as they could.
>
> In a study of the top dozen heaviest spenders among special-interest political committees, both labor and the professions appeared to outrank business in the amount spent, but the business world is gearing up to regain its position in 1978. So we face a kind of escalating political arms race to see who can paper Congress with the most currency. . . .[38]

But even though interest-group contributions to congressional candidates increased by 62 percent (controlling for inflation) from 1974 to 1976, it is not clear that this increase had a great impact on the behavior of the 95th Congress, as opposed to the 94th. The influence of labor, the largest contributor, actually seemed to decline, as evidenced by labor's defeat in the attempt to enact a common situs picketing act in 1977.[39] Probably the most egregious instance of special-interest money was the donation of $900,000 by maritime unions and corporations to congressional campaigns. But the attempt by the maritime industry to mandate that 10 percent of imported oil be carried in American flagships was defeated after the press, using Common Cause data, publicized the extent of the industry's campaign contributions.

During the 1970s, incumbents in the House were reelected 93 percent of the time.[40] This retention of incumbents was offset, however, by a large number of retirements and resignations from the House. Thus, there was a significant turnover rate in a large number of House seats. For example, 70 House seats changed hands in 1976, a 16 percent turnover rate.[41] From 1972 to 1980, more than half of the House members were replaced. This turnover significantly limits the number of alliances that the incumbents may have with special-interest groups.

Other factors mitigate the argument for public funding of congressional elections. One reason for caution in adopting public funding is the lack of understanding of its effects on state and local party organizations. Many political scientists believe that local parties promote the candidacies of politicians inclined to bargain, compromise, take part in the politics of give-and-take— the politics of the pragmatic center. This is because local party organizations must please a majority of voters in order to win elections. The money raised by local parties is an incentive to pragmatic behavior by congressmen. If interest-group and local party funding of candidates is eliminated through complete public funding of congressional campaigns, it is thought that the politics of ideology would become more important. Republicans would have an increasing tendency to stress right-wing appeals and Democrats to stress leftist appeals in their primaries because "extremist" voters often turn out in primaries in higher proportions than do centrist voters. Many observers question the value of such an increase in ideological politics, and hence criticize the worth of public funding of congressional elections. Further, raising money for congressional candidates is one of the more important functions of local parties, and such parties might atrophy if this function was denied to them.

Another argument against public funding of congressional campaigns is that future congressmen might be tempted to manipulate the system to the advantage of incumbents by inserting unduly low spending limits. For example, the Supreme Court has stated that if candidates accept public funds, Congress can set expenditure ceilings for campaigns. Yet it is well understood that challengers to incumbents often need to spend considerable sums just to get themselves known to the electorate.[42] A low ceiling for campaign spending would help incumbents and hurt challengers. In fact, the House tried to manipulate expenditure ceilings in 1974.

At that time, Common Cause understood the problems a low ceiling would cause and preferred a ceiling of $100,000 for campaigns for the House plus an additional 20 percent allowance for fund-raising costs. The Senate passed a $90,000 plus 20 percent ceiling; the Hays Administration Committee recommended $75,000 plus 25 percent. But the House lowered this figure to $60,000, in an amendment that passed 240-175. The eventual outcome of the Senate-House conference was a figure of $70,000 plus 20 percent as a ceiling for campaigns for the House.[43] The particular ceilings on congressional campaign expenditures in the 1974 law were invalidated by the Supreme Court's 1976 *Buckley* v. *Valeo* decision, but certain types of congressional campaign ceilings would be permitted if Congress legislated them.[44] This sequence of events is disturbing. There is no guarantee that some future Congress might not manipulate the law to the benefit of incumbents.

There are three main differences between the decision to fund presidential elections and the decision to fund congressional elections. First, there was a clearly demonstrable evil in the 1968 and 1972 presidential elections. In 1968, the rules for funding gave Richard Nixon an important advantage over Hubert Humphrey; in 1972 the rules played a big part in the Watergate scandal. In recent congressional elections, on the other hand, it is difficult to show that the rules for funding had any great impact on the subsequent behavior of members of Congress.[45] Second, although a presidential election is very big and important, its structure is simpler than the 535 legislative races taken together. In fact, one aspect of the presidential reforms which eluded the understanding of Common Cause is the item that is central to congressional races—the role of autonomous state and local parties. Third, congressmen in both parties have a common interest in manipulating the campaign rules to give an advantage to incumbents, just as state legislators of both parties have a common interest in gerrymandering districts to help incumbents.[46] Congressmen do not have a strong common interest in manipulating the rules for funding presidential races.

A new factor in this issue is that the 1974 act set ceilings on contributions by interest groups to federal election campaigns. The ceilings were $5000 for organizational contributions to each primary, runoff, and general election campaign for Congress. An interest group can give $5000 to each congressional campaign, but it cannot give more than that to a single campaign. This gives latitude for a score of unions to contribute $5000 each to one candidate or for several corporations in the same industry to give $5000 each. But the disclosure provisions of the law ensure that such contributions are publicized during the campaign, which acts as a control on the behavior of candidates. In some districts, publicizing a candidate's acceptance of campaign contributions from corporations in an unpopular industry (e.g., oil companies or producers of nuclear power) could cost a candidate votes.

Influential congressional committee chairmen sometimes get large contributions from the industries, professions, or organized workers they regulate. Common Cause makes this argument for the public funding of congressional elections, but its force is lessened by the new capacity of House members to vote out chairmen who are a discredit to the House.

In 1982, few conservative Republicans supported the public funding of congressional elections. Such a measure has little chance of passing a Republican-controlled Senate or being signed by Ronald Reagan or any succeeding conservative Republican President. Nevertheless, the issue of spending on congressional elections is likely to continue, and public funding may undergo a revival in a few years.

There are signs that congressional policy on public funding will proceed on a step-by-step basis with a good deal of caution. There are advantages to a cautious approach. The leading campaign finance bills of the late 1970s provided for something like 25 percent public funding for congressional races, granted in a way to match small contributions, with primaries exempted from the matching-grant provision.[47]

If unexpected problems occur, amendments can be made or the reform can be dropped entirely; in the meanwhile, the problems will be less serious with 25 percent funding, primaries excluded, than if everything were funded with public money. On the other hand, if partial funding proves a success, there will be a more solid basis for proceeding to a more thoroughgoing change.

Gubernatorial elections in some states may present a stronger case for public funding than congressional elections. In Massachusetts, Illinois, and Maryland, for example, contributions to gubernatorial candidates may buy favors for racetrack owners, construction firms, architectural firms, and liquor retailers.[48] Public funding could be financed through $1 check-off provisions on state income taxes in a manner similar to the federal system. Action at the state level is perhaps more needed than action at the congressional level, but Common Cause is expected by its supporters to give priority to federal elections.

This chapter has discussed the first priority of the Common Cause platform during the 1970s: the passage of legislation to establish public financing for major candidates in national elections. I have argued that public financing of presidential elections constitutes a significant change in American politics, and that the adoption of partial public financing for congressional elections might also have significant effects on our political system.[49]

NOTES

1. Murray Edelman, *The Symbolic Uses of Politics* (Urbana: University of Illinois Press, 1964).
2. Herbert E. Alexander, *Money in Politics* (Washington, D.C.: Public Affairs Press, 1972), 198-229.
3. "Only one successful prosecution—that of an oil company lobbyist twenty years ago— has been brought under existing law." Richard L. Lyons, "House Struggles to Pass Lobbying Disclosure Bill," *Washington Post,* 29 September 1976, A11.
4. The word "joke" is frequently applied to the 1946 lobby registration act: "The 1946 lobby registration act, called a 'joke' and a 'fraud' by Ribicoff and House support-

ers of legislation to tighten it, has no workable enforcement provisions." Richard L. Lyons, "Last-Minute Senate Move Kills Lobby Control Bill," *Washington Post*, 1 October 1976, C4. Another example: "The lobby disclosure bill approved by the House 307 to 31 would replace present requirements that the bill's floor manager Rep. Walter Flowers, D-Ala., called 'a joke.' " "House Approves Public Disclosure Bill for Lobbyists," *Washington Star*, 29 September 1976, 1.

5. "Testimony of Fred Wertheimer, Vice President, Common Cause, on Lobbying Disclosure Reform Legislation before the House Judiciary Subcommittee on Administrative Law and Governmental Relations: Wednesday, 6 April 1977," Common Cause memorandum, 2, 3.

6. Traditionally, Marxist theorists did not consider political institutions worthy of extensive study. Nor did theorists of elite control in the 1950s consider American political institutions to be very significant in their effects on outcomes. See C. Wright Mills, *The Power Elite* (New York: Oxford University Press, 1956); Floyd Hunter, *Community Power Structure* (Chapel Hill: University of North Carolina Press, 1953). For a criticism of the position of elite theorists on this question, see Nelson W. Polsby, *Community Power and Political Theory*, rev. ed. (New Haven: Yale University Press, 1979).

In the 1950s and 1960s, sociologists in the Parsonian tradition, then the dominant school of thought, were unlikely to consider the details of political institutions important objects of study in comparison to social values, which they saw as determining social structure and public policy. Such positions seem to be changing. During the 1970s, a number of Marxists and other leftist writers, influenced by the writings of Antonio Gramsci, among others, became interested in the theory of the state and its role in imposing the "hegemony" of capitalism upon the rest of society. Such an outlook implies that such political reforms as regulation of lobbies and campaign financing might be significant objects of study. See Ralph Miliband, *The State in Capitalist Society* (New York: Basic Books, 1968). Similarly, G. William Domhoff, an influential writer in the Millsian tradition, exhibits some interest in the role of political institutions, as shown by his interest in the question of the relationship of campaign contributions to control of the national political parties. See G. William Domhoff, *Who Rules America?* (Englewood Cliffs, N.J.: Prentice-Hall, 1967).

7. "Not only was Hubert Humphrey badly outspent in 1968, but his funds came too late in the campaign to be effectively used. [Herbert E.] Alexander does not say so, but the reader [of *Financing the 1972 Election*] comes away with the impression that 1968 was an election that money did decide. In 1972, however, no amount of additional spending could have saved George McGovern's ill-fated candidacy." David Adamany, "Money, Politics, and Democracy: A Review Essay," *American Political Science Review* 71 (March 1977): 290.

8. On 6 October 1968, a *New York Times* survey of political leaders of both parties in all 50 states indicated that Nixon was ahead in states having a total of 380 votes, Wallace was ahead in states having 66 votes, and Humphrey ahead in states having 28 votes.

9. *Common Cause et al.* v. *Finance Committee to Re-Elect the President et al.*, C.A. 1780-72.

10. This is indicated by the number of articles indexed under "Campaign Funds" in

the *Reader's Guide to Periodical Literature,* volumes of which do not correspond exactly to the calendar year but are instead organized by a March through February period.

Years	Number of Articles
March 1966—February 1967	32
1967-68	28
1968-69	25
1969-70	5
1970-71	19
1971-72	26
1972-73	51
1973-74	65
1974-75	87

11. Herbert E. Alexander, *Financing Politics* (Washington, D.C.: Congressional Quarterly, 1976), 193-94.
12. See Delmer Dunn, *Financing Presidential Campaigns* (Washington, D.C.: Brookings Institution, 1972), for a discussion of proposals to regulate expenditures for television advertising for presidential campaigns.
13. John Gardner, *In Common Cause* (New York: Norton, 1972), 33. By permission of W.W. Norton & Company, Inc. Copyright © 1972 by John W. Gardner.
14. Ibid., 33-34.
15. Ibid., 36.
16. Ibid.
17. Ibid., 70.
18. Ibid., 37.
19. Ibid.
20. Ibid., 69.
21. Ibid., 55.
22. Ibid., 38-39.
23. Ibid., 55.
24. Ibid., 56.
25. Robert L. Peabody, Jeffrey M. Berry, William G. Frasure, and Jerry Goldman, *To Enact a Law: Congress and Campaign Financing* (New York: Praeger, 1972), 184.
26. David Adamany and George Agree, "Election Campaign Financing: The 1974 Reforms," *Political Science Quarterly* 90 (Summer 1975): 207. For a discussion of the National Committee for an Effective Congress, see Harry M. Scoble, *Ideology and Electoral Action* (San Francisco: Chandler, 1967).
27. For a summary of the cloture vote, see *Congressional Quarterly Almanac, 1974* (Washington, D.C.: Congressional Quarterly, 1975), 30: 617.
28. In Congress the most frequently criticized portions of recent changes in regulations of federal election campaigns are those permitting the increase in the number of corporate political action committees (PACs), branches of corporations permitted to donate money to campaigns, an action that is legally prohibited to the corporation itself. The legislation clarifying the role of corporate PACs was a result of labor lobbying and a series of court decisions, not a result of Common Cause

lobbying efforts. Common Cause was very active in 1979 in lobbying for a ceiling on the total amount that a congressional candidate could receive from all PACs (corporate, labor, associational). See Edwin M. Epstein, "The Emergence of Political Action Committees," in Alexander, *Political Finance*, chap. 6.

29. See the summary of the Supreme Court's *Buckley* v. *Valeo* decision on the constitutionality of the 1974 campaign reform act, in *Congressional Quarterly Almanac, 1976* (Washington, D.C.: Congressional Quarterly, 1977), 32: 461-62.

30. *Common Cause et al.* v. *Shultz et al.*, C.A. 433-73 (D.C.D.C.).

31. *Congressional Quarterly Almanac, 1974,* 30: 616.

32. Ibid., 630-31.

33. This is based on an estimate of $2,750,000 total expenditures for Common Cause litigation from 1972 to 1982, and the observation that about two-thirds of this effort was related to lawsuits involving public funding of elections, free congressional franking, and special-interest spending in elections.

34. See the summary cited in note 29.

35. Such widespread agreement is indicated by the unanimous passage in Congress of amendments to allow state and local political parties to spend unlimited amounts on voter registration drives and campaign paraphernalia. See *Congressional Quarterly Almanac, 1979* (Washington, D.C.: Congressional Quarterly, 1980), 35: 558.

36. Ibid., 558-61.

37. One such person was Eugene McCarthy, one of the plaintiffs in *Buckley* v. *Valeo,* the unsuccessful suit to overturn the Federal Election Campaign Amendments of 1974: *Buckley et al.* v. *Valeo et al.,* 424 U.S. 1 (1976), *per curiam.*

38. John W. Gardner, "Campaign Finance: The Quiet Revolution," *Washington Post,* 7 December 1976.

39. Mary Eisner Eccles, "House Rejects Labor-Backed Picketing Bill," *Congressional Quarterly Weekly Report* 34 (26 March 1977): 521-24. The common situs picketing act "would have allowed unions with a grievance against a single contractor to picket and potentially close down an entire building site, overturning a 1951 Supreme Court ruling that such practices constituted an illegal secondary boycott." *Congressional Quarterly Almanac, 1977* (Washington, D.C.: Congressional Quarterly, 1978), 33: 122.

40. John F. Bibby, Thomas E. Mann, and Norman J. Ornstein, *Vital Statistics on Congress, 1980* (Washington, D.C.: American Enterprise Institute, 1980), 14.

41. See Richard E. Cohen, "Don't Expect a Republican Congress," *National Journal* 11 (20 October 1979): 1755.

42. Indeed, Professor Gary Jacobson has marshaled evidence that indicates that public financing of congressional campaigns would usually favor incumbents. See his "Public Funds for Congressional Campaigns: Who Would Benefit?" in Alexander, *Political Finance.* The reader interested in scholarship about public financing of elections will want to read other articles in this useful volume. See also Jacobson's excellent study, *Money in Congressional Elections* (New Haven: Yale University Press, 1980).

43. *Congressional Quarterly Almanac, 1974,* 30: 613, 629-30, 632.

44. See notes 29 and 37.

45. See Michael J. Malbin, "Of Mountains and Molehills: PACs, Campaigns, and Public Policy," in *Parties, Interest Groups, and Campaign Finance Laws,* ed. Michael J.

Malbin (Washington, D.C.: American Enterprise Institute, 1980), 152-84. See also the commentary on Malbin's paper by Fred Wertheimer, ibid., 192-205.

46. Malcolm Jewell, *The Politics of Reapportionment* (New York: Atherton, 1962).

47. For example, HR 1 of 1979 provided for up to $60,000 in matching grants to a candidate, who would be limited to an expenditure ceiling of $220,000, no more than $25,000 of which could come from the candidate's own funds. See *Congressional Quarterly Almanac, 1979* (Washington, D.C.: Congressional Quarterly, 1980), 35: 554.

48. See Bill Prochnau, "Corruption in Massachusetts: 'A Way of Life,' " *Washington Post,* 1 January 1981, 1: "Yesterday a new two-year study of construction contracts concluded that 'corruption has been a way of life' in Massachusetts. Bribes and political favoritism may have left as many as 76 percent of the public buildings constructed since 1968 with 'significant defects,' that is, a structural defect that threatens safety.

". . . Yesterday, Massachusetts' latest corruption panel [the Special Commission on State and County Buildings], which issued a 12 volume, 2,500 page report after its two-year study, said . . . 'alleged payoffs were disguised as campaign contributions and the quid-pro-quo was so ingrained that not an incriminating word had to pass between giver and taker.' "

This observation is also based on the reporting of Maryland politics in the *Washington Post* and on the reporting of Illinois politics in the *Chicago Sun-Times* and the *Chicago Tribune.*

49. Others, of varying political outlooks, would agree that the adoption of public financing for electoral candidates has important effects on the conduct of politics. See for example, the collection of essays in Malbin, *Parties, Interest Groups, and Campaign Finance Laws.*

8. The Program: Procedural Reform

In addition to its drive to reform political campaigns, Common Cause has put a great amount of its resources into the attainment of several other changes in political procedures. These reforms suggested by Common Cause have had some effect on the political process. This chapter discusses such reforms as the regulation of lobbyists and sunshine laws. In addition, because the Vietnam issue was the main priority of Common Cause in the first two years of its history, its impact on that issue is treated here.

Getting Information about Decision Making

Since 1971, Common Cause has pushed hard for what it calls the OUTS reforms: public funding of federal elections and regulation of contributions to electoral campaigns plus disclosing the scope of lobbyists' activities, requiring open meetings of congressional and executive decision-making committees, and requiring that high-level federal officials disclose sources of their outside income. The disclosure ideas are different from campaign regulations; they are meant to make the public aware of activities in the public sector and thus limit special-interest influence.

One cannot assume that passing a set of regulations will bring about important changes in human behavior. Efforts to pass international treaties in the 1920s to outlaw war probably did more harm than good by taking attention away from the underlying causes of war. Similarly, it would do little good to open a congressional committee meeting to the public at which all attending lobbyists signed a register and the major outside income sources of the attending congressmen were revealed. Such information would have no effect on political outcomes. The importance of such information derives from its use by political groups in lobbying and in changing public opinion.

Information about what congressional committees and executive commissions are doing, gained from attendance at open meetings, can be valuable to reform lobbyists, who otherwise might not get information that is important for the formulation of lobbying tactics. Similarly, laws requiring lobbyists to register can give useful information about the alignment of forces on a bill or provide data that can change public opinion. For instance, contrasting the size of the extremely effective National Rifle Association lobby with that of the opposing gun-control lobbies might persuade some apathetic believers in gun control to contribute to the lobbying effort on that side. And the extension of disclosure provisions to cover most sources of income over $100 and assets over $1000 might deter public officials from making investments that would cause conflicts of interest. Common Cause has lobbied for all three of these measures at the state level and has contributed to the passage of reform legislation in all fifty states.

The Government in the Sunshine

Sunshine legislation, signed by President Gerald Ford in September 1976, was described by *Congressional Quarterly* as follows:

> Called the "Government in the Sunshine Act," HR 11656 required some 50 federal agencies — almost all but the Cabinet departments — to meet regularly in open session. The only exceptions would be for discussion of ten specified matters, such as national security or personnel business, and meetings could be closed then only by majority vote of the agency. Clear legal remedies were provided in the bill for enforcement of the requirements.
>
> In a separate title, HR 11656 barred for the first time informal — *ex parte* — contacts between agency officials and interested outsiders to discuss pending agency business. Calling that provision a sleeper, legal observers suggested that it could have far-reaching effects on what had come to be an accepted practice before regulatory agencies in Washington. . . . The unprecedented open-door requirements embraced regulatory agencies, advisory committees, independent offices, the Postal Service. . . .[1]

Since closed meetings could still be held on ten kinds of matters, a major criticism of the bill was that it would not change political outcomes by much. One reason why there was little congressional opposition to this legislation in its final form was that by 1973 both the House and the Senate had eliminated most of their closed committee meetings. Most congressmen had evidently concluded that it did not make a whole lot of difference whether their committee meetings were open or not. Some members of Congress were moderately critical of congressional sunshine laws, however, claiming that during publicly attended committee meetings congressmen tended to show off for their audience, rather than attend to business. Proponents of the sunshine act argued that congressmen came to committee meetings better prepared and were more attentive to committee business with an audience present.

Common Cause had made "government in the sunshine" part of its program in 1971, and from 1971 to 1974 its lobbying for this goal concentrated on getting more open committee meetings in Congress. By 1975 only 3 percent of House committee meetings were closed and only 15 percent in the Senate.[2] Even the House Democratic and Republican caucus meetings were open to the public. After November 1975, the public could attend meetings of the hitherto secret Senate-House conference committees.[3]

In the fall of 1974 a Common Cause questionnaire showed that a majority of the next House of Representatives would endorse the idea of a sunshine bill that would apply to both Congress and the executive branch. In the post-Watergate atmosphere, almost no congressman wanted to go on record as opposing open decision making in the federal government. A vote against government in the sunshine could become a centerpiece of a challenger's campaign in 1976. Further, Congress in 1973 and 1974 increased the number of open committee meetings. There was no political basis for opposing sunshine laws, which the new legislators knew would be unpopular with both their conservative and liberal constitutents. And congressmen with an active Common Cause organization at home knew that a vote against sunshine laws would lead to protest among their constituents, including hostile newspaper and television editorials. The media, by its very nature, is strongly supportive of open meetings in government. Thus, almost all members of Congress voted for sunshine bills, which passed 86-0 in the Senate in November 1975 and 390-5 in the House in July 1976.

Some political maneuvering in September and October indicated that a thoroughgoing open meeting law would surely pass. Senator Robert Byrd of West Virginia, then the Democratic Whip, put through a sudden amendment to the sunshine law in the Senate Rules Committee. The amendment struck out the mandatory application of the bill to the Senate and would have permitted Senate committees to decide whether to open their meetings to the public. The amendment was proposed without any warning so that proponents of sunshine legislation could not organize an opposition in committee. But the advocates of the legislation (including Common Cause) soon organized to defeat Byrd on the Senate floor by the laughable margin of 16-77, and the provision applying the legislation to the Senate was reinstated.[4]

Sunshine legislation would have passed the House earlier than July 1976 except for a jurisdictional dispute between the House Government Operations Committee and the Judiciary Committee. Both committees could cite precedents to claim that the legislation was within their purview, and thus the bill had to be passed by the Government Operations Committee and then sent to the Judiciary Committee, which made seventeen changes in the bill.

Common Cause had similar problems with the lobbyist registration bill and the financial disclosure bill in 1976. Both had to clear the Judiciary Committee and then the Committee on Standards of Official Conduct in the House. Such legislation is subject to congressional committee jurisdictional disputes,[5] which gives opponents of the bills an extra advantage. If they can stall the legislation in one of two committees, there may not be enough time to vote on the bills before the final adjournment of Congress in September or October of an election year. Thus congressional reorganization plans that would clarify jurisdiction over good-government legislation would have an important effect on political outcomes by eliminating the need for novel legislation to pass two or three substantive committees.

Ordinarily it is difficult to assess the effects of open congressional committee meetings on a legislative issue. An observer usually must have extensive knowledge of the politics of a single bill before he can decide whether the outcome would have been different if the committee meeting had been closed. On one kind of legislation, however, a reasonable hypothesis can be made that open meetings have a significant effect: the politics of trading exceptions to the tax code in the Senate Finance Committee. Stanley Surrey, formerly assistant secretary of the Treasury, reported that the trading of tax exceptions is an important part of the activity of the Finance Committee at the end of a legislative session.[6] This is the politics of "I'll let you put through a tax exception for some of your constituents, and I'll expect you to let me do something for mine."

In July 1976 Senator Russell Long, chairman of the Finance Committee, clearly desired to hold a closed meeting while tax exceptions were being traded, but he could no longer do so. He thus resorted to the expedient of talking in a very low voice to other committee members and staff, who similarly responded without electronic amplification. The reporters who were present in the same room could not hear the proceedings. Through this procedure, a score of measures was added to the 1976 amendments to the tax code. When the infuriated reporters complained, and congressional tax reformers such as Senator Edward Kennedy criticized the procedure, Long relented and reconsidered the tax bill in committee, a most unusual event.[7] The point is that Long did not want an open meeting with its attendant publicity, and such publicity forced him to reduce the number of tax exceptions in 1976.

The most sophisticated criticism of open meeting legislation is that necessary negotiation and compromise are prevented by public discussion. Critics note that special-interest lobbyists are now able to attend bill-writing sessions of the Senate Finance and the House Ways and Means committees. Such lobbyists can scrutinize the activities of their tax-writing congressional friends, who with open meetings lose the opportunity of dropping a special-interest tax exception in a closed meeting and telling a white lie to a lobbyist friend about what happened behind closed doors. One Ways and Means Committee member told me that he sees "lots of lobbyists" at open committee meetings, but he "doesn't see lots of housewives coming down from the suburbs."

From the Common Cause perspective, this is not the point. While public-interest lobbies encourage citizens to attend meetings of congressional committees, Common Cause is primarily concerned that a few reporters as well as a Common Cause volunteer be present at important committee meetings. Then, if a committee does somethng unexpected, such as granting tax exceptions to friends of committee members, news of this event will appear in Common Cause bulletins and influential newspapers. Common Cause volunteers attend most meetings of congressional taxation and appropriations committees and report to the organization's lobbyists if there is a sudden move to grant political favors.

To many people, a sufficient argument for sunshine laws is that government should act in a way that corresponds to widespread public beliefs about fairness. Among at least part of the population, it does not seem fair to close committee meetings where a high proportion of important congressional decisions are made.[8] Nor does it seem fair, for instance, to close the meetings of the Interstate Commerce Commission, which sets transportation prices. Few things are more irritating to a politically active citizen than to be told that he cannot observe an important meeting of government decision makers.

Lobbying Disclosure Legislation

There seems to be widespread agreement among politically attentive Americans that Washington lobbyists should be legally compelled to register, to state how much they spend, and to state their legislative goals.[9] This opinion was represented in the 1946 Federal Regulation of Lobbying Act, but the act was vaguely written and seldom enforced, and so even frequent Common Cause opponent Representative Walter Flowers referred to it as "a joke."[10] *Congressional Quarterly* described the Senate Government Operations Committee's report on the 1976 lobbying disclosure bill as follows:

> The report stated that "the witnesses who appeared before this committee's hearings on lobbying legislation were in full agreement that the present law was vague, ineffectual and unenforceable. A study done by the General Accounting Office for this committee found enforcement of the act to be practically nonexistent. . . . The result is a law which is in effect no law at all."
>   The committee cited testimony that "only 2000, or 20 percent to 40 percent, of the 5000 to 10,000 persons who should register as lobbyists actually do so un-

der the present law. One estimate brought to the committee's attention suggests that not more than one-tenth of 1 percent of the total amount spent on lobbying is reported under the 1946 act."

The panel said a tougher lobby law would give members of Congress a better understanding of "the actual nature and source" of lobbying on an issue, would help ensure public confidence in government and would better inform both the public and Congress about "which views are most represented before Congress" and how much money is spent to influence legislation. In addition, the committee said a new law "will enhance the lobbying profession by removing the secrecy surrounding its activities."[11]

Under the 1946 law organizations were supposed to register as lobbies if their "principal purpose" was attempting to influence the course of legislation. For example, until the early 1970s, the National Rifle Association (a lobbyist's lobby) and the National Association of Manufacturers did not register as lobbies because they claimed that a predominance of their organizational effort was devoted to activities other than lobbying.[12] Another omission of the 1946 act was its vagueness in defining the lobbying expenses to be filed. Thus the 20 to 40 percent of Washington lobbies that actually registered usually did not record their entire lobbying expenses, including such items as lobbyists' full salaries and secretarial assistance. Some lobbies recorded only such obvious costs as cab fare to the Hill and luncheons with congressional staff. Thus, when Common Cause registered its full lobbying costs, it looked like the biggest lobby in Washington just sixteen months after its founding.[13]

Reform of the 1946 lobbying regulation act was an obvious program for Common Cause, which took up the idea in 1971 and made it a top priority program in 1973. Support for a new law was part of the campaign to get public commitments from congressional candidates in 1974. At that time, 317 of 345 representatives who responded and won election, plus 49 of 58 responding senators, agreed to support a new law. As with the open meeting laws, the time for a new lobbying regulation act appeared to have arrived.

But a lobbying regulation act did not pass the 94th Congress. The legislation was stalled in Representative Flowers's subcommittee of the House Judiciary Committee (see chapter 6). Such legislation eventually passed the House on 19 September 1976, at the end of the 94th Congress, by a vote of 301-31. But there was not enough time to hold a conference before adjournment with the Senate, which had passed a stricter set of regulations on 15 June 1976 by a vote of 82-9.[14]

The high tide of support for political reforms had begun to recede, and Common Cause was able to get only one more floor vote on a lobbyist regulation act, which passed the House 259-140 in 1978.[15] During the early 1980s, there was little chance that such legislation would be enacted. But the idea of strengthening reporting requirements for lobbyists might achieve renewed popularity in Congress in the future.

Why was Common Cause defeated in its campaign to achieve the regulation of lobbyists? First and foremost, such legislation was opposed by almost all lobbyists. Even many public-interest lobbies were critical of the legislation.[16] Second, regulating lobbyists means regulating some of the best friends of a member of Congress. Third, journalists and other leaders of public opinion seemed more concerned about other items on the reform agenda—sunshine laws, conflict-of-interest codes for members of Congress, and fair campaign practices. Regulating lobbyists in Washington was backed by Common Cause, the League of Women Voters, and certain reform leaders in Congress, but it received effective political support from practically no one else.

In retrospect, it is easy to see that Common Cause erred in its lobbying strategy to regulate lobbyists. During the 94th Congress, a relatively modest bill to require accurate reporting by larger lobbies might have passed. Such a bill might, for instance, have demanded that organizations spending more than, say, 50 percent of their budgets to influence Congress register as lobbies. A modest bill might have been restricted to lobbies with budgets in excess of, say, $500,000. In addition, such lobbies might have been required to file their actual expenditures (including rent, lobbyists' salaries, legislative research) rather than minimal expenditures (lunches, gifts, etc.).

Nevertheless, Common Cause tried to get Congress to pass a relatively strict bill to regulate lobbyists. The legislation would have applied to smaller lobbies, would have required the reporting of *sources* of income in addition to expenditures, and might even have included requirements for members of Congress to log contacts with lobbyists in an official record. Common Cause proved willing to compromise, but not before a great deal of political resistance to lobbyist regulation had been created. Such resistance slowed down the consideration of lobbyist regulation in Congress.

Financial Disclosure Legislation

From 1973 to 1978, financial disclosure legislation for the federal government was one of the main lobbying goals of Common Cause. "Financial disclosure" refers to the goal of requiring top federal government officials to publicly disclose their principal sources of income and investment. In 1974, support for financial disclosure legislation was a subject of Common Cause's campaign to get public commitments from congressional candidates.

Financial disclosure legislation in the federal government has been a success for Common Cause, at least in the sense that most of what the organization leaders wanted in 1973 was enacted in the Ethics in Government Act of 1978. Yet it is difficult to say how much credit Common Cause can take for the passage of the ethics law. It was supported by the Carter administration and many of the reformers in Congress, and gained momentum by an upsurge in skepticism among the press and the public about the quality and motivations of congressmen and federal "bureaucrats."[17] Common Cause was active in lobbying for financial disclosure legislation, gave it top priority, and used all its lobbying techniques in behalf of such legislation. The League of Women Voters and Nader's Public Citizen organization also actively lobbied for financial disclosure legislation, but only a few other interest groups were active lobbyists.

In 1968 both the Senate and the House established disclosure requirements in the wake of the censure of Senator Thomas J. Dodd (Dem-Conn.) for pocketing campaign contributions. In the Senate these regulations had little effect because in practice honoraria and gifts were frequently received by senators' campaign committees rather than personally by the senators. However, the Federal Election Campaign Amendments of 1974 restricted the amount of honoraria to be received by a senator and his campaign committees to $15,000 a year, a costly restriction for several senators (the ceiling was raised in 1976 to $25,000 per year, was suddenly eliminated in 1981, and will probably change every few years). Senators had to file a copy of their tax forms with the comptroller general—the head of the General Accounting Office, an agency subordinate to Congress—but no one was permitted to look at these returns except members of the Senate Committee on Standards and Conduct. In the early 1970s House members were required to file a list of any interests worth more than $5000 or sources of income of more than $1000 from companies doing substantial business with the government or subject to federal regulatory agencies. In addition, representatives had to file lists of sources of noncongressional income of more than $5000, capital gains of more than $5000, honoraria of more than $300, and sources of unsecured loans of more than $10,000.[18] However, the amounts of money involved were not filed. The lists were available to the public and were summarized annually by Congressional Quarterly Weekly Reports.[19]

Common Cause backed more detailed disclosure requirements for top federal officials. As an example of the legislation Common Cause supported, the Senate in 1976 passed a bill that would have required disclosure of the amount and source of all income over $100, all assets valued at more than $100, and gifts-in-kind more valuable than $500. The comptroller general would audit a sample of 5 percent of the reports filed by the top 15,000 federal officials covered in the bill.[20]

The House in 1976 delayed the passage of a disclosure bill by an eighteen-month stall in Flowers's Judiciary subcommittee and the requirement that the bill pass both Judiciary and Standards of Official Conduct committees. Unexpectedly in early 1977, however, much of the aim of disclosure legislation was enacted by other means. Strict financial disclosure measures were contained in separate House and Senate ethics codes that applied to the finances of congressmen and their top aides.[21] Similarly, President Carter demanded a complete disclosure of financial holdings of several hundred of his top appointees.

Both Presidents Ford and Carter, as well as former Majority Leader Byrd and House Speaker Tip O'Neill, believed that if Congress was to receive a pay increase in early 1977, the Senate and the House should pass "ethics codes" regulating controversial aspects of the personal finances of congressmen and other aspects of the conduct of the congressional office, such as office funds, the use of the franked mail, and the acceptance of gifts. Both Byrd and O'Neill were well aware of the decreasing respect for Congress among the public, which might well have decreased further if congressmen's finances had not come under public disclosure in 1977. Accordingly, disclosure provisions for members of Congress were speedily enacted.[22]

Consequently, by the middle of 1977, disclosure of sources of income and financial holdings was the practice for members of Congress and high-level officials of the Carter administration. But in both cases disclosure was a matter of compliance with a set of rules not formally enacted into law. In June 1977, by a vote of 75-5, the Senate passed its version of the Ethics in Government Act, providing for disclosure by federal employees at the level of GS-16 and above and tightening and extending from one year to two years the statutory ban on former government officials' representing private interests before the agency in which they had been employed. The enactment of similar legislation by the House was delayed for a year, principally because of jurisdictional disagreements among the four committees with authority over the legislation. In September 1978, however, the House passed its version of the Ethics in Government Act by a vote of 368-30. The conference committee's version easily passed both houses the next month.[23]

The 1978 Ethics in Government Act has become the basic law in its field. As noted, it provides for disclosure of sources of income and holdings of property by the President, members of Congress, executive branch officials at level GS-16 and above, and federal judges. The law restricts for a two-year period the dealings of former government employees with their former agencies. Civil but not criminal penalties have been enacted. This law also has established a mechanism for court appointment of a special prosecutor to investigate criminal allegations against high-level government officials.[24]

Enactment of this legislation was an important part of the Common Cause platform. In March 1979, however, Common Cause had a minor setback when the Senate, in a surprise, hurried move, delayed for four years the date of initiation of a measure to put a lower ceiling on the amount of honorarium income (mostly from speeches) a senator could receive while holding office.[25] The 1976 Federal Election Campaign Act had established a ceiling of $25,000 for such income, which would have been cut to $8625 by the Senate's ethics code in January 1979. In March 1979, however, at the behest of Minority Whip Ted Stevens (Rep-Alaska), a resolution was passed to delay this limitation until January 1983: "The resolution was debated for less than five minutes, with only about six senators on the floor at the time of the vote. . . ."[26] But according to the Congressional Quarterly Almanac, 1979, a "public outcry" forced the Senate to hold another vote on this matter, and the delay was ratified for a second time on 28 March 1979, by a vote of 54-44. The 1979 Almanac reported: "Common Cause worked to keep the issue in the public eye. President David Cohen called the delay the Senate's version of 'take the money and run and the public be damned.' He said the Senate had 'turned its back' on the 1977 ethics code, and accused Byrd of allowing 'the Senate to quietly gut the code without following orderly procedures of committee consideration and advance notice.' "[27] Such strong language by David Cohen indicated that Common Cause would be aggressive in lobbying to defend the 1978 Ethics in Government Act. The Senate handed Common Cause still another defeat on the issue of limiting honoraria, however, when it voted 45-43 in October 1981 to abolish entirely the $25,000 yearly limit on the amount a senator could receive from honoraria. The limit of $2000 for a single speaking engagement remained in force.[28]

Disclosure laws seem to be a useful deterrent against conflicts of interest in policy-making situations. The requirement to report income and property holdings gives civil servants, members of Congress, and judges an incentive to avoid making public decisions in areas in which their private interests could conflict with public interests. Yet it is not apparent that the enactment of disclosure laws has had a great impact on political outcomes at the federal level. Probably most Common Cause leaders would agree with Grant McConnell that the slanting of policies because of long-standing friendships among lobbyists, high-level civil servants, and congressmen — Gardner's unholy trinity — is a far greater problem in the federal government than the outright venality that disclosure legislation seeks to deter.[29]

An important argument to justify the disclosure of financial holdings by top-level federal officials in the late 1970s is that such regulations are desired by the public (in the opinion of congressmen, at least) in an era of widespread skepticism about the honesty of Congress and the integrity of the federal bureaucracy. Disclosure laws can play a small part in increasing public respect for government. Such laws can easily be amended by later political generations that may regard disclosure of finances as an unnecessary restriction on public officials.

The Sunset Proposal for Administrative Reform

By January 1975, the national leadership of Common Cause foresaw a time when the basic national OUTS program would be enacted into law. Gardner, Cohen, and the staff thought that public funding of congressional elections, a lobbyist regulation act, a disclosure law, and a far-reaching sunshine bill would all be passed by the 94th Congress, majorities of which had indicated approval of these ideas in Common Cause questionnaires. In addition, most provisions of the congressional reform program were being enacted, step-by-step, every two years at the beginning of each new Congress. As it turned out, the 94th Congress passed only the sunshine law of the OUTS program, although both houses of Congress enacted substantial reforms in their procedures in 1975.

Expecting the enactment of the basic national OUTS program, the staff began looking for new lobbying goals in early 1975. In this situation several reasons made it natural for the staff to begin developing a program to reform the executive branch of the national government. First, holding to the values of individualist liberalism,[30] Americans have been particularly critical of the power of government bureaucracy. A program of making the executive branch more "accountable" would thus be popular. Second, in the wake of the Watergate scandals, supporters of Common Cause were particularly concerned about the exercise of unchecked power by executive agencies of the government in Washington. Third, Gardner and other leaders of Common Cause had witnessed firsthand the importance of bureaucratic decisions in their careers before joining Common Cause. Fourth, Common Cause leaders soon realized that reforms of the executive branch could be a way of taking action in complicated, controversial areas of substantive policy. For example, most energy issues are controversial, but Common Cause could please virtually all of its members, and act on energy policy, by advocating such measures as changing the Interior Department's procedures in leasing federal lands for oil or coal production; the logging of nongovernmental contacts by top officials of Interior; and abolishing the Congressional Joint Committee on Atomic Energy, which favored the nuclear lobby.[31]

The Common Cause staff readily located a number of ideas for reforming the federal executive branch, ideas that were accepted by the membership with near unanimity. But for a few months the staff did not develop any administrative reform proposals that could stir great enthusiasm from the organization and its members. This was to be the function of the sunset proposal.

In October 1975 the national policy research staff recommended to the governing board that Common Cause lobby for the initiation of sunset laws:

> No issue speaks more directly to government size and efficiency than executive branch organization. The executive bureaucracy—departments, agencies, boards, commissions—has become too complex, cumbersome, and fragmented to deal effectively with modern issues. Jurisdictional rivalries, bureaucratic concerns for narrow parochial interests, and piecemeal approaches to problem-solving abound. Responsible management of social and economic programs is often undermined by outmoded structures and arrangements. Some executive branch institutions appear to have outlived their original purpose.
>
> During Campaign '76, too many candidates will respond to these real issues with rhetoric and generalities about a government that is "too big." As evidence of their commitment to act on the issues of executive branch size and effectiveness, *presidential candidates would be asked to endorse a "sunset" mechanism whereby departmental and regulatory functions and programs are periodically and automatically reviewed, modified and certified for continuation* [emphasis in the original].[32]

Basically, a sunset law specifies a cutoff date for an agency or program; after this date, it has to be reauthorized to continue to exist. A justification for sunset laws is that government agencies or programs sometimes work to the benefit of particular interests but do not yield a benefit to the general public commensurate with their cost. In such situations, those who do benefit from the program form a coalition to prevent its overall assessment. Such coalitions frequently prevent an overall evaluation from being considered by a legislature. The sunset mechanisms provides a legislative procedure by which those interested in overall evaluation might defeat the opposing coalition. For example, some congressmen would like the chance to vote to abolish the Interstate Commerce Commission because they think it helps the trucking industry at the expense of the public. A sunset mechanism would provide a procedure for such a vote.

The campaign for a sunset law was originated by Craig Barnes, a leader of the Colorado Common Cause organization, in late 1974. Actually, the idea dates back to the late 1930s when William O. Douglas suggested to Franklin D. Roosevelt that regulatory agencies be subject to automatic termination. The President laughed off the idea.[33] In 1969 political scientist Theodore J. Lowi put forth this idea in *The End of Liberalism,* but it was not immediately picked up by congressmen.[34] Barnes dubbed the concept of automatic termination a "sunset" law, a term that heightened its appeal in an age of salesmanship. The Colorado group sold the sunset plan to its state legislature, and in early 1976, it enacted a sunset mechanism for the state's thirty-nine regulatory agencies. Colorado Common Cause suggested the idea to the national board in April 1975, and the board endorsed the sunset proposal in October of that year.

Common Cause lobbyists began informing members of Congress about the new proposal. The time seemed right for the automatic termination idea. In the wake of Watergate, liberal Democrats, who formerly were not aggressive critics of the federal bureaucracy, now joined their more conservative colleagues in denouncing "big government." Few innovative legislative proposals have initially gained such rapid acceptance on Capitol Hill. Six months after Common Cause endorsed the proposal, 166 members of the House and 48 senators joined the list of sponsors of various sunset bills. The Senate Government Operations Committee held hearings on a sunset bill sponsored by two of its members, Senators Edmund Muskie (Dem-Maine) and William Roth (Rep-Del.).[35] Of the 435 representatives elected in the fall of 1976, 300 indicated on Common Cause questionnaires that they supported the sunset idea. Apparently, the rapid appearance of the sunset law on the congressional agenda was largely a result of the activities of Common Cause.

The sunset proposal appealed to Americans in the 1970s, but even a little reflection indicates its many problems. First, how does a legislature evaluate programs under the sunset plan? A few federal agencies ought to be abolished, in the opinion of many people from a variety of political persuasions. But there would be intense disagreement about the performance of many other agencies. And it is frequently argued that the measurement of governmental performance is very difficult.[36] Second, legislators have no experience with sunset measures, and thus their rapid implementation could pose unexpected problems. Third, there is no guarantee that measures intended to serve the welfare of the general public will not be used by special interests for their own benefit. During those times when public concern for reform wanes, groups with particularlistic interests might have an easy time abolishing consumer and environmental protection agencies under the provisions of sunset laws. Fourth, the introduction of sunset laws provides an incentive for groups opposing the goals of a new agency to sabotage its program by tactics such as cutting its appropriations and initiating dilatory lawsuits. If the implementation of a new program can be slowed down by such tactics, a new agency may show a poor performance record by the time its sunset evaluation occurs. Then the opponents can move to ax the agency. Fifth, even in happier circumstances for agencies, sunset provisions could encourage an agency to devote an excessive amount of its manpower resources to the politics of getting reauthorized, thereby diverting tax dollars from programs to bureaucratic politics. Finally, the widespread application of sunset provisions would greatly increase the workload of legislatures, which might be called upon to evaluate the performance of two or three dozen agencies a year. Much debate would have to take place on the floor, rather than in committee, since it would be unfair to terminate ongoing governmental programs on the vote of a legislative committee, which could very well be unrepresentative of the legislature as a whole. And certainly other objections to the sunset proposal could be made.

Drawbacks to the sunset proposal were sufficiently apparent to the staff of Common Cause that the summer 1976 edition of *In Common* stated: "If Sunset is to work, however, it must take effect step-by-step, with prime emphasis on good evaluation processes."[37] At that time, Common Cause also stated that evaluation questions ought to be standard from agency to agency, that sunset provisions ought not to arbitrarily limit the rights of citizens by canceling all the obligations of an agency, that aid be given to those who would lose their jobs by the termination of an agency, that sunset discussion and debates be open to the public, and that the congressional committee system be reorganized so that sunset evaluations could be conducted effectively.[38] David Cohen stated that sunset measures had to be considered with deliberation and that Common Cause should not rush to lobby them through Congress.

The above criticisms of sunset laws, especially the prospective increase in the congressional workload, have been influential in Congress. Accordingly, while in the mid-1970s there was a great deal of congressional interest in passing a generalized sunset law that would apply to a large number of agencies, by 1980 the popularity of this concept seemed to be receding. In October 1978 the Senate passed a sunset measure by a vote of 87-1. But it passed only a few days before the adjournment of the 95th Congres, when there was no possibility of having a similar vote on the floor of the House.[39] The *Congressional Quarterly Almanac, 1978* referred to the Senate's passage of the sunset measure as "a symbolic vote."[40]

During the 96th Congress, a sunset measure of wide applicability was buried in a subcommittee of the House Rules Committee. In the Senate, such a measure was reported favorably by the Government Operations Committee, but it was then referred to the Senate Rules Committee, which reported a watered-down version on 4 September 1980 — so late in the year as to reduce significantly the probability of another vote on the Senate floor in 1980. This Rules Committee version was a far cry from the original concept of Common Cause. The Rules Committee bill made the sunset measure optional at the discretion of a Senate committee. At the beginning of a Congress, a committee would select agencies, and their existence would be reviewed by the committee within the time span (two years) of that Congress. The sunset choices of the committees would be consolidated into a sunset agenda, which would be considered by the full Senate at the end of the two-year period.[41] This measure was not considered by the Senate before it adjourned.

By the 96th Congress (1979-80), support for a generalized sunset measure seemed to be waning, but there was considerable interest in attaching specific sunset measures to bills. For instance, in 1979 a number of bills containing provisions for a mandatory review of new legislation was passed by the Senate or the House. Bills containing such sunset provisions included an act passed by the Senate to authorize the payment of attorneys' fees in some instances of successful private suits against the government;[42] the Child Health Assurance Bill as passed by the House;[43] and a bill passed by the House specifying the need to authorize the Office of Personnel Management and two related personnel agencies.[44] An amendment to establish a sunset provision in the law establishing the Department of Education was narrowly rejected in the Senate by a vote of 46-48.[45] In 1979 there was an unsuccessful major effort to insert a sunset provision in existing tax legislation—the provision in the tax code that permitted municipalities to sell tax-free bonds to provide funds to lend to individuals for home mortgages.[46] One major Senate bill that did not pass, a measure to set limits on price increases charged by hospitals, contained a provision providing for its mandatory review.[47] Indeed, Common Cause originated in 1977 the idea of specific sunset provisions by advocating a mandatory review of tax exceptions inserted in the federal tax code.

Another derivation from the original sunset concept was advocated by Senator Edward Kennedy and was labeled "high noon." This concept would simply mandate the review of an agency or regulation at a certain time, but would not provide for automatic termination in the event of a congressional failure to reauthorize. This provision was part of a regulatory reform bill sponsored by Kennedy in 1979.[48]

By 1984, it seemed that a sunset measure of wide applicability would not be passed by Congress in the immediate future. On the other hand, mandatory review and automatic termination clauses were legislative devices used with some frequency. Also, thirty-three states had passed sunset laws, and nine more had adopted specific sunset clauses to apply to particular legislation.[49] There is, however, no clear view of the effectiveness of such laws at the state level.

Reform of the House of Representatives

The House of Representatives has changed greatly since 1969, when Democratic committee chairmen, other senior members, and the Democratic leadership pretty much controlled the institution. Since that time, the House, particularly the Democrats within that body, has enacted a substantial degree of reform, which has reduced the power of senior members.[50] As noted, committee chairmen are now elected by the Democratic Caucus, which at the beginning of the 94th Congress (January 1975) deposed three chairmen: Wright Patman of Banking and Currency, W.R. Poage of Agriculture, and F. Edward Hebert of Armed Services. Appropriations subcommittee chairmen, who have as much power as most full committee chairmen, can also be removed by the caucus. In January 1977, the Democratic Caucus deposed Robert L.F. Sikes as chairman of the Military Construction subcommittee of the House Appropriations Committee.

The power of appointing Democrats to committees was removed from the Democrats on Wilbur Mills's Ways and Means Committee and given to the Democratic Steering and Policy Committee, part of which is picked by the leadership and part of which is elected.[51] (Mills, the most powerful congressman in the late 1960s and early 1970s, lost his influence in a personal scandal.) A substantial increase in congressional pensions, the greater workload, a flood of citizen complaints and demands, a decrease in the rewards of seniority, and the despair of House Republicans of ever gaining power have meant more retirements from the House. Since 1977, about half the members of the House have been in office three terms or less, most of them replacing members who retired.[52] There has been a great increase in the number of open committee meetings in the House, and the voting of committee members, in contrast to the former practice, is now usually recorded. More votes on the floor are also recorded by name, as opposed to simply announcing the numbers for and against some measure. Thus senior members have lost influence, junior members have become more independent, and the proceedings of the House have been much more open to public scrutiny.

The organizing of liberals within the House Democratic party has been the main immediate cause of these changes, but Common Cause has been the major outside lobby working to get such reforms.[53] Common Cause lobbyists have exercised significant influence in the direction of reform.

First, the Common Cause "Campaign '74" questionnaires indicated that a majority of the House Democrats were on record as favoring the transfer of the committee appointment power for Democrats from the Ways and Means Committee to some more representative committee. This information surprised almost all observers of Congress and paved the way for the enactment of that reform.

Second, a Common Cause booklet analyzing the House committee chairmanships had an important effect on the voting of new Democrats in the selection of chairmen for the 94th Congress.

Third, two of the more striking exercises of power by the newly significant House Democratic Caucus occurred partly in reaction to determined lobbying by Common Cause. In March 1975, the caucus voted to instruct the Rules Committee to report a tax bill with a rule permitting an amendment to repeal the oil depletion allowance.[54] And in June 1976 the caucus voted to instruct Walter Flowers's Administrative Law and Governmental Relations Subcommittee of the Judiciary Committee to hold hearings and report out financial disclosure legislation introduced in early 1975.[55] In both cases, the committees complied with the caucus. The oil depletion allowance was immediately repealed (with exemptions for small oil companies); but financial disclosure legislation was not enacted until 1978.

Fourth, Common Cause played a central part in the "Sikes affair." Congressman Robert Sikes of Florida was an influential member of the House who had served since 1940 and held a coveted post — chairman of the Military Construction subcommittee of the House Appropriations Committee. In late 1975 and early 1976, investigative reporting by the *St. Petersburg Times* disclosed that Sikes had used his influence to further his financial position in ways that were legal but seemed unethical. Sikes had (1) successfully sponsored a measure that lifted federal restrictions on developing Gulf Coast property in which he had invested; (2) induced the navy to permit the location of a bank in which he had an interest on the Pensacola Naval Base, contrary to the navy's policy; and (3) invested $40,000 in Fairchild Industries stock while he was making appropriations decisions affecting the company's financial status. As the Sikes case began to attract national attention, Common Cause decided to lobby for a congressional sanction against Sikes, something the House ordinarily does not do in such a situation. The House has a Committee on Standards of Official Conduct, popularly known as the ethics committee, which was formed in 1968 as a result of the controversy arising from an attempt to expel Representative Adam Clayton Powell. But no boat rockers were appointed to this committee, and by 1976 it had not investigated the conduct of a single congressman.

The Standards Committee would not investigate Sikes's actions unless it was pressured. Common Cause lobbyists at first could not induce a single congressman to make a complaint, because even the most antiestablishment Democrats feared the retribution of senior Democrats in the House against a member who complained about Sikes. But Common Cause lobbyists worked from July 1975 until March 1976 to get a group of members to complain to the Standards Committee. Finally, 44 House members jointly complained about Sikes's behavior to the Standards Committee. The committee held hearings and was forced by the evidence to recommend that Sikes be reprimanded by the full House, which did so in July 1976 by a 381-3 vote.[56] The reprimand carried no sanction other than the expression of disapproval. Sikes was the linchpin of the economy in his district, in which the Department of Defense spent $500 million per year. Pensacola voters would not turn out of office a man who had successfully maintained such a high level of defense expenditures in their area.

In December 1976 a group of reform congressmen launched a drive among House Democrats to vote Sikes out of his subcommittee chairmanship.[57] Common Cause actively supported this effort and produced a great deal of mail about the issue. To the surprise of Washington political observers, Sikes was unseated by the overwhelming margin of 189-93 in the Democratic Caucus.[58]

If Common Cause had not been in existence, Sikes probably would have escaped congressional sanction for conflict of interest. The House Committee on Standards of Official Conduct had not criticized a member of the House during the first eight years of the committee's existence. Common Cause had to work for nine months to get a group of congressmen to complain. No individual member of the House would have been willing to act.

By 1977 strong deterrents to the use of congressional office for personal financial reward were institutionalized. The ethics codes of both houses of Congress included provisions for full disclosure of assets, which is an important deterrent to using the office for financial gain, since it makes it difficult to keep the results of questionable financial activity off the public record without outright lying. And if such lies are discovered by journalists and electoral opponents, they can end a congressional career. And even if a congressman can be reelected in such a situation, the Sikes case demonstrates that the House will punish even powerful members whose conflicts of interest bring the House into disrepute. Decreasing the actual incidence and the appearance of congressional venality is probably important for the maintenance and enhancement of public respect for Congress. Common Cause's active lobbying for regulating conflicts of interest in the House has helped prevent future scandals that would have further discredited Congress in the era of the Abscam scandals.

The Senate has not been so dominated by its senior members as the House, and so Common Cause has not been as active in pressing for reform of the Senate. Common Cause did lobby for the reduction of the number of senators necessary to cut off filibusters from two-thirds of those present to three-fifths of the total number of senators, a measure adopted in March 1975.[59] Common Cause also lobbied for the reduction of the number of senatorial committees and subcommittees because it thought that numerous committee and subcommittee memberships dissipated the time and legislative attention of senators.[60]

State-Level Reforms

Since 1970, all state legislatures have passed one or more reforms of the sort proposed by Common Cause: disclosure of the financial holdings of state officials, conflict-of-interest rules, sunshine laws, regulation of lobbyists, and regulation of campaign finances. According to Common Cause, its state organizations have played a major role in passing 160 reform bills in 46 states.[61]

An analysis and evaluation of Common Cause-sponsored reforms at the state level are beyond the scope of this study. Much time is required for such a project because state governments vary. In states like California, decisions are generally made in a public manner, lobbyists do not command inordinate power, and there is not much graft. The same could be said for Colorado and Florida. On the other hand, New Jersey, Maryland, Illinois, and Texas have powerful lobbyists and, by some accounts, considerable graft.[62] The effect of a sunshine law or a lobbyist regulation act might also vary according to the nature of a state's politics. In some states, such measures might have little effect on state government; in other states, enacting and enforcing the OUTS measures would revolutionize the state government. Thus, a thorough analysis of the effects of state-level OUTS legislation would require considerable study.

I hope that one result of the present study will be to arouse the interest of political scientists and those who grant research funds so that there will be a way of analyzing the effects of enacting institutional reforms at the state level.[63] Otherwise citizens, government officials, and scholars will never understand the effects of enacting such reforms. If farmers in all fifty states started using a new insecticide on apple trees, a million dollars would be spent analyzing the effectiveness of the insecticide. A similar amount of attention ought to be given to the effects of enacting several hundred political reform measures.

Antiwar Lobbying: 1971-72

Vietnam was Common Cause's main priority in 1971-72. Early polls of the membership indicated a greater concern about ending the Vietnam war than about any other issue. This concern was in accordance with the beliefs of John Gardner and other staffers, and so Common Cause launched an antiwar lobbying drive in the House in January 1971.

Antiwar leaders and other liberals urged people to write their senators in support of the McGovern-Hatfield Amendment, which called for the withdrawal of American troops from Indochina, and the Cooper-Church Amendment, which would cut off funds for the war by the end of 1971. Almost half of the senators were critical of American involvement in Vietnam, including the Senate's Majority Leader, Mike Mansfield (Dem-Mont.). The Senate considered the McGovern-Hatfield, Cooper-Church, and variations of these amendments on the floor of the full Senate, where all Senators could vote on them. The measures were voted down in close votes. The so-called Mansfield amendment, calling for withdrawal of American troops by some set date shortly after the release of American prisoners of war, passed four times but was thrown out by House conference committee members three times. President Nixon was forced to sign a defense appropriations bill containing a Mansfield amendment on 17 November 1971, but Nixon called the amendment "without binding force or effect."[64]

The situation regarding antiwar amendments was much different in the House. Here, the Democratic party leadership, the Rules Committee, the Foreign Relations Committee, the Appropriations Committee, and the Armed Forces Committee were on balance opposed to antiwar amendments in January 1971. The Democratic leadership of the House was opposed to the idea of voting on antiwar measures by the full House, and succeeded in preventing such votes until the spring of 1971. Opponents of the Vietnam war were forced to express themselves in such indirect ways as opposing the entire defense budget, opposing a resolution commending Nixon's efforts to negotiate with the North Vietnamese (1969), and voting for measures prohibiting appropriations for American troops in parts of Indochina other than South Vietnam (1970).[65]

Direct votes on the war were taken in the House in 1971. This was the prime Common Cause lobbying objective at that time. In a halfway confrontation in March, the House rejected, 122-260, an amendment offered by Donald Fraser (Dem-Minn.) that provided that no person drafted after 31 December 1971 could serve in Indochina.[66] A direct confrontation was held in June on the Nedzi-Whalen amendment, analogous to the Cooper-Church amendments in the Senate, which would have cut off funds after 31 December 1971 for the war in Indochina. Although the Nedzi-Whalen amendment was rejected, 254 to 158, gaining 158 votes against continuing the war was generally interpreted as an important victory for antiwar advocates.[67] Another amendment to the overall defense procurement bill, analogous to the Mansfield amendment, was offered by Claude Pepper (Dem-Fla.) but was defeated 147-237.[68]

Other antiwar votes were held in the House in 1972. In a new departure for the House Democratic Caucus, it voted in April to instruct the Foreign Affairs Committee to report a bill mandating a specific date for the end of the war. The measure passed its key vote in the caucus, 135-66. After rejecting an antiwar measure in June by 19-18, the Foreign Affairs Committee in August included such a measure, 18-17, as part of the foreign aid bill. The measure was voted out of the foreign aid bill, however, getting 177 votes in favor and 229 votes against.[69] This vote was nevertheless interpreted as indicative of a growing strength of war opponents in the House. Before this vote, the House in June had voted down, 152-244, a measure by Congressman Michael Harrington (Dem-Mass.) to cut off appropriations for the war.[70] A later measure to cut off appropriations was offered in September by Congressman Joseph Addabbo (Dem-N.Y.) and was voted down, 160-208.[71]

David Cohen and Fred Wertheimer say that in 1971-72, Common Cause was the leading antiwar lobby in the House. This is probably an accurate statement, partly because only a few professional lobbyists were working for antiwar measures at that time. The *Congressional Quarterly Almanac* reports that in 1972, "among groups that lobbied for an end to the war were Common Cause, Americans for Democratic Action, Vietnam Veterans Against the War, National Student Lobby, and the National Peace Alert."[72] Common Cause's effort probably was greater than those of other groups, although Vietnam Veterans Against the War staged effective antiwar demonstrations. Wertheimer recalls that less than ten professional lobbyists, other then Common Cause lobbyists, were available for antiwar lobbying in the House. Most of them were from labor unions.[73] A testimony to the effectiveness of Common Cause comes from Congressman Phillip Burton, quoted as saying in regard to the passage of a cutoff date measure by the Democratic Caucus in 1972: "Many outside groups and members of Congress participated in this effort, but particular credit goes to Common Cause and its members, under the leadership of John Gardner, for mobilizing and coordinating public concern for passage of the resolution."[74] Common Cause described their lobbying effort as follows:

> We played a key role in the Democratic Caucus action. In a span of four days we put in over 2000 hours on the issue. We alerted our phone chains on Sunday, April 16, to prepare for a phone and telegram barrage to House Democrats. On Monday, our D.C. staff and volunteers telephoned all Democratic House offices to learn if the Representative planned to attend the Caucus (obtaining a quorum to conduct business was a crucial initial problem). We sent a dozen Washington staffers, who had registered as lobbyists, to visit nearly 200 of the more than 250 Democratic offices in the House. Their purpose was to gauge the Representative's sentiment on adoption by the Caucus of a strong antiwar resolution. Then we telephoned to Common Cause members in the districts of Congressmen who needed pressure brought on them either to attend the Caucus or to vote to end the war. In the short space of two days this effort produced dramatic feedback from members in all states. Congressmen reported many communications, including phone calls to their homes at night.[75]

The phone chains now in place at Common Cause were not well organized at that time, but the enthusiasm of active members for antiwar issues was extraordinary. No doubt Common Cause lobbyists were briefed by antiwar congressmen about which of their Democratic colleagues, undecided on the cutoff date issue, were most moved by receiving large numbers of letters from their districts.

It can be argued that antiwar votes in the House had no effect on the Nixon administration, which was trying to withdraw from Vietnam anyway. But perhaps these measures increased the motivation of the administration to end the war in Vietnam because the White House was forced to expend some of its political resources in vigorously lobbying against antiwar measures in the House.

Possibly the main effect of the antiwar votes was on the institution of the House of Representatives. Some liberal Democrats were angered by the opposition of many senior Democrats to holding debates and voting on the war. This opposition discredited the seniority system, while the caucus victory for the antiwar forces gave impetus to efforts by the liberal Democratic Study Group to modify the system.

On the issue of the Vietnam war in the House, Common Cause had a significant effect on a substantive issue, as opposed to the procedural issues of government reform. As noted, Common Cause also achieved major successes in substantive areas in lobbying against the construction of the SST (the supersonic airliner) and against the continuation of the oil depletion allowance for large oil companies.

In sum, two parts of the Common Cause platform "to open up the system" have been enacted by the federal government: sunshine legislation and the mandatory disclosure of personal finances of top federal officials. Among organizations outside the government, Common Cause was the leading lobbyist for these measures. Common Cause pioneered the concept of sunset legislation, but the enactment of a sunset law by the federal government does not seem likely. However, the U.S. Congress now applies the concept to specific legislation with some frequency. In addition, thirty-three states have enacted sunset laws. Common Cause was also the coordinator of interest groups that lobbied against the war in Vietnam in the House of Representatives.

NOTES

1. Ted Vaden, "Government in the Sunshine Approved 390-5," *Congressional Quarterly Weekly Report* 34 (31 July 1976): 2067.
2. *Congressional Quarterly Almanac, 1975* (Washington, D.C.: Congressional Quarterly, 1976), 930.
3. Ted Vaden, "Senate Votes 'Sunshine' Rules for Committees," *Congressional Quarterly Weekly Report* 33 (8 November 1975): 2413-14.
4. Ibid.
5. See Walter J. Oleszek, "Multiple Referral of Legislation in the House" (paper presented at the annual meeting of the American Political Science Association, Washington, D.C., 28-31 August 1980). The problem of the referral of a single bill to multiple committees is discussed in the report of a House of Representatives self-study com-

mittee. See U.S. House of Representatives, *Final Report of the Select Committee on Committees, (report of the Patterson Committee), H. Rept. No. 96-866, 96th Cong. 2nd sess.* (Washington, D.C.: Government Printing Office, 1980).

6. Stanley S. Surrey, "How Special Tax Provisions Get Enacted," in *Readings in American Political Behavior,* ed. Raymond E. Wolfinger, 2nd ed. (Englewood Cliffs, N.J.: Prentice-Hall, 1970), chap. 16.

7. Thomas P. Southwick, "Tax Debate: Slow Progress in Senate," *Congressional Quarterly Weekly Report* 34 (31 July 1976): 2061-62.

8. I do not know of poll data to this effect, but apparently members of Congress consider sunshine legislation to be popular with the public as evidenced in the passage of such legislation by votes of 390-5 in the House and by 86-0 in the Senate. See note 1.

9. Congressmen avoid voting against measures to regulate lobbyists because they think that such votes would be unpopular with their constituents. See note 48, chap. 6.

10. "House Approves Public Disclosure Bill for Lobbyists," *Washington Star,* 29 September 1976, 1.

11. Al Gordon, "Tougher Lobbying Disclosure Act Reported," *Congressional Quarterly Weekly Report* 34 (1 May 1976): 1047.

12. See *Congressional Quarterly Weekly Report* 30 (19 August 1972): 2068.

13. Ibid.

14. "Time Ran Out for Lobby Revision Bill," *Congressional Quarterly Almanac, 1976* (Washington, D.C.: Congressional Quarterly, 1977), 477-86.

15. *Congressional Quarterly Almanac, 1978* (Washington, D.C.: Congressional Quarterly, 1979), 782-87.

16. See, for example, *Congressional Quarterly Almanac, 1976, 477, 482.*

17. *Congressional Quarterly Almanac, 1978, 835-50.*

18. "Disclosure Requirements for House and Senate," *Congressional Quarterly Weekly Report* 34 (31 July 1976): 2051.

19. For example, see ibid., 2050-60.

20. "Watergate Reform," *Congressional Quarterly Almanac, 1976, 422-26, esp. 426.*

21. Thomas P. Southwick, "Senate Adopts New Code of Ethics," *Congressional Quarterly Weekly Report* 35 (2 April 1977): 591-99; and "House Adopts Tough Ethics Code," *Congressional Quarterly Weekly Report* 35 (5 March 1977): 387-90.

22. *Congressional Quarterly Almanac, 1977* (Washington, D.C.: Congressional Quarterly, 1978), 763-81.

23. Ibid., 578-82; *Congressional Quarterly Almanac, 1978, 835-50.*

24. Ibid., 836.

25. *Congressional Quarterly Almanac, 1979* (Washington, D.C.: Congressional Quarterly, 1980), 578-80.

26. Ibid., 571.

27. Ibid.

28. "Congress Votes Itself New Pay Benefits," *Congressional Quarterly Almanac, 1981* (Washington, D.C.: Congressional Quarterly, 1982), 287-89.

29. Grant McConnell, *Private Power and American Democracy* (New York: Knopf, 1966).

30. I am referring to the type of thesis advanced by Louis Hartz, *The Liberal Tradition in America* (New York: Harcourt, Brace, 1955).

31. Andrew S. McFarland, *Public Interest Lobbies: Decision Making on Energy* (Washington, D.C.: American Enterprise Institute, 1976), chap. 4.

32. Common Cause, "Memorandum to the Governing Board: Campaign '76—Executive Branch Reform Issues," October 1975, 6-7.

33. "The great creative work of a federal agency must be done in the first decade of its existence if it is to be done at all. After that it is likely to become a prisoner of bureaucracy and of the inertia demanded by the Establishment of any respected agency. That is why I told FDR over and over again that every agency he created should be abolished in ten years. And since he might not be around to dissolve it, he should insert in the basic charter of the agency a provision for its termination. Roosevelt would always roar with delight at that suggestion, and of course never did do anything about it." William O. Douglas, *Go East, Young Man* (New York: Random House, 1974), 297.

34. Theodore J. Lowi, *The End of Liberalism* (New York: Norton, 1969), 309-10.

35. " 'Sunset' Legislation," *Congressional Quarterly Almanac, 1976,* 504-6.

36. See for example, Aaron Wildavsky, *The Revolt Against the Masses* (New York: Basic Books, 1971), chaps. 10, 15, 18, 22.

37. *In Common* 7 (Summer 1976): 12.

38. Ibid., 12-13.

39. *Congressional Quarterly Almanac, 1978,* 850-52.

40. Ibid., 852.

41. Alan Murray, "Prospects Dim for 'Sunset' Legislation as Senate Panel Waters Down Original Bill," *Congressional Quarterly Weekly Report* (6 September 1980): 2645-46.

42. *Congressional Quarterly Almanac, 1979,* 402.

43. Ibid., 499.

44. Ibid., 583.

45. Ibid., 469.

46. Ibid., 326.

47. Ibid., 513.

48. Ibid., 580.

49. *The Book of the States, 1980-1981* (Lexington, Ky.: Council of State Governments, 1980), 23: 122-24. See also 168: "In legislative reviews mandated by sunset laws, Kansas in 1979 abolished four state agencies, Florida continued 19 of 20 reviewed, and Colorado continued seven of nine health professional licensing boards and two of three commissions."

50. See Lawrence C. Dodd and Bruce I. Oppenheimer, "The House in Transition," in *Congress Reconsidered,* ed. Dodd and Oppenheimer (New York: Praeger, 1977), 21-53; and Charles O. Jones, "Will Reform Change Congress?" in ibid., 247-60.

51. *Congressional Quarterly Almanac, 1975,* 27.

52. John F. Bibby, Thomas E. Mann, and Norman J. Ornstein, *Vital Statistics on Congress, 1980* (Washington, D.C.: American Enterprise Institute, 1980), 18, 53, 54.

53. For information about the House Democratic Study Group, the main organizational expression of liberal Democrats in the House, see Arthur G. Stevens, Jr., Arthur H. Miller, and Thomas E. Mann, "Mobilization of Liberal Strength in the House, 1955-70: The Democratic Study Group," *American Political Science Review* 68 (June 1974): 667-81.

54. *Congressional Quarterly Almanac, 1975,* 101.

55. Bruce Freed and David Loomis, "Financial Disclosure: Little Now, More Later?" *Congressional Quarterly Weekly Report* 34 (31 July 1976): 2050.

56. *Congressional Quarterly Almanac, 1976,* 30-31.

57. According to Common Cause, these Democrats were Andrew Maguire of New Jersey (who stuck his neck out the farthest), Max Baucus of Montana (who managed the debate against Sikes), Richard Bolling of Missouri, Phillip Burton of California, Butler Derrick of South Carolina, Dante Fascell of Florida, Thomas Luken of Ohio, Matthew McHugh of New York, Abner Mikva of Illinois, Norman Mineta of California, Parren Mitchell of Maryland, Leon Panetta of California, and Richardson Preyer of North Carolina. See *Frontline* 3 (January-February 1977): 3.

58. Thomas P. Southwick, "Sikes Ousted as Subcommittee Head," *Congressional Quarterly Weekly Report* 35 (29 January 1977): 159-60. Sikes retired from Congress in 1978.

59. *Congressional Quarterly Almanac, 1975,* 35-38.

60. In other words, Common Cause supported the original report of the temporary Select Committee to Study the Senate Committee System, the so-called Stevenson Committee after its chairman (Dem-Ill.), before it was compromised to meet political necessities. See Thomas P. Southwick, "Senate Approves Committee Changes," *Congressional Quarterly Weekly Report* 35 (12 February 1977): 279-84.

61. It is certainly plausible to argue that the lobbying of the state organizations has had a major effect on state government. For instance, a handbook of state government, *The Book of the States: 1980-81,* 80-81, 122-24, states that 33 states had passed some form of sunset legislation by 1980. We know that no states had such legislation before it was initiated by Common Cause in Colorado in 1975, and we know that the state organizations have been active in lobbying for sunset legislation since it became a priority issue in 1976.

    Writing in *The Book of the States: 1980-81,* Richard G. Smolka says: "The wave of election reform legislation passed in the states during the 1970s was almost over by 1978. Laws requiring disclosure of campaign contributors were passed in almost every state. Limits on individual contributions to candidates were imposed in about one-half the States, and 17 states passed legislation allowing public funding of campaigns in one form or another" (52). Again one might plausibly suppose that state lobbies often had a major role in passing such legislation, part of the reform platform, although of course this point remains to be proven.

62. These are my observations based on residence in California for twelve years, from 1962 until 1974. California did have very powerful lobbyists of the state legislature in the 1940s, but during the 1950s their power waned. Petty graft apparently was uncommon in California during the 1960s and 1970s.

    Common Cause staff members in the 1970s regarded Florida and Colorado as states in which "good government" legislation was becoming more extensive. This was particularly true in Florida under Governor Reubin Askew (1971-79), who was active in support of procedural reform legislation in Florida. The concept of sunset legislation was initiated in Colorado.

63. A beginning for the analysis of state institutional reforms can be found in Herbert E. Alexander, ed., *Campaign Money: Reform and Reality in the States* (New York: Free Press, 1976); Karen J. Fling, "The States as Laboratories of Reform," chap. 9 in *Political Finance,* ed. Herbert E. Alexander (Beverly Hills, Calif.: Sage, 1979);

Ruth S. Jones, "State Public Financing and the State Parties," in *Parties, Interest Groups, and Campaign Finance Laws,* ed. Michael J. Malbin (Washington, D.C.: American Enterprise Institute, 1980).

64. *Congressional Quarterly Almanac, 1971* (Washington, D.C.: Congressional Quarterly, 1972), 305.

65. *Congressional Quarterly Almanac, 1969* (Washington, D.C.: Congressional Quarterly, 1970), 857; *Congressional Quarterly Almanac, 1970* (Washington, D.C.: Congressional Quarterly, 1971), 388.

66. *Congressional Quarterly Almanac, 1971,* 266.

67. Ibid., 310-13. The Nedzi-Whalen amendment was sponsored by Lucien Nedzi (Dem-Mich.) and Charles Whalen, Jr. (Rep-Ohio).

68. Ibid., 313.

69. *Congressional Quarterly Almanac, 1972,* 469-71.

70. Ibid., 409.

71. Ibid., 807.

72. Ibid., 1077.

73. Interview, 26 September 1975.

74. *Common Cause: Report from Washington* 2 (May 1975): 1.

75. Ibid., 2.

9. Will Common Cause Endure?

Networks of Reform: The Logic of Organization

The Common Cause organization, and the theory underlying it, has a logic with an almost mathematical fascination. Let us review the core of the structure.

1. A mass membership is attracted through computerized mailings. This membership provides the basic organizational resources of money and legitimacy.

2. Recruitment messages stress the civic balance belief system.

3. This civic balance is formulated into a program through the platform of structure and process reforms. It is argued that these reforms are fundamental for achieving better governmental representation and policies.

4. The structure and process reforms are the organization's top priority. Most of the lobbying resources are used to promote these reforms.

5. Common Cause's leadership, activists, and contributors adhere to the values of the structure and process program.

6. The Common Cause leadership is aware that members will quit the organization if it lobbies on many issues that depart from the government reform program. A minority veto, expressed in polls of the membership, is sufficient to prevent activity on new issues. The organization remains very unified, but may seem a bit dull.

7. A complex structure is maintained through congressional district committees and state units. Good communication is established via telephone.

8. The organization can be broken into subunits for lobbying purposes. Phone chains can be activated in the specific districts of congressmen who may be swing votes on critical committee decisions, state units can activate members for lobbying legislatures, and so forth. A multitude of combinations of district and state units can be called into being. Each unit can be described as a "network of reform."

9. The leaders of the organization teach political pragmatism to activists in the networks.

10. The formation of state units to lobby for reforms in state government is a consequence of the logic of the organization. But this leads to periodic

conflict among the national and state leaders over limited organizational resources.

11. Common Cause is so successful in lobbying for procedural reform that it tends to exclude the formation of other, similar national lobbies, which would compete for scarce resources.

12. This basic logic of Common Cause is understood by many. Accordingly, if the present organization disappears or changes radically, somebody else will probably start a similar reform lobby.

The Creator of the Logic

This organizational logic was in place when John Gardner resigned the chairmanship. Gardner did not have all these points clearly in mind when he started Common Cause in 1970. Nor did he create the organizational structure, in the sense of day-to-day working on details. But he did know what he wanted for Common Cause. He wanted an effective lobbying organization in Washington, and he understood that this meant organizing the constituencies of Congress and hiring excellent personnel—among them, Jack Conway, David Cohen, Tom Mathews, and Fred Wertheimer.

In 1970 conditions were ripe for the creation of a lobby such as Common Cause. But without John Gardner, that lobby would not have been as successful. It takes a rare person to launch successfully a general-purpose public-interest lobby. We noted in chapter 3 that Andrew Maguire and some of his friends had a similar idea at about the same time as Gardner, but they were relieved to merge their effort with Gardner's. Ralph Nader did not think that a public subscription drive for members would succeed. Fred Harris in 1972 and George Romney in 1973 tried to start public-interest lobbies, but failed.

More than anything else, Gardner wanted to influence American society for the better. In the late 1960s Gardner was everyone's ideal college president—he was an intellectual, interested in the education and moral development of youth, with experience in management, fund raising, and public speaking, who had headed a bureaucracy that was a leading source of outside funds for colleges. A Washington joke at that time was: "John Gardner gets so many requests to apply for college presidencies that he answers them with a form letter." But Gardner preferred to head a public-interest group—the Urban Coalition.

Gardner was astute enough not to run for public office. A liberal Republican, he was not likely to ever get a Republican nomination for President. Switching to the Democratic party and running in the 1972 presidential primaries would have been a long shot, at best. Liberal Republican John Lindsay tried this and got nowhere. Gardner might have run for the Senate in 1970 by challenging J. Glenn Beall, Jr., of Maryland, for the Republican nomination and then taking on the incumbent senator, Joseph Tydings. Beall was a conservative who came from a locally prominent political family. Conservatives tend to predominate in Maryland Republican primaries, and the idea of Gardner courting the support of suburban Agnewites for the Republican nomination is ridiculous. There was little point in Gardner's attempting to become a 58-year-old freshman member of the House in 1971.

Gardner preferred the lobbying activities of the Urban Coalition Action Council to the organization's other efforts, such as fund raising, promoting discussions among a city's leaders to devise plans to meet urban crises, and organizing the poor. But the tax law of 1969 prohibited the funding by foundations of lobbies. Gardner had to look for a new source of funds. He had been impressed by the work of civil rights and conservationist lobbies while he was secretary of HEW. And Tom Mathews, one of Gardner's associates, pointed out the success of the Center for the Study of Democratic Institutions in raising funds by mass mailing. At one point, the Urban Coalition discussed the concept of acquiring members. These ideas came together in the concept of a general-purpose public-interest lobby funded by public subscription.[1]

Gardner was an ideal figure to launch such a group. He was looking for a political niche where he could influence events without running for office. He found his constituency among upper-middle-class professionals living in the Northeast and on the West Coast, people who were most willing to contribute to the new lobby. Gardner was greatly respected among this group. He had impressed and inspired them by writings that stressed the values of striving for excellence and avoiding the stagnation and rigidity of personality encouraged by many modern organizations. Gardner was a sincere, intelligent idealist, and he knew something about the workings of Washington. To his new constituency, he was a man who would fight the congressional establishment without going overboard, as many people felt Ralph Nader did.

When 100,000 people joined Common Cause in six months, Gardner and everyone else were amazed. But Common Cause would have been short-lived without Gardner's skill in establishing and maintaining an effective organization. A key to his success was his ability to relate the "morale function" of an organization to its "task function."

Social scientists have found that groups often develop two leaders: one maintains the group's morale and is typically a liked and admired person; the other directs the group toward the achievement of its goals, which frequently involves unpleasant labor and discipline.[2] Michael Lipsky has described a protest group that disintegrated because the morale leader was uninterested in the tasks of maintaining the organization.[3] This is a familiar phenomenon. Another problem occurs when the inspiring public figure who leads the organization sporadically intervenes in decisions about the techniques of attaining the group's goals, that is, when the morale leader does not realize his ignorance of techniques.

Gardner consciously split the morale function from the task function by assuming the morale leadership and selecting "a strong right arm" to assume the task leadership. This was the function that Jack Conway and then David Cohen assumed at Common Cause. Thus Gardner concentrated on public speaking, writing policy statements, planning for the organization, presiding over staff and governing board meetings, and bolstering staff morale. Conway or Cohen guided the details of lobbying and of establishing and maintaining an effective field organization.

Common Cause respects technical expertise. Gardner, basically a generalist and a morale builder, knew the importance of technique and made sure that the specialists in his employ felt that what they were doing was important. Gardner was extremely talented at picking the right people for the right jobs, a skill that many publicly impressive leaders lack. Jack Conway performed excellently at developing the Common Cause field organization, David Cohen was superb in establishing the lobbying operation and relating it to other aspects of the organization, Tom Mathews set up an extremely effective network of relationships with the press, and Fred Wertheimer adapted the organization's strategies to the problems posed by the Reagan administration.

Continuing without Gardner

Gardner founded Common Cause at the age of fifty-seven and never intended to remain as chairman for the rest of his life. He knew it would not be good for Common Cause to become too dependent on one man. Accordingly, in January 1975 he indicated to the governing board that he would step down in two or three years. During this time, he delegated most of the decision-making authority to Common Cause's number-two man, David Cohen, who gained valuable experience in running an organization (he had started as a lobbyist). It became apparent that Common Cause could survive without Gardner.

Who would be the next chair of Common Cause? There was no obvious heir to Gardner. Cohen was satisfied to be the manager of the organization. To the extent he wanted to engage in public speaking or writing for Common Cause, he could do so in his capacity as president. Moreover, it was apparent that Cohen had enough influence with other Common Cause leaders so that they would not select a chairman antagonistic to Cohen.

Many thought that Gardner's successor would be a national celebrity similar to Gardner. Liberal Republicans, Watergate heroes, former Justice Department leaders, and environmentalists were mentioned. In fact, discussions about the chairmanship were held with Archibald Cox (who was elected to the governing board in April 1976), Russell Train (head of the Environmental Protection Agency under Gerald Ford), John Doar (minority counsel to the Republicans during the House Judiciary Committee's impeachment investigation), and Burke Marshall (head of civil rights enforcement in the Justice Department under John Kennedy and Lyndon Johnson). These men already had full career commitments, however, and none of them at that time was extremely enthusiastic about presiding over Common Cause.

The leaders of Common Cause began to think that a famous chairperson was not a necessity for the organization. Gardner had indicated a desire to stay on as chairman emeritus with an office in the same building as Common Cause's national headquarters, and it was thought that his continued presence would be an asset. Some judicious advice from Gardner might prevent mistakes on the part of a new chairperson. Moreover, Gardner could continue to sign Common Cause's mailed solicitations for members, along with the signature of the new chairperson. It gradually became apparent that a leading member of the Common Cause governing board might be a good selection to replace Gardner.

In February 1977 a committee of ten board members was appointed to nominate a successor. The nominating committee chose Nan Waterman, who was unanimously elected at the April board meeting.

Waterman then resided in Muscatine, Iowa, and had been active on the Common Cause national governing board for five years. Also active in the League of Women Voters, of which she had been a vice president, she had shown a masterful understanding of the processes of consultation and communication within a political organization of voluntary participants. This talent, which the League of Women Voters frequently develops in its leaders, had proven of great value to Common Cause as Waterman helped develop the network of relationships among national headquarters, the governing board, district steering committees, and state organizations. Waterman also had a great deal of experience in maintaining good relationships between state and national units.

It was decided that the job of chair of Common Cause would be a part-time one, about two days a week. This was sufficient because the chairperson would be the leading public speaker for Common Cause, and would lead the policy-making discussions, but would not be involved in the day-to-day management. The impression was widespread that Waterman and other future chairpersons might not hold the post for too long—three or four years was seen as a typical length of service.

Waterman served as chairperson of Common Cause from April 1977 until February 1980. Under Waterman, the Common Cause organizational networks continued to function well. The chairwoman's major talent was what might be termed "organizational leadership"—maintaining the morale of Common Cause volunteers and reconciling the national-state conflicts that inevitably arise. David Cohen and other staff leaders maintained a strong lobbying effort. But neither Waterman nor Cohen was particularly adept at "the public leadership" function—increasing enthusiasm among the general public for Common Cause through speeches and articles and through symbolically representing the organization in one's public persona. Waterman did not become a well-known person, even to those who follow Washington politics closely.

Waterman's relative anonymity would not have mattered much if Common Cause had not suffered a serious drop in the number of its members—from 225,000 in 1977 to a low point of 203,000 in 1979. This meant that Common Cause lost 10 percent of its budget during a time of persistent inflation. In the fall of 1979 Common Cause headquarters was forced to cut back its subsidies to the state organizations. Budget problems caused staff salaries to lag behind government salaries. The public interest in Common Cause reforms was not high during this period; even a famous leader might not have been able to halt the decline in the membership. But on balance it seems that a leader of Common Cause has to fulfill the public function if Common Cause is to reach its full potential of members and financial resources.

In the fall of 1979, Archibald Cox indicated his availability for the chairmanship of Common Cause and was unanimously elected by the governing board in February 1980. Cox is a Watergate hero; he is the special prosecutor Elliott Richardson and William Ruckelshaus refused to fire at President Nixon's order, thereby precipitating the "Saturday Night Massacre." The Common Cause leadership may have hit upon a successful tripartite formula for their organization: Wertheimer for the lobbying function, Waterman and other leaders for the organizational function, and a respected celebrity for the public leadership role.

Pragmatism, the Concept of Representation, and Political Survival

Common Cause has organizational problems peculiar to the task of organizing middle-class reformers who adhere to a civic balance belief system. Often, groups of reformers have not been successful in practical politics because their moralism, distance from everyday politics, engagement in abstract debates, and lack of a long-standing political commitment have crippled their effectiveness.

The national leadership of Common Cause has usually followed a pragmatic course of action, but to retain the political effectiveness of its lobbying effort, Common Cause must continually educate new activists in the virtues of pragmatism.

An example of a conflict between the pragmatic national leadership and the less flexible views of an activist occurred at a national board meeting in October 1977. A spokesman for a group of members wanted the board to change its position of opposing the Carter-Mondale plan to eliminate most of the Hatch Act's restriction on political participation by federal civil servants. The spokesman argued that by its opposition, "Common Cause is agreeing with Barry Goldwater and other politicians who are usually much to the right of Common Cause." The argument was totally inappropriate, not only because Goldwater and others on the right agree with Common Cause part of the time, but also because the national leaders want to maintain a pragmatic political organization. Pragmatism means to them that "Common Cause has no permanent friends, and no permanent enemies." It means that Common Cause is happy to work in coalition with anyone who agrees with a Common Cause position, to let "bygones be bygones." Pragmatism means to the Common Cause leaders that their organization not be rooted, either in fact or in the perceptions of congressmen, in one part of the ideological spectrum. Such a pragmatic attitude increases Common Cause's effectiveness in influencing Congress and recruiting members.

The leaders are probably correct in these beliefs. But such an outlook and its virtues are not immediately comprehensible to many activists, who join Common Cause because of a skepticism about the quality of government and the politicians who govern. Thus, one of the tasks of the post-Gardner management is to maintain a politically effective organization by teaching the new activists and leaders how Common Cause has been effective in the past. In other words, a constant effort is needed if Common Cause is not to reflect the politically ineffective moralism and loquaciousness that is common among the reformers.

There is a second reason why Common Cause must emphasize a pragmatic outlook. The main goal of Common Cause is to achieve better political representation. But, as we saw in chapter 5, the meaning of "representation" is complex and paradoxical. In its pursuit of better representation from one standpoint, in lobbying for a particular bill Common Cause often confronts some other conception of representation, which conflicts with the Common Cause concept but may have equal validity. With its major procedural reform issues, Common Cause lobbies for better representation as the idea is widely understood from one perspective.

For example, Common Cause works for opening executive branch meetings to public attendance. But pushing for representation on one score (such as open government) may lessen representation on another score (making it more difficult for an administration to represent the public by drawing up controversial programs). In drawing up a complicated proposal, such as an annual budget or an anti-inflation package, secrecy can be useful to prevent adversaries from attacking a controversial point out of context, a common strategy to discredit an entire package. If all the cuts in agency requests made by the Office of Management and Budget (OMB) were immediately known to congressional friends of each agency so reduced, it would not be possible to present the President's annual budget.[4]

Similar paradoxes occur in other areas of representation. On the one hand, it may promote better representation to pressure electoral candidates to take clear stands on as many issues as possible. But on election, if such a candidate stands fast to the entire body of promises, he may inflexibly resist subsequent changes in opinion by his electoral supporters, and such opinion changes may reflect important changes in the world. For instance, Common Cause attempted to get presidential candidates to declare their future federal budget during the primary campaign in 1976. A candidate might do this, reflecting a prior concern with an unemployment problem; then, after the election, spiraling inflation might be a much greater problem. On the one hand, getting detailed promises may promote better representation. On the other hand, it may not.

As an organization that puts forth proposals to improve the quality of political representation, Common Cause can frequently be caught in political debate arising from such paradoxes. There is no way to foresee the paradoxes that may arise from proposed structure and process reforms. Consequently, Common Cause's reforms are sure to be criticized by many who are concerned by a meaning of representation not reflected in a Common Cause proposal.

Because of the paradoxes, Common Cause may aggressively push forward some plan to improve representative government but then see a need to revise the plan in the light of political arguments arising from another perspective on representation. For example, plans for the public financing of congressional elections may be revised to take into account the maintenance of local political parties. If the Common Cause organization is too set on legislating its original proposals intact, it may lose political support by offending proponents of another perspective on representation. Successful improvements in political representation are complex and multifaceted—"give a little bit to open government here, but restrict the number of primaries in favor of stronger political parties over there. . . ." To get such plans legislated and successfully implemented requires a very flexible attitude on the part of Common Cause.

Two conclusions can be drawn. Because of the paradoxes, the structure and process reforms advocated by Common Cause sometimes will not be as appealing to the general public as the Common Cause management expects. Second, in pursuing the structure and process reforms, Common Cause performs a "thought forcing" function. Because it is concerned with representation, and because it is sufficiently influential to put its proposals on legislative agendas, Common Cause forces politicians, journalists, and political scientists to consider what is meant by better representation in American politics.

The Future

Common Cause or a similar organization is now a fairly durable force on the American political scene. An interest in reforming political institutions has endured among middle-class professionals throughout the twentieth century. Now that Gardner and his associates have demonstrated that this interest in reform can be organized for lobbying in Washington, it is likely that other reformers of the future will follow the Common Cause model even if the present organization disintegrates.

Perhaps Common Cause is subject to a cycle of issues in the way that third parties are in American politics. Third parties often bring up new issues, and when these issues get favorable public attention, they become part of the program of the major parties. Much of FDR's New Deal was first advocated by socialists and populists; George Wallace's antibureaucracy positions of 1968 were mainstream positions in the 1976 and 1980 elections. In bringing up its OUTS program, Common Cause acted like a third party in that established leaders of the two big parties tended to oppose such measures (except for sunset laws). When Common Cause demonstrated the popularity of government reform issues, ambitious politicians began to advocate them. We must expect this. Such reforms then become mainstream issues, advocated by many congressmen, perhaps even by the President and other national leaders. The Common Cause effort may in time seem superfluous.

Another cycle of issues may affect the strength of Common Cause. For example, a scandalous or unpopular situation occurs; Common Cause makes an issue out of it; the public is demonstrably concerned about it; the President or other political leaders advocate the Common Cause solution, which may be adopted or rejected; and Common Cause looks for a new issue to interest its membership.

Issue cycles place an important check on the power of a citizens' lobby. In general, the more successful the lobby, the more eager politicians will be to support its program. And after the adoption of a number of reforms, aggrieved citizens will usually lose interest in pressing for further reforms, as they think the original problem is solved or alleviated. In this situation, it is difficult for a lobby such as Common Cause to maintain a high level of membership.

There is a countervailing tendency to the cycle. Most political reforms have to be passed by Congress. And when such reforms involve the behavior of congressmen, they may not behave like political entrepreneurs, eager to advocate a popular new issue. They may resist the adoption of the reform, as some congressmen resisted the control of campaigns by the Federal Election Commission and the restrictions on their free postage privileges. Such resistance keeps Common Cause in business.

A cautious conclusion is that Common Cause or similar organizations will have considerable power perhaps one year out of three. When a backlog of feasible and popular government reform measures builds up, it will take perhaps six years (comparable to 1972-78) for an organization to initiate them and get them passed by Congress. An estimate is that such a reform period will be followed by another period, perhaps twice as long, when popular interest in government reform dwindles (1978-90?). Finally, if political scandals and governmental ineptitude precipitate another widespread demand for reform, much of that reform will be initiated by a citizens' lobby. But only an exceptionally inventive and politically talented leadership will permit the present Common Cause to maintain its organizational strength through the 1980s.

The Effectiveness of Middle-Class Reform Movements

One reason I expect a national citizens' lobby to continue to be influential is that it is a particular reflection of a more general phenomenon: the harnessing of a middle-class social movement to skilled political tactics. Since the mid-1960s, we have witnessed the women's movement, the environmentalist movement, the peace movement, the good-government movement, the consumer movement. All have been basically white middle-class political activities. The women, the environmentalists, and the government reformers have achieved a degree of success that would have surprised virtually anyone twenty years ago. The political effectiveness of the consumer and peace movements is more controversial, but surely a strong case can be made for the effectiveness of both of them. And while the civil rights movement drew support from all sectors of black society, middle-class ministers, students, and intellectuals were the dominant leaders.

The initiation of a political program by a middle-class social movement, and the implementation of the program through skilled political tactics, is now a frequently traveled road to social change in America. Women, environmentalists, and government reformers have shown considerable political skill in forming pressure groups, lobbying Congress, lobbying state governments, initiating lawsuits, injecting their issues into electoral campaigns, getting their points of view broadcast through the media, organizing demonstrations, and persuading people to support the movement. The national leadership of such social movements generally is aware of the importance of a continuing political organization and does not believe that the formalities of passing a bill, establishing an agency, or instituting "scientific administration" will end the movement.

The recent history of middle-class social movements indicates that rapid political and social change is possible in America. Such change is more readily attained in social and cultural realms than in the economic area because the American middle class is not especially dissatisfied with the workings of the capitalist system. Also, it must be observed that other such movements can be traditionalist or antidemocratic. For example, the McCarthyism of the early 1950s can be viewed as a middle-class social movement led by politicians who saw the possibility of changing American institutions in an authoritarian direction.[5]

The basic point is that middle-class social movements, using sophisticated tactics, can cause major social change. But disparate elements among the American middle class could initiate very different programs, and one should not draw hasty conclusions about the effects of this social process. In any event, the connections between social movements, their political strategies and lobbying tactics, and social change is an important topic for further study.[6]

NOTES

1. In 1976 Mathews left Common Cause and with Roger Craver of the Common Cause membership recruitment division formed Craver & Mathews, a consulting firm in Washington that has an active business advising liberal public-interest groups about recruiting members by "direct mail." In 1980 Mathews was finance director of the Anderson for President campaign.

2. Sidney Verba, *Small Groups and Political Behavior* (Princeton: Princeton University Press, 1961), chaps. 6-7.

3. Michael Lipsky, *Protest in City Politics: Rent Strikes, Housing and the Power of the Poor* (Chicago: Rand-McNally, 1970).

4. Allen Schick has observed that the change from closed to open bill mark-up sessions of the appropriations committees has made it more difficult for committee members to resist pork-barrel spending requests; Allen Schick, *Congress and Money: Budgeting, Spending, and Taxing* (Washington, D.C.: Urban Institute, 1980), 428-29.

5. Michael Paul Rogin, *The Intellectuals and McCarthy* (Cambridge, Mass.: MIT Press, 1970).

6. See Maurice Pinard, *The Rise of a Third Party* (Englewood Cliffs, N.J.: Prentice-Hall, 1971); Jo Freeman, *The Politics of Women's Liberation* (New York: McKay, 1975); Paul Sabatier, "Social Movements and Regulatory Agencies: Toward a More Adequate—and Less Pessimistic—Theory of 'Clientele Capture,' " *Policy Sciences* 6 (September 1975): 301-42. A sociological perspective that attempts to integrate social movement theory and interest-group theory may be found in John D. McCarthy and Mayer N. Zald, "Resource Mobilization and Social Movements," *American Journal of Sociology* 82 (May 1977): 1212-41. See also Anne N. Costain, "The Struggle for a National Women's Lobby: Organizing a Diffuse Interest," *Western Political Quarterly* 33 (December 1980): 476-91; Robert Cameron Mitchell, "From Elite Quarrel to Mass Movement," *Society* 18 (July/August 1981): 76-84; Anne N. Costain and W. Douglas Costain, "The Women's Lobby: Impact of a Movement on Congress," in *Interest Group Politics,* ed. Allan Cigler and Burdett A. Loomis (Washington, D.C.: Congressional Quarterly, 1983), 191-216; Andrew S. McFarland, "Public Interest Lobbies Versus Minority Faction," in ibid., 324-53. Mary Douglas and Aaron B. Wildavsky, *Risk and Culture* (Berkeley: University of California Press, 1982), can be viewed as applying to the environmentalist movement.

Index